The Human Tradition in America

CHARLES W. CALHOUN
Series Editor
Department of History, East Carolina University

The nineteenth-century English author Thomas Carlyle once remarked that "the history of the world is but the biography of great men." This approach to the study of the human past had existed for centuries before Carlyle wrote, and it continued to hold sway among many scholars well into the twentieth century. In more recent times, however, historians have recognized and examined the impact of large, seemingly impersonal forces in the evolution of human history—social and economic developments such as industrialization and urbanization as well as political movements such as nationalism, militarism, and socialism. Yet even as modern scholars seek to explain these wider currents, they have come more and more to realize that such phenomena represent the composite result of countless actions and decisions by untold numbers of individual actors. On another occasion, Carlyle said that "history is the essence of innumerable biographies." In this conception of the past, Carlyle came closer to modern notions that see the lives of all kinds of people, high and low, powerful and weak, known and unknown, as part of the mosaic of human history, each contributing in a large or small way to the unfolding of the human tradition.

This latter idea forms the foundation for this series of books on the human tradition in America. Each volume is devoted to a particular period or topic in American history and each consists of minibiographies of persons whose lives shed light on that period or topic. Well-known figures are not altogether absent, but more often the chapters explore a variety of individuals who may be less conspicuous but whose stories, nonetheless, offer us a window on some aspect of the nation's past.

By bringing the study of history down to the level of the individual, these sketches reveal not only the diversity of the American people and the complexity of their interaction but also some of the commonalities of sentiment and experience that Americans have shared in the evolution of their culture. Our hope is that these explorations of the lives of "real people" will give readers a deeper understanding of the human tradition in America.

Volumes in the Human Tradition in America series:

Ian K. Steele and Nancy L. Rhoden, eds., *The Human Tradition in Colonial America* (1999). Cloth ISBN 0-8420-2697-5 Paper ISBN 0-8420-2700-9

Nancy L. Rhoden and Ian K. Steele, eds., *The Human Tradition in the American Revolution* (2000). Cloth ISBN 0-8420-2747-5 Paper ISBN 0-8420-2748-3

Ballard C. Campbell, ed., *The Human Tradition in the Gilded Age and Progressive Era* (2000). Cloth ISBN 0-8420-2734-3 Paper ISBN 0-8420-2735-1

Steven E. Woodworth, ed., *The Human Tradition in the Civil War and Reconstruction* (2000). Cloth ISBN 0-8420-2726-2 Paper ISBN 0-8420-2727-0

David L. Anderson, ed., *The Human Tradition in the Vietnam Era* (2000). Cloth ISBN 0-8420-2762-9 Paper ISBN 0-8420-2763-7

Kriste Lindenmeyer, ed., *Ordinary Women, Extraordinary Lives: Women in American History* (2000). Cloth ISBN 0-8420-2752-1 Paper ISBN 0-8420-2754-8

Michael A. Morrison, ed., *The Human Tradition in Antebellum America* (2000). Cloth ISBN 0-8420-2834-X Paper ISBN 0-8420-2835-8

Malcolm Muir Jr., ed., *The Human Tradition in the World War II Era* (2001). Cloth ISBN 0-8420-2785-8 Paper ISBN 0-8420-2786-6

Ty Cashion and Jesús F. de la Teja, eds., *The Human Tradition in Texas* (2001). Cloth ISBN 0-8420-2905-2 Paper ISBN 0-8420-2906-0

Benson Tong and Regan A. Lutz, eds., *The Human Tradition in the American West* (2002). Cloth ISBN 0-8420-2860-9 Paper ISBN 0-8420-2861-7

Charles W. Calhoun, ed., *The Human Tradition in America from the Colonial Era through Reconstruction* (2002). Cloth ISBN 0-8420-5030-2 Paper ISBN 0-8420-5031-0

The Human Tradition in the
AMERICAN WEST

The Human Tradition in the
AMERICAN WEST

No. 10
Human Tradition in America

Edited by
Benson Tong
and
Regan A. Lutz

A Scholarly Resources Inc. Imprint
Wilmington, Delaware

First published 2002
Printed and Bound in the United States of America

Scholarly Resources Inc.
104 Greenhill Avenue
Wilmington, DE 19805-1897
www.scholarly.com

Library of Congress Cataloging-in-Publication Data

The human tradition in the American West / edited by Benson Tong and Regan A. Lutz.
p. cm.—(Human tradition in America ; no. 10)
Includes bibliographical references and index.
ISBN 0-8420-2860-9 (alk. paper)—ISBN 0-8420-2861-7 (pbk : alk. paper)
1. West (U.S.)—Biography. 2. West (U.S.)—History—Anecdotes. 3. Pioneers—West (U.S.)—Biography. I. Tong, Benson, 1964– II. Lutz, Regan A., 1954– III. Series.

F590.5 .H86 2001
920.078—dc21

2001031068

⊗ The paper used in this publication meets the minimum requirements of the American National Standard for permanence of paper for printed library materials, Z39.48, 1984.

For our mentor and friend,

Gerald Thompson (1947–1998),

who taught us the significance of the U.S. West

About the Editors

BENSON TONG, assistant professor of history at Wichita State University, Wichita, Kansas, is a scholar of U.S. immigration history and ethnicity. His published works include *Unsubmissive Women: Chinese Prostitutes in Nineteenth-Century San Francisco* (1994), *Susan La Flesche Picotte, M.D.: Omaha Reformer and Tribal Leader* (1999), *The Chinese Americans* (2000), and several journal articles related to American Indian history.

REGAN A. LUTZ, associate professor of history at Greensboro College, Greensboro, North Carolina, specializes in nineteenth-century U.S. history. Her award-winning teaching extends beyond her specialty field and encompasses Native American history, U.S. women's history, North Carolina history, U.S. foreign policy, and Latin American history. Professor Lutz has written book reviews and presented conference papers on various topics.

Acknowledgments

The authors deeply appreciate the assistance of those who helped make this book a reality. A special thank-you is extended to L. G. Moses for presenting them with the opportunity to pursue this project; the volume's contributors for their professionalism and patience; Stephen Ford, reference librarian at Greensboro College, who found things no one else could locate; Melanie Decker, secretary for the Humanities Division at Greensboro College, for her clerical assistance and for her invaluable emotional support and friendship; Benson Tong's companion, John, for his unflagging support and deep affection; and Regan Lutz's husband, Lon, for his loving support and amazing computer expertise.

Contents

Introduction
The American West in Its Many Incarnations

Benson Tong and Regan A. Lutz

An old Japanese immigrant poem begins with the following lines: "Chasing them in dreams, / Mountains and rivers of home."[1] Evoking memories of origins, the poem echoes the aspirations of newcomers to the American West, both past and present. Migrating westward—or eastward for those from Asia or northward for those from Central and South America—to that place has been a story of fanciful desires, alluring promises, and human foibles. But it has also been one of developing new ties while nurturing old roots. A story of departures, a narrative of arrivals—this is the imaginable and contestable West.

Peopled by many ethnic groups, the historical West, the crossroads of multiple cultures, shaped a continent and forged a nation, and for the actors, it was the stage on which their lives were reshaped. From the meandering, humid Mississippi to the sunny, kitschy Hawaiian Islands, from the riotous colors of the Tejano culture in arid Texas to the gurgling oil rushes in frigid Alaska, and from the expansiveness of the grassy ancient Great Plains to the soaring majesty of the Continental Divide, there have been many Wests. Covering nineteen U.S. states and encompassing five time zones, the region in its many incarnations boasts of varying landscapes and climates, racial and ethnic diversity, many economies, and multiple regional histories. The numerous subregions are topographically, economically, and socially different from one another. Yet what unifies them and what sets them apart from the rest of the republic is obvious: diversity.[2] Unlike the East, with its seemingly deterministic Puritan heritage, and the South, saddled by the burden of slavery, the U.S. West defies a monocausal explanation for its development. Such is the contemporary, "New Western" image of the region and its cast of thousands. Since its emergence in the early 1980s, New Western history has broken a fresh trail for the study of this region. Inclusive, non-Eurocentric, and pointedly pessimistic about the past, New Western works seem a marked contrast to the well-known Turnerian literature, which is, in part, intellectually rooted in the almost oratorical prose of Frederick Jackson Turner.

In July 1893 a young Turner, then a historian at the University of Wisconsin, presented a turgid paper at a professional meeting. On that sweltering late afternoon, he addressed a disinterested audience of his peers in the heart and soul of his beloved Midwest, Chicago. In what would become perhaps the seminal essay about U.S. history, Turner claimed that the American national identity—unique and unwedded to European roots—was primarily the outcome of shifting frontiers advancing westward across the continent over time.[3] Building on the democratic ideals of Thomas Jefferson and Andrew Jackson and invoking the triumphalist tone of Manifest Destiny, Turner declared in a larger work that "American democracy . . . came out of the American forest, and it gained new strength each time" Euramerican civilization encountered "savagery."[4] The rigors of the frontier experience turned settlers into rugged defenders of democracy and freedom, possessing minds at once idealistic and practical. Such ideal qualities, however, hinged on the availability of "free" or abundant land, a notion Turner fashioned from the English radical seventeenth-century faith that political independence hinged on landed proprietorship. Yet the end of the frontier in 1890, as proclaimed by the Bureau of Census, seemed to suggest that a descent into social chaos would soon ensue. The disappearance of the frontier—defined as land with a population density of two or fewer persons per square mile—meant that the West could no longer serve as a safety valve to ease the pressure of industrial forces and open opportunities. Neither immigration restrictions nor further territorial expansion could offset the loss of the American frontier. Scholars and the literate audience of that period found much to approve and little to reject in Turner's work. Writing at the end of one age and the dawn of another—a time when the disappearance of both the agrarian frontier and America's self-sufficiency seemed to be the reality, together with the emergence of industrial strife and unassimilable immigrants—Turner spoke to the Gilded Age nostalgia for an optimistic past and the simultaneous fear of an unknown future.[5]

The frontier theory drew from the past in order to validate the present. As Richard White has argued, Turner, like the Wild West show performer Buffalo Bill Cody (who was also in 1893 in Chicago for the Columbian Exposition), played up popular representations of the West. Using great military icons, Cody's Wild West exhibitions dramatized the conflicts between valiant whites and "rapacious" Indians that ended in retreat for the former; by contrast Turner's works, using the cabin icon, painted a picture of advancing farmers conquering nature. Though each man told a certain, differing narrative of the American frontier, both reflected the age-old definition of American national identity, one that embodied morality and civilization.[6]

More conceptual than empirical, more imaginative than factual, the Turner thesis drew scathing criticism after the end of the Great War. A sense of disillusionment swept through the American intelligentsia, and along with that came a more critical study of celebratory nationalist interpretations of the past. Class conflict, some scholars charged, determined the American national character far more than the moving frontier line did. So, too, did immigration and the transplanted cultures, along with urban growth. At the same time, the American connection to European roots remained. By the 1920s, scholars were considering economic determinism, ethnic influences, psychological factors, and race as major determinants of the American experience.[7]

One outcome of the U.S. involvement in World War I was a heightened awareness of internationalism. In the context of receding isolationist sentiments, historian Herbert Eugene Bolton extended the Turner thesis from a nationalist to an internationalist perspective. The frontier, Bolton argued in several classics, was first shaped by Spanish conquistadores encountering Native Americans in the American Southwest. Moving from south to north these early European explorers left a cultural and geopolitical legacy on the Spanish borderlands. Since Spain possessed the whole trans-Mississippi West from 1762 to 1800, any attempt to trace that region, reminded Bolton, had to include these antecedents. As scholar Sucheng Chan has claimed, Bolton was the first to emphasize the multicultural nature of western American history.[8]

Both Turner and Bolton saw the West as a process of social evolution unfolding in stages. So did historian Walter Prescott Webb. However, western American history—as explored in Webb's masterpiece, *The Great Plains* (1931)—played out within definite geographical boundaries. Webb eschewed Turner's "to-the-region" approach in favor of an "in-the-region" one. Yet, like Turner, who betrayed his Midwestern sensibility when he made agrarianism the wellspring of democracy in his thesis, Webb, in claiming that aridity defined the West, asserted his affinity for the dry Plains, his birthplace and home. Thus, rather than faithfully accept nineteenth-century explorer John Wesley Powell's identification of the land west of the one-hundredth meridian as subhumid America, Webb moved the line eastward to the ninety-eighth meridian so that it was just outside

Austin, Texas, the city where he lived. This subhumid America, he declared, was the West, a region where the annual rainfall measured less than twenty inches and where few trees grew.[9]

Even as Webb departed from Turner on the veracity of the frontier theme, he converged with the latter in accepting environmental determinism. In Webb's story the absence of timber and plentiful rain forced pioneer settlers to live and innovate within the limits of the environment. However, unlike Turner, who claimed the flowering of a national character in this pastoral garden, Webb only perceived unique lifeways thriving in this desertlike area, wholly unconnected to the rest of the republic.[10]

Like Turner, Webb also came under fire for his geographical determinism. The critics charged that he ignored cultural continuities and that he and Turner both exaggerated the degree to which settlers' lives changed when they moved westward. Furthermore, people changed the land as much as the latter changed them.[11] Both Turner and Webb, though separated by one generation, mined an old American faith, existing since the days of Daniel Boone and Leatherstocking, about the transformation that resulted from the confrontation between a human and an unknown landscape.

American studies scholar Henry Nash Smith perceptively made that observation in his classic work, *Virgin Land: The American West as Symbol and Myth* (1950). In this book, which borrowed from cultural psychology and plumbed highbrow texts and popular fictional works, Smith explained that the transformation attributed to that confrontation was born of human desire projected on the landscape. Language—words and image—affected historical change; thus, the American West "is an idea that became a place." Ideas about the West that engendered deeds revolved around three major myths: the West as "Passage to India," as home of the "Sons of Leatherstocking," and as "The Garden of the World." In the days of Thomas Jefferson the region was simply a gateway to an aspired empire in Asia. The empire, however, under the sway of Manifest Destiny, contracted eastward to America itself. The western figure in dime novels also became more complex: both civilized and in need of civilization. The West was wild and yet fertile, an agricultural utopia that Euramericans were ordained to own. Turner's thesis, Smith boldly revealed, was simply a manifestation of this mythical understanding of the region.[12]

The beleaguered frontier theory was not without its share of defenders. Perhaps foremost in assiduously maintaining the credibility of the theory was Ray Allen Billington. In several sweeping sagas—*Westward Expansion: A History of the American Frontier* (1949) being the most ambitious—Billington defended the notion that democracy was born in the western wilderness. He admitted that the working class encountered a barrier in accessing frontier opportunity and that democracy preceded European colonization of America, but he still asserted his faith in a thesis that for him was a natural law. Though his narratives took readers to different subregions of varying peoples, Billington never tested the thesis.[13]

The post–World War II critique of the Turnerian school often built on the earlier Progressive Era challenge to the frontier thesis. Historian Earl Pomeroy, echoing the claims made by scholars in the 1920s, argued in several works that western settlers typically adopted old lifeways brought from the eastern seaboard or Europe, rather than adapting to the new landscape by innovating. Pomeroy's emphasis on continuity was echoed in Webb's *The Great Frontier* (1951). Webb wrote that "what happened in America was but a detail in a much greater phenomenon" that had taken place in Europe during the prior four centuries of expansion. In casting this global framework on the significance of the West, Webb lay a basis for comparative frontier studies. Yet, like Turner, Webb was pessimistic about the future that would follow the end of this four-hundred-year boom.[14]

Pomeroy and later Gerald Nash shared Webb's definition of the West as a place rather than a process. But Pomeroy and Nash departed from Webb's (and Turner's) preoccupation with the frontier's closing. They saw the twentieth century, complete with its urban growth, as a period that deserved scholarly inquiry. In his *The American West in the Twentieth Century* (1977), Nash also offered an expansion of writer Bernard DeVoto's argument, first made in the 1930s, that the West was a "plundered province," one that nonwestern capitalists had exploited for self-interests. The twentieth-century West, Nash contended, could be divided into two eras: the colonial period preceding World War II and a postwar period during which the region became a pacesetter for the nation. The shift from one to the other stemmed from economic changes set in motion by the defense industries that had sprung up since World War II and government investments, particularly in dams and irrigation projects.[15] The most recent survey of the twentieth-century West—*The American West: A Twentieth-Century History* (1989) by Michael P. Malone and Richard W. Etulain—accepted Nash's periodization but reminded its readers that the postwar West blends pacesetting and imitative tendencies, breaking from as well as adhering to the patterns of the nation. Like Nash, the authors also defined the regional West as a place that is arid, shares a history of colonialism, and has strong ties to the federal government. The surveys also had two other commonalties: they excluded Hawai`i and Alaska, and they relegated racial ethnic minorities to a separate chapter.

In the last few decades the New Western history has remapped the study of the West. Hawai`i and Alaska are now part of the West; even areas beyond U.S. boundaries are tied to this past, when image making and the global economy are factored in. The frontier theory was tailored to fit Turner's Portage, Wisconsin, and in spite of its sense of movement, it simply trimmed out the story of intercultural collisions along with transnational ties across the Pacific. It was geographically limiting, even as it purported to be continentwide. New Western history, to paraphrase historian Elliott West, has given scholars shifting angles of vision and a widened embrace.[16]

But New Western history is, in fact, not all new. The incorporation of race, class, gender, and sexuality as central foci of an analysis of certain western topics is simply the mirroring of the thrusts of modern American historiography. Moreover the rejection of 1890 as the magical dividing line between a developing West and a settled West found resonance among scholars soon after the appearance of the frontier theory. Historian Gerald Thompson believed that Turner would have agreed with the New Western historians' privileging of conquest as a major historical theme, since Turner wrote "the first ideal of the pioneer was that of conquest . . . vast forests . . . and a fierce race of savages, all had to be met and defeated."[17] Turner's conquest, however, is a triumphal one; the New Western historians' is tragic, with no clear victors. The theme of conquest, as explored in syntheses such as those offered by Patricia Nelson Limerick and Richard White, presents the story of the West as a process of dispossession, one perpetrated by Euramericans on peoples of color and women.[18] In privileging such a theme—one that hints of economic determinism—the agency and the voices of the victimized became muted. A selective rendering of the past, in spite of an eschewing of the heroic exploits of white male figures, still pervades these more contemporary understandings of the region. The New Western history, however, has gone a long way toward recovering the stories of non-Euramericans and women, those that Turnerians neglected. Monographs and anthologies written by women's and ethnic historians are often framed by the assumption that power was distributed in relationships of race, class, and gender. Since such social experiences were ever changing, the so-called marginalized also at times resisted and redefined such relationships.[19]

New Western history works also often remind one of Turner's legacy in other ways. Environmental historian William Cronon claimed that Turner, like New Western historians, conceived western history as the interplay of scarcity and abundance that exists throughout space and time, which in turn produced diversity and conflict in this region. Turner's interest in putting ordinary people at the center of the story—hunters, traders, farmers, and workers—also presaged the incorporation of social history into the study of the West, although women's historian Glenda Riley contravened that Turner was more interested in masses of people or types rather than individuals. The new environmental history—which spatially has mostly been in the West—is an updated version of Turner's environmental interpretation.[20]

Or so it seems, Richard White reminded his readers. Frontier historians, he pointed out, see "wilderness"—land unaffected by human use—on one side of the frontier line and "civilization," having conquered nature, on the other. But the "real" West, as Elliott West chimed, was not a simple story of pioneers moving into a storyless land but one that involved the merging of intertwined tales, of the deep and recent past with victors and victims on both sides of the cultural divide. Even as different contesting groups competed for limited resources, all of them were embroiled in a dialectical relationship between nature and culture. Another historian, Donald Worster, has argued that regardless of who controlled land use, the exploitation of land was the end result. Aridity in the West forced the rise of a hydraulic culture or water empire that involved irrigated agriculture, reclamation, and dams for water supply, all of which demanded dependency on the government and capitalism, a situation Turner predicted in his writings. Turner, however, as Worster noted, refused to admit that such conditions would destroy American democracy along with the lands.[21]

Turner came up short on analysis and details, but historians are still turning to him for the "rhetorical structure," to borrow Cronon's phrase.[22] The fact that he envisioned his frontier thesis as part of a larger frontier-sectional theory provides some explanation for its persistent influence on historians. Turner saw the frontier as a momentary process and the section as an enduring fact of U.S. history. The passing of the frontier in the 1890s, he argued, was followed by pioneers settling in new homelands, which in turn gradually became separate sections or regions. His idea of sectionalism was the basis for the present-day understanding of regionalism; both purport to explore interrelationships of social, geographical, political, cultural, and economic forces in the development of the American society.[23]

Whether one understands the West to be "to-the-region" or social evolution "in-the-region," the reality is that for those who lived it, past and present, it was far more than an intellectual abstraction or individual thesis. It has been written that "a place as varied as the West and a process as complex as its history can never be captured in a single definition or paradigm."[24] Perhaps that realization informed the writing of the latest edition of *The American West: A New Interpretive History* by Robert V. Hine and John Mack Faragher. Published in February 2000 this survey surpasses those by Limerick and White in terms of its chronological coverage and perhaps its theoretical framework as well. Not only does the volume begin with the first Columbian contacts between indigenous peoples and Europeans, it also presents the West as both frontier and region, an area that embraced many places but all involving a tale of conquest and yet also survival and the merging of peoples and cultures. The "history of the frontier," wrote Hine and Faragher, "is a unifying American theme, for every part of the country was once a frontier, every region was once a West."[25] Whether one views the West as a process, a place, or a combination of the two, few scholars today consider it as a particular period in time. Only survey textbook publishers, who grant it a partial chapter falling somewhere between Reconstruction and late-nineteenth-century politics, or the John Fords of Hollywood seem stuck forever in a Gilded Age time warp.

Those whose life stories fill the pages of this volume are living proof to refute that understanding. Chronologically, these actors in the drama of the West range from an eighteenth-century Spanish borderlands historiographer to a late-twentieth-century San Francisco gay activist-cum-politician. Their lives coincided with dramatic turning points in American history: early European contact with Native Americans, the overland trails of the antebellum period, the gold rush of the mid-nineteenth century and the settlement of the West, Progressive Era reforms, the Great Depression, World War II, postwar prosperity, and the sociopolitical protests of the 1960s and 1970s. Their stories, however, were not simply replications of those in the East or South; theirs were regionally distinctive. What made them distinctive was the shifting pattern of mixing and interaction in a much divided space.

Most of the figures covered in this volume hailed from somewhere outside of the trans-Mississippi West, and yet they set deep roots in their new "home." Itinerancy has always been an important force in shaping western lives. Moving into the region, they then moved around within it. Even when they left the region for brief periods, the West still held an alluring appeal for them.

In terms of ethnicity the story presented in the pages that follow is partly one of unsung black, yellow, and red heroes whose varied exploits shaped the contours of the West. However, it is also the more conventional story of white men and women who left their mark on the West. The deeds of African American pioneer Henry Ossian Flipper at the turn of the last century's Southwest paralleled those of white mining journalist Henry De Groot during the Colorado River gold rush of 1862; both men enriched our understanding of the physical landscape and its connection to human ecology. Their writings on the promise of this region, though, built essentially on the works of people such as the Mexican Jesuit priest Francisco Javier Clavijero. Even though African American William Jefferson Hardin was a reluctant territorial legislator in Wyoming and, in contrast, Eugene C. Pulliam was a self-serving booster of postwar Phoenix, Arizona, both encouraged the emergence of governmental, economic, and social institutions that replicated those on the eastern seaboard. The theme of cultural continuity, first expounded by Progressive historians, clearly found expression across space and time even as the merging of worlds led to new human imaginings and actions.

The theme of the inseparability of the environment from human society runs throughout this volume. Blackfeet politician Joseph W. Brown and Lakota Sioux activist Robert Burnette when compared to U.S. Supreme Court Justice William O. Douglas seemed to share little in common. Yet all of these public figures had their fortunes shaped by the central government, which administered large amounts of public land in the West. They believed in the nurturing stewardship of western resources; Douglas fought for the environment through his writings and judgments, whereas Brown and Burnette fought for tribal control of the landscape via political lobbying and community work. These individuals in discrete locations told distinct tales, but together they vocalized a singular story of visionary expectation, thus suggesting that the West could be placed on both an experiential and a spatial continuum.

Because power was unequally distributed in the transient West, the struggle for empowerment often led to an interrogation of personal and national identity. Of course, identity formation was gendered as well as racialized. During the heyday of the overland trails, Eliza Hart Spalding answered the call to serve God in the Indian-populated Oregon country of the late 1830s but also the challenge to expand women's roles beyond the home, in spite of the sway of the prescriptive ideology of domesticity that upheld the superiority of white culture over all others. Along the way, she helped to close the racial gap between two vastly different worlds, even as she herself came to appreciate better the humanity of the "other." Clara True, through her labors among the Pueblo Indians during the height of the federal government's assimilation policy at the turn of the last century, also strove to gain female empowerment, though at the expense of the

Native Americans' cultures. Unlike Spalding, who worked within an informal setting where authority was fluid and in a time of a faith in the unity of humanity, True operated in an institutionalized context of strident assimilation, designed to preserve the homogeneity of the republic against the tide of immigration and non-Anglo values. Clearly, then, to neglect gender in western history—which was passive and thus irrelevant in Turner's masculinized version—is to miss power relations along the axis of race, culture, and nationalism.

María Amparo Ruiz Burton and Margaret Chung were also caught between dominant ideologies and a conflict-ridden reality. Though they entered the public realm in separate eras—Burton in the aftermath of the Mexican War of 1846–1848 and Chung mostly during World War II—these women found themselves playing the role of the cultural broker, one who tried to improve the quality of human life while fostering mutual understanding across the racial divide. Shaped by two lifeways—the dominant Euramerican culture and her own ethnic culture—each of these individuals lived in a cultural borderland of fluid relations and identities. In their respective efforts to be part of a community and nation, each had to contend with racial oppression, the pressures of Americanization, and the pulls of ethnicity. Along the way, they challenged the hegemonic association of birthright with "whiteness." The story of the West, to borrow Richard White's words, has been one of movement, contact, and exchange.[26]

Perhaps the life story of camera-store owner turned politician Harvey Milk, covering mostly the turbulent 1960s and 1970s, is the appropriate reminder of the significance of the West in the United States. The sexuality that Milk was part of and his bloody murder remind us of the open and violent images of the West. During the period of Spanish colonization, ritualized Native American homosexuality was noted in the records kept by conquistadores and padres. Then homosexual subcultures flourished during the days of the gold rush, with its skewed sex ratios, and beyond. Throughout this history, society made intermittent official and popular vigilante attempts to police the boundaries of "decency" and defend "law and order." Yet gay utopians never gave up the attempt to be part of the West's vaunted opportunities. The western fork of the long road to gay liberation reminds us that the settling of the lands beyond the Mississippi has been about boundary setting, state forming, and self-shaping.[27]

Such processes suggest that "much of western history has been about ceasing to be west" or "making the long transition from frontier to region."[28] The West may be a place, but it is also the experience of getting there. When peoples and cultures encountered one another, they were forced to mutually concede, adapt, and borrow from one another. Turner's understanding of the American national identity and how it was forged in the frontier was chauvinistic, but a regional identity, as he had predicted, did eventually develop. His vision was simply narrowed by the cultural blinders of his generation. Where he saw Daniel Boone standing astride the Cumberland Gap gazing at a "virgin land," today's New Western historians see the land and the peoples beyond the gap.

Perhaps a hundred years from now, a new generation of scholars of the West will look back at the New Western historians and conclude that they, too, saw what their generation was conditioned to see or perhaps wanted to see. Whereas Turner and Theodore Roosevelt and their Gilded Age compatriots saw white male heroes, Limerick, White, and their baby boomer generation saw a multicultural society that was far more complex than the one Turner perceived a century earlier. His was a simpler age, with simpler answers. Will our own age be judged the same a century hence?

In 1891, Frederick Jackson Turner wrote that "each age tries to form its own conception of the past. Each age writes the history of the past anew with reference to the conditions uppermost in its own time."[29] If that is true, then we present you with the West as viewed from the millennial divide that we stand astride today. As the editors of this collection, we believe that the lives of the westerners herein portrayed unequivocally demonstrate that the Turner thesis and the New Western history are not mutually exclusive. The fortunes of our biographical figures attest to the fact that the boundaries of the region were not naturally determined but were politically and socially set. Since geography did not define the boundaries of the West, history created them, and thus, a fluid definition is required to answer the often asked question, "Where is the West?"

A recent biographer of Turner, historian Allan G. Bogue, has written that "the West is less than a perfect representation of, and more than a regional variation on, American history, life, and character." Neither uniquely American nor mundanely the same as other parts of the United States, the West is a "fragmented unity," at once a place and many places, a process and many processes. In the following pages, readers will come to know this complex and puzzling region through the lives of a remarkable group of people—multiracial, multicultural, of both genders, from varying sexualities and divergent worlds—who were all part of a process in a place that was and is "hope's native home."[30]

Notes

1. Kazuo Ito, *Issei: A History of Japanese Immigrants in North America* (Seattle: Japanese Community Service, 1973), 49.

2. Michael C. Steiner and David M. Wrobel, "Many Wests: Discovering a Dynamic Western Regionalism," in *Many Wests: Place, Culture, & Regional Identity,* ed. Michael C. Steiner and David M. Wrobel (Lawrence: University Press of Kansas, 1997), 10–12.

3. Frederick Jackson Turner's paper was entitled "The Significance of the Frontier in American History." It was first published in the *Annual Report of the American Historical Association for the Year 1893* (Washington, DC: GPO and American Historical Association, 1894), 199–227.

4. Martin Ridge, "Frederick Jackson Turner, Ray Allen Billington, and American Frontier History," *Western Historical Quarterly* 19 (January 1988): 9; quote in Frederick Jackson Turner, *The Frontier in American History* (New York: Henry Holt, 1920), 293.

5. Sucheng Chan, "Western American Historiography and Peoples of Color," in *Peoples of Color in the American West,* ed. Sucheng Chan, Douglas Henry Daniels, Mario T. Garcia, and Terry P. Wilson (Lexington, MA: D. C. Heath, 1994), 2.

6. Richard White, "When Frederick Jackson Turner and Buffalo Bill Cody Both Played Chicago in 1893," in *Does the Frontier Experience Make America Exceptional?* ed. Richard W. Etulain (Boston: Bedford/St. Martin's, 1999), 46–57.

7. Gerald D. Nash, *Creating the West: Historical Interpretations, 1890–1990* (Albuquerque: University of New Mexico Press, 1991), 19–20, 28.

8. The work that marks Herbert Eugene Bolton as the pioneer in the field of Spanish borderlands history is his *The Spanish Borderlands: A Chronicle of Old Florida and the Southwest* (New Haven: Yale University Press, 1923). For an assessment of Bolton's scholarly contributions, see Donald E. Worcester, "Herbert Eugene Bolton: The Making of a Western Historian," in *Writing Western History: Essays on Major Western Historians,* ed. Richard W. Etulain (Albuquerque: University of New Mexico Press, 1991), 193–214; see also Chan, "Western American Historiography," 4.

9. Donald Worster, "New West, True West: Interpreting the Region's History," *Western Historical Quarterly* 18 (April 1987): 146–47.

10. Elliott West, "Walter Prescott Webb and the Search for the West," in *Writing Western History: Essays on Major Western Historians,* ed. Richard W. Etulain (Albuquerque: University of New Mexico Press, 1991), 172, 174.

11. Ibid., 175.

12. Lee Clark Mitchell, "Henry Nash Smith's Myth of the West," in *Writing Western History: Essays on Major Western Historians,* ed. Richard W. Etulain (Albuquerque: University of New Mexico Press, 1991), 254–56; quote in Clyde A. Milner II, "Introduction: America Only More So," in *The Oxford History of the American West,* ed. Clyde A. Milner II, Carol A. O'Connor, and Martha A. Sandweiss (New York: Oxford University Press, 1994), 3; Richard W. Etulain, *Re-imagining the Modern American West: A Century of Fiction, History, and Art* (Tucson: University of Arizona Press, 1996), 161–62.

13. Other major works by Ray Allen Billington include *The Far Western Frontier, 1830–1860* (New York: Harper and Row, 1956), *America's Frontier Heritage* (New York: Holt, Rinehart and Winston, 1966), and *Frederick Jackson Turner: Historian, Scholar, Teacher* (New York: Oxford University Press, 1973).

14. See Earl Pomeroy, "Toward a Reorientation of Western History: Continuity and Environment," *Mississippi Valley Historical Review* 41 (March 1955): 579–600, and *The Pacific Slope: A History of California, Oregon, Washington, Idaho, Utah, and Nevada* (New York: Alfred A. Knopf, 1965); quote in Walter Prescott Webb, "Ended: Four Hundred Year Boom—Reflections on the Age of the Frontier," *Harper's* 203 (October 1951): 26.

15. Nash, *Creating the West,* 63, 116; see Gerald D. Nash *The American West in the Twentieth Century: A Short History of an Urban Oasis* (Albuquerque: University of New Mexico Press, 1977), and *The American West Transformed: The Impact of the Second World War* (Bloomington: Indiana University Press, 1985).

16. Elliott West, "A Longer, Grimmer, but More Interesting Story," in *Trails: Toward a New Western History,* ed. Patricia Nelson Limerick, Clyde A. Milner II, and Charles E. Rankin (Lawrence: University Press of Kansas, 1991), 103.

17. Gerald Thompson, "Another Look at Frontier/Western Historiography," in *Trails: Toward a New Western History,* ed. Patricia Nelson Limerick, Clyde A. Milner II, and Charles E. Rankin (Lawrence: University Press of Kansas, 1991), 92–93; Turner, *Frontier in American History,* 289.

18. See Patricia Nelson Limerick, *The Legacy of Conquest: The Unbroken Past of the American West* (New York: W. W. Norton, 1987); Richard White, *"It's Your Misfortune and None of My Own": A New History of the American West* (Norman and London: University of Oklahoma Press, 1991).

19. For examples, see Elizabeth Jameson and Susan Armitage, eds., *Writing the Range: Race, Class, and Culture in the Women's West* (Norman: University of Oklahoma Press, 1977); Valerie J. Matsumoto and Blake Allmendinger, eds., *Over the Edge: Remapping the American West* (Berkeley: University of California Press, 1999).

20. William Cronon, "Revisiting Turner's Vanishing Frontier: The Legacy of Frederick Jackson Turner," *Western Historical Quarterly* 18 (April 1987): 157–76; Glenda Riley, "Frederick Jackson Turner Overlooked the Ladies," in *Does the Frontier Experience Make America Exceptional?* ed. Richard W. Etulain (Boston: Bedford/St. Martin's, 1999), 65.

21. Richard White, "Trashing the Trails," in *Trails: Toward a New Western History,* ed. Patricia Nelson Limerick, Clyde A. Milner II, and Charles E. Rankin (Lawrence: University Press of Kansas, 1991), 28, 37; Elliott West, *The Contested Plains: Indians, Goldseekers, and the Rush to Colorado* (Lawrence: University Press of Kansas, 1998), XXII–XXIV; see Donald Worster "New West, True West," 141–56, and *Rivers of Empire: Water, Aridity, and the Growth of the American West* (New York: Pantheon Books, 1985).

22. Cronon, "Revisiting Turner's Vanishing Frontier," 170.

23. Wilbur R. Jacobs, *On Turner's Trail: 100 Years of Writing Western History* (Lawrence: University Press of Kansas, 1994), 13–14. Turner explored his concept of sectionalism in *The Significance of Sections in American History* (New York: Henry Holt, 1932) and then framed his narrative in *The United States, 1830–1850: The Nation and Its Sections* (New York: Henry Holt, 1935).

24. Anne F. Hyde and William Deverell, "Reintroducing a Re-envisioned West," in *A New Significance: Re-envisioning the History of the American West,* ed. Clyde A. Milner II (New York: Oxford University Press, 1996), 301.

25. Robert V. Hine and John Mack Faragher, *The American West: A New Interpretive History* (New Haven: Yale University Press, 2000), 11.

26. White, "Trashing the Trail," 38.

27. William Cronon, "Becoming West: Toward a New Meaning for Western History," in *Under an Open Sky: Rethinking America's Western Past,* ed. William Cronon, George Miles, and Jay Gitlin (New York: W. W. Norton, 1992), 3–27.

28. Ibid., 26.

29. Turner quoted in Richard Hofstadter, *The Progressive Historians: Turner, Beard, Parrington* (New York: Alfred A. Knopf, 1968), 84.

30. Bogue quoted in William Deverell, "Fighting Words: The Significance of the American West in the United States," in *A New Significance: Re-envisioning the History of the American West,* ed. Clyde A. Milner II (New York: Oxford University Press, 1996), 33; second quote in Milner, "Introduction," 2; third quote in Wallace Stegner, *Where the Bluebird Sings to the Lemonade Springs: Living and Writing in the West* (New York: Penguin Books, 1992), xv.

1

Francisco Javier Clavijero and the Founding of the Literary West

John F. Crossen

Francisco Javier Clavijero (1731–1787), a Jesuit priest, was one of the first to write authoritatively on what would become the American Far West. Born in the city of Veracruz in New Spain (present-day Mexico), Clavijero was an extremely well-educated criollo (native-born white Hispanic) who yearned for an ecclesiastical placement in Baja California but instead remained within the university setting in his native Mexico.

After the Jesuits were expelled from the so-called New World in 1767, Clavijero lived the rest of his life in exile in Italy, writing best-selling books about the land he had both loved and lost. In the process, he opened up the Spanish borderlands to both European and American scholars. As Professor Crossen explains in this essay, Clavijero's works ultimately influenced generations of leading figures, including Thomas Jefferson, Alexander von Humboldt, William H. Prescott, George Bancroft, and John Steinbeck.

Crossen offers further evidence that the representation of the American West—expansive, "virgin," and even mysterious—has been shaped, in part, by citizens of other nations who visited the West as well as by those who perceived it only from afar. Furthermore, a duality ran through the period covered by this essay: some saw the region as inviting and alluring, yet others saw it as primitive and threatening. Ultimately the mastery of nature was the aim of those who sought to know this region, and in that effort, Clavijero played a part.

John F. Crossen is an assistant professor of Spanish at Mansfield University, Mansfield, Pennsylvania. He recently completed a manuscript entitled "A Tale of Two Exiles: Losing, Recalling, and Inscribing the Landscape of Mexico in the *Historias* of the Jesuits Francisco Javier Clavijero (1731–1787) and Andrés Cavo (1739–1803)." He also has published essays in the *Romance Languages Annual* and *The Encyclopedia of Mexico.*

Before the great American westward expansion of the nineteenth century, the first "explorer" of the U.S. West was the American imagination. This imagination needed a literature—letters, reports of encounters with the indigenous inhabitants, memoirs, and oral histories—to feed its ambition and romantic dreams of the opportunities that lay beyond the rivers, plains, and mountains and in unknown places. The documentation was often exaggerated, contradictory, or fantastic in its claims, but it served as a textual template on which the political and scientific intelligence of the infant United States could map its territorial claims to the American West.

However, the majority of the texts available to American readers in the late eighteenth and early nineteenth centuries were written by European critics and were controversial in nature. Several were by writers who had never even visited the Americas. Others—largely authored by missionaries to the Indians—had a sectarian purpose and were frowned on by the "enlightened," more secular mind of the age. They were not considered scientific. Of the many authors who presented the American imagination with a textual vision of the West, perhaps only one stands out as an authority respected by scientist and politician alike: the Mexican Jesuit and savant Francisco Javier Clavijero.[1] Though he was a Catholic author, his histories of Mexico and the Southwest were eighteenth-century "best-sellers" and admired by European and American scholars as diverse as Edward Gibbon, William Robertson, and Thomas Jefferson. His work became the foundation of a "literary" West—a West depicted in a series of books by Clavijero and those he inspired that illustrated the wilderness awaiting American frontiersmen and settlers; a West whose physical and natural aspects were described in every imaginable detail; a West that could be truly seen in the mind as ambitious men and women prepared to pace its limits.

The son of a Spanish government official, Francisco Javier Clavijero displayed ability in languages and music at an early age. His father had a diverse library in the home, and the young Clavijero became familiar with ancient and modern authors: Greeks and Romans, philosophers and historians. Under his father's tutelage, he became fluent in French and Italian. His mother, a criolla, taught him how to read music and play several instruments. Since his father held a variety of posts in New Spain, Clavijero also developed an interest in indigenous language and culture and learned to speak Nahuatl in his early years.[2]

In 1748, Clavijero entered the novitiate of the Jesuits (the Society of Jesus) at Tepozotlán. Completing his philosophical and theological studies with honors, he was ordained a priest in 1754. As a priest his primary responsibilities involved teaching theology and philosophy to other seminarians. He served as a professor at Jesuit schools in Valladolid (today's Morelia) and Guadalajara. Though he deeply desired to be assigned mission work in Lower (Baja) California, his superiors valued his intellectual gifts and refused to place him outside a university setting.

From José de Jesús Velaz'quez San'chez, ed., *Almanaque nacional iconografico* (Mexico, D.F.: Editorial Porrúa, 1982), 374.

Clavijero's passion for indigenous history and culture was fed by his exposure to Mexica-Azteca ruins in Mexico City, where he studied and taught for a time, and also by the famous manuscript collection of the seventeenth-century Mexican polymath Carlos Sigüenza y Góngora. He began to establish a reputation as a preacher and poet. In addition, he wrote devotional works (including a commentary on Saint Francis de Sales) and translated Christian prayers in native Mexican languages. He also taught the first complete course of modern philosophy in Mexico, highlighting René Descartes, Francis Bacon, Isaac Newton, Jean-Jacques Rousseau, Benedict de Spinoza, Benjamin Franklin, and others, many of whom had been prohibited a general readership in the Americas by the Inquisition.[3]

In 1767 the Bourbon king of Spain, Charles III, issued a *Pragmatic Sanction* ordering the expulsion of the Jesuits from all Spanish territory. Bourbon monarchs, who exercised a centralist authority, were suspicious of any agency that seemed to operate as a "state within a state," and they claimed the right to direct not only secular activity but also church missions. Since the Jesuits took a vow of obedience directly to the pope, they were seen as a threat to the monarchs' control over their possessions and subjects. The Jesuits, moreover, had long been considered troublemakers by many Europeans. Seen as dissemblers and intriguers who could be disloyal to God and Crown, they were believed to be secretly withholding Indian gold and other treasures from the king. So, like other Bourbon monarchs in Portugal and France, Charles III decided to banish the Jesuits from his lands.

The greatest number of exiled Jesuits from Mexico were criollos; thus, the king's decree of expulsion disrupted the criollo families in Mexico and elsewhere. This move would fuel a deep-seated resentment among that class toward the *gachupines,* or Spanish-born rulers, ultimately empowering independence movements in the first years of the nineteenth century. As one critic noted, "The Jesuits, more than any other order, had encouraged the *criollos* in their aspirations to an independent cultural identity."[4] The violent expulsion of the Jesuits had not only disrupted the social order of Mexico but also torn some of the country's most talented intellectuals away from the land they loved. Among these criollo exiles was Francisco Clavijero.

However, this physical defeat eventually turned into an intellectual triumph. Settling in the papal states of Italy, many of the Jesuit exiles began to write histories and memoirs of their lost homelands. The city of Bologna became the center of Mexican Jesuit activity, and Clavijero would live there until his death in 1787, assembling materials for books about the natural history of his native country, the conquest of the Mexica-Aztecas in 1521, and the founding of Jesuit missions. He and other exiled Jesuit writers would become the "literary precursors of American nationalism."[5] He wrote to relieve his homesickness, to feel connected to his distant homeland, and to defend the dignity of the Americas and thus reaffirm the value of his criollo identity in the midst of European strangers.[6]

The prime motivator behind Clavijero's literary work was what historian Antonello Gerbi referred to as the "dispute of the New World," a philosophical debate that had been raging in Europe since the discovery of the Americas in 1492.[7] In the eighteenth century this debate had become a major literary enterprise generating dozens of books that criticized the New World as being younger in age than the Old World, more underdeveloped, and thus inferior in every way. Many of the critiques were bitter and even insulting, depicting the Americas as a degenerative place that sapped the vitality out of anyone daring to venture there. One critic, the French naturalist Georges Louis Leclerc Comte de Buffon, explained why there was so much degeneration and impotence in America: "There is thus, in the combination of the elements and other physical causes, something antagonistic to the increase of living nature in this new world. [Everything] is here reduced, shrunken beneath this ungenerous sky and empty land."[8] The impact of the climate, he continued, could affect plants, animals, and even the Native American, whom Buffon claimed was "feeble and small in his organs of generation . . . he lacks vivacity, and is lifeless in his soul; the activity of his body is less an exercise or a voluntary movement than an automatic reaction to his needs."[9]

What irritated Clavijero most about this insulting picture was that none of the controversial writers in Europe (abbé [Guillaume-Thomas-François] Raynal, Buffon, Corneille De Paw, Robertson, Voltaire) had actually visited Mexico or any other part of the Americas, yet they wrote as those who had "true knowledge."[10] This injustice spurred the Mexican exile to insert his own "voice" into the dispute through the publication of his monumental *History of Mexico* in 1780–1781. Writing with boldness and a powerful sarcasm aimed at the critics of the Americas, Clavijero armed himself with an encyclopedic knowledge of previous histories of Mexico and synthesized various (and usually conflicting) accounts of the conquest of the Mexica-Aztecas. He added experience to reason, persuasive qualities in a scholar of the Age of Enlightenment: "I resided thirty-six years in that extensive kingdom; acquired the Mexican language, and for several years conversed with the Mexicans, whose history I write."[11] The result was a book that one scholar claimed "proved to be the most popular, certainly the most influential, history of Mexico."[12]

What immediately distinguished Francisco Clavijero's book from other histories was its organization. Unlike earlier Hispanic chroniclers of Mexico, Clavijero arranged his book as a modern-looking natural history text—beginning not with the Indians but with the geography and geology of the land. From there, he went on to describe in detail the plants, animals, and finally the humans. Clavijero moved seamlessly from the inanimate to the animate, the simple to the complex. Building on this scheme, he presented a three-dimensional picture in words of the Mexican landscape—a vibrant and dynamic space from which glorious civilizations emerged.

Clavijero alternated between a detached, descriptive voice, as if he were narrating a documentary, and a polemical one, never missing an opportunity to remind abbé Raynal, Buffon, De Paw, and others of their ignorance. For example, after a lengthy discussion of American birds, he responded to erroneous reports that they could not sing: "It is more difficult for Europeans to hear the Mexican birds than to see them."[13] In other passages the exiled criollo tenderly recalled the beauty of the land:

> The purity of the atmosphere, the smaller obliquity of the solar rays, and the longer stay of this luminary upon the horizon in winter, in comparison of other regions far removed from the equator, concur to lessen the cold, and to prevent all that horror which disfigures the face of nature in other climes. During that season, a serene sky and the natural delights of the country, are enjoyed. . . . No less causes, combine to temper the heat of the summer. The plentiful showers which frequently water the earth after mid-day . . . the high mountains continually loaded with snow, scattered here and there through the country of Anahuac; the cool winds which breathe from them in that season; and the shorter stay of the sun upon the horizon, compared with the circumstances of the temperate zone, transform the summer of those happy countries into a cool and cheerful spring.[14]

Such lyrical writing transcended the factual reporting of the text and captured the imagination, imparting a magic to Mexico that both informed and enticed the reader. Through Clavijero's text, Mexico became irresistibly attractive.

The Mexico that he described encompassed territory extending from parts of present-day Central America to the American Southwest. The overall effect was to give an unfinished or undefined feel to the landscape—ambiguous and pliable. This quality would invite later authors to build on Clavijero's text and clarify it, trying to define what was Spanish and later Mexican—and even later Anglo-American. His writings on Mexico fueled the imagination of future generations of American writers. Clavijero's *History of Mexico* had established a textual frontier in the literary West.

Though the history of Mexico was his best-known work, Clavijero also wrote *History of California,* published posthumously by his brother Ignacio in 1789. In this book, he took up where he left off in the *History of Mexico,* relating events surrounding the exploration and evangelization of Baja California up to the expulsion of the Jesuits in 1767. He opened the text with a natural history of the geology, flora, and fauna of the regions around the Sea of Cortez (Gulf of California). He also discussed the landscape of what would become New Mexico and Arizona Territory, devoting generous space to his Jesuit hero—the "Apostle of the Southwest," Father Eusebio Kino, who founded missions and contributed to the cartography of the Spanish borderlands in the eighteenth century. Clavijero strove to be more scientific in this volume, indicating Latin names as well as indigenous ones for the creatures inhabiting the area. He invoked the Swedish botanist Carolus Linnaeus, father of the modern system of classification by genus and species, to give a more scientific dimension to his text.[15] The book was also a more personal work, recalling Clavijero's youthful desire to serve in the Californian missions.[16]

On his death in Bologna in April 1787, Clavijero left behind several manuscripts, among them detailed descriptions of the mines, agricultural projects, and various towns and shrines in Mexico. Some of these documents may have constituted his working notes for an unrealized "Geographical and Ecclesiastical History of Mexico."[17] Honored as an American naturalist of the first rank by Europeans and Anglo-Americans, Francisco Javier Clavijero continued to live and speak through his history of Mexico. Even in death, he would be a guide to the western frontier.

Published in Italian in 1780–1781, *History of Mexico* was a book that every intellectual had to have in his or her library. The original text was written in Spanish but not published in that language until 1945, for as an exiled Spanish American Jesuit, Clavijero was unable to obtain permission for its publication in Spain from the Bourbon monarchy. The Italian translation, however, gave him a wider reading audience in Europe and beyond. In 1787 an English translation was prepared, and the book was also translated into German. American editions appeared in Richmond, Virginia, in 1806 and in Philadelphia, Pennsylvania, in 1817. With such a frequent and constant press run, Clavijero was familiar, in one language or another, to intellectuals on both sides of the Atlantic. In the United States, he would become a key authority for the first imagining, planning, and writing of westward expansion into the territories beyond the Ohio Valley contested by Britain, France, New Spain, and the United States.

At first, it may seem odd that a history of Mexico would serve as an authority for the American imagination's incipient forays into the West after the Revolution in 1783. It must be remembered, however, that no one in the eighteenth century really knew how far off Mexico or, for that matter, the South Sea (the Pacific Ocean) was. What lay to the west of the Ohio River and into the Louisiana and Arkansas Territories was largely unknown, and maps were either inaccurate or nonexistent. The West, in sum, was far beyond anything that one could conjure. Thus, Clavijero filled in the empty space with what seemed to be the most accurate description—a picture of alternating deserts and plains, of rich agricultural fields and high volcanoes, of unusual animals (including horned toads and jaguars) and the exotic descendants of the Aztec Empire. The vivid conception he presented seemed imaginable and therefore reachable.

In the earliest phase of U.S. history in the eighteenth century, the architects of the new republic dreamed of adventures to pursue and acquisitions to be gained in the West. For reasons related to geopolitics and nationalist pride, early American patriots such as Thomas Paine, Alexander Hamilton, and Thomas Jefferson fixed their eyes and imaginations on the borderlands shared with the Spanish Crown. Though the term had yet to be coined, the implications of "Manifest Destiny" were clear even in those early days.

Of the Anglo-Americans looking west at this time, the most scientific in his aspirations for the republic was Thomas Jefferson (1743–1826). In fact, he published a book in 1782, *Notes on the State of Virginia,* that attempted to describe the region with as much natural detail as Clavijero's *History of Mexico.* Though Jefferson had not read the Mexican's work before writing his *Notes,* it is fascinating to see the parallels between the two authors' texts. Jefferson organized his book in much the same way, beginning with a survey of the topography and geographic features of the land and moving into discussions of the mineral, vegetable, and animal resources. He then added commentary on the climate and the indigenous peoples. Jefferson even responded to European criticism of the Americas as degenerate, though in a less polemical voice than Clavijero had used. His response was less biting than the Jesuit's, but it still underscored the need for actual observation and accurate measurements in comparing the animals of the New and Old Worlds. Of Buffon's reliance on reports from outsiders to support his arguments of degeneracy, Jefferson gently but sardonically inquired: "But who were these travellers? . . . Was natural history the object of their travels? Did they measure or weigh the animals they speak of? Or did they not judge them by sight, or perhaps even from report only?"[18]

In the published edition of the *Notes,* Jefferson quoted from *Noticias americanas* (1772) by the Spanish officer Antonio de Ulloa, a book he prized for its geographic detail on South America.[19] However, in his personal copy of the British edition of the *Notes* (published by John Stockdale in 1787), he began inserting additional comments and annotations in the margins, citing other authorities as he came on them while assembling his book collection. Chief among them was Francisco Clavijero.[20]

While serving as ambassador to France in 1789, Jefferson was able to obtain several copies of the best works of natural history. He was especially eager to procure any books that mapped out in detail the lands to the west of the Ohio River, most importantly Mexico. After reading Clavijero's history in Italian, Jefferson was enthusiastic, even if he somehow mistakenly took the Mexican to be an Italian: "Clavigaro [*sic*], an Italian also, who has resided thirty-six years in Mexico, has given us a history of that country, which certainly merits more respect than any other work on the same subject."[21] Later, Jefferson added over ten references to Clavijero in the margins of his *Notes,* taking special interest in his physical descriptions of the land and quoting him on the origins of the *papa,* or potato.[22]

Despite his familiarity with Clavijero and others who wrote about Spanish lands in the New World, Jefferson remained ignorant of what actually lay to the west. In 1803 the purchase from France of the Louisiana Territory (at one time a territory of Spain) enabled him to actively plan research and mapping trips throughout the region. The most famous of these would be the Lewis and Clark Expedition of 1804–1806. However, Jefferson's hopes to know the West encompassed more than Louisiana, since he envisaged expeditions to the southwestern and northern areas in addition to the Lewis and Clark drive up the Missouri. He apparently wanted to learn as much as possible about the features of the western land and its inhabitants in the event of war with Spain.[23]

Jefferson's handpicked leader of the grand expedition to the West was Meriwether Lewis. The president supervised the explorer's education and sent him to Philadelphia to receive careful preparation in the natural sciences. In the early nineteenth century, Philadelphia was not only the largest city in the United States but also its chief scientific center. There, Benjamin Franklin had founded the American Philosophical Society (in which Jefferson served as third secretary), and the artist Charles Willson Peale opened a museum in 1794 to popularize science. The first novel and first textbook in the United States were published in Philadelphia, and the city had a flourishing book industry. Lewis's tutors included the best intellectuals of the age. Among these were Benjamin Smith Barton and Jedidiah Morse, both admirers of Francisco Clavijero.[24] Undoubtedly Lewis's reading list included the Jesuit's *History of Mexico.*

In his instructions to Lewis and Clark, Jefferson asked them to note carefully everything, including plants and animals, "especially those not known in the U.S."[25] Specimens were to be sent back to Philadelphia. One of the most intriguing creatures the explorers encountered was the horned toad, which was sent to the scientist Benjamin Barton.[26] Among the authorities Barton consulted was Clavijero, who had included an illustration of the animal in his history of Mexico.[27] The Mexican had described it as an "inoffensive animal, [which] seems to take pleasure in being handled."[28] Barton had the chance to find out for himself.

As the epic journey of Lewis and Clark captured the American imagination in a dramatic way, the hunger for more accurate knowledge mounted. Most of the western territories, however, remained isolated and alien—a mysterious otherworld that could not be entered because the Spaniards feared Anglo-American intentions. Once again, those who tried to imagine the Far West could only visit it in the literature of the time, most especially through the work of one man who relied heavily on Clavijero to write his own descriptions of Mexico and the Southwest and refine his predecessor's observations: Alexander von Humboldt (1769–1859).

In the first half of the nineteenth century, Humboldt was a bona fide celebrity scientist, the "Indiana Jones" of his generation. A German aristocrat, he obtained in 1798 permission from the Bourbon king of Spain, Charles IV, to explore Spanish America and to draw up maps and take notes for an up-to-date and careful natural history of the Western Hemisphere. Between 1799 and 1804, Humboldt made the grand tour of South America, culminating in a visit to New Spain, where he was made an honorary citizen of the realm by the viceroy.

Of the works produced from his experiences in the Americas, three were major sellers: *Political Essay on the Kingdom of New Spain* (first published in French in 1811, in English in 1822), *Aspects of Nature* (1808), and *Personal Narrative* (1834), which described his travels. In *Political Essay,* Humboldt organized his material according to the style of previous natural histories written in the late eighteenth century, but he seems to have followed Clavijero most closely. As one critic noted, he became familiar with the *History of Mexico,* "on whose authority he relied more than was customary at the time."[29] He augmented and refined Clavijero's data and in the footnotes frequently compared his findings with the Jesuit's.[30] Citing Clavijero's "judicious observations" on the nature and habits of the ancient peoples in Mexico, he repeated many of the priest's assertions.[31]

In regard to Humboldt's lengthy plotting and description of the various towns and geographic features in New Spain in the third volume of *Political Essay,* it is curious to note how closely his text followed that of several manuscript pages written by Clavijero (which may have been working notes for a geographic history that the Jesuit never finished). Compared to the duration of his stay in South America, Humboldt's visit to Mexico was brief, lasting less than a year. Shortly after his return to Europe in 1804, he traveled to Italy to see his brother and to consult manuscripts in Rome,

Bologna, Modena, and Milan.[32] Did he seek out Clavijero's notes and other unpublished information on Mexico to flesh out his hasty, incomplete observations of the landscape? Since Bologna was one of his key destinations, that conclusion seems very likely. In *Political Essay,* he paid tribute to Clavijero as the pathfinder of his own physical geography. Humboldt fulfilled the Jesuit's unrealized history.

With Humboldt's *Political Essay,* a work inspired by Clavijero's verbal map of Mexico, Anglo-American readers had the best source of information on the Southwest yet. After the establishment of an independent Mexico in 1821, the book provided accurate bearings for speculators on the border with the United States. Through the work of Humboldt, Clavijero continued to influence new writing on the West.

After the Texas Rebellion of 1835–1836, it became the fashion for journalists and literati to tour the newly opened wilderness of the former Mexico. That activity led to more writings on those lands. In the late 1830s the writer William H. Prescott (1796–1859) was hard at work on his own book about the Spanish conquest of Mexico. Prescott's guiding authors were Francisco Clavijero and, building on the Jesuit's geography and ethnography, Alexander von Humboldt. It was the American historian's goal to create an "epic in prose" and to inject blood, thunder, and glory into the tale of the Spanish defeat of the Mexica-Aztecas.[33] The result was one of the most popular books ever published in the United States, *History of the Conquest of Mexico* (1843).

From the start of his research, Prescott relied on Clavijero's list of sources in the *History of Mexico* to locate as many manuscripts on the conquest as possible. In a letter dated 1838, he urged his agent in Spain to search for certain documents named by the Jesuit author.[34] Though critical in his book of Clavijero's assertions on Mexican geography, he nevertheless considered the exile worthy of an immediate tribute: "I have conformed to the limits fixed by Clavigero. He has, probably, examined the subject with more thoroughness and fidelity than most of his countrymen."[35] Discussing his sources, Prescott indicated to the reader that Clavijero was a frequently cited authority in his text, and he added a lengthy paragraph of commentary on the life, struggles (especially as an exile), and literary achievement of the criollo:

> [On] the whole he seems to have conducted [his] discussion with good faith; and if he has been led by national zeal to overcharge the picture with brilliant colors, he will be found much more temperate, on this score, than those who preceded him, while he has applied some sound principles of criticism, of which they were incapable. In a word, the diligence of his researches has gathered into

> one focus the scattered lights of tradition and antiquarian lore, purified in a great measure from the mists of superstition which obscure the best productions of an earlier period.[36]

Prescott's book was a classic and read by a U.S. population eager to rid the continent of the supposed Mexican tyranny that in 1836 had led to the assault on the Alamo and the death of an American hero, Davy Crockett. When war came soon after the annexation of Texas by the United States in 1845, sales of *History of the Conquest of Mexico* increased. It became the Americans' primer on what to expect in the harsh world in the Southwest. As a friend of Prescott's wryly noted, "The *past* Conquest of Mexico [now] foretold the *future* one."[37]

Prescott was horrified at the thought that his book had stimulated hostility toward Mexico. But the years 1846–1848 were witness to a vicious war of Manifest Destiny—considered the fulfillment of the Anglo-American duty, as determined by Providence, to expand westward and to possess the whole continent. Volunteer and professional soldiers carried Prescott's book into battle and the occupation of Mexico. Historian Robert W. Johannsen pointed out that the volume "not only served to provide the Americans . . . with a sense of historical purpose but it also served in a more practical way as a guidebook to the sights along the route to the Mexican capital."[38]

It is an irony in the history of the literary West that a book largely based on a patriotic Mexican exile's celebration of his homeland would become the guiding text in the invasion and dismantling of his country. Clavijero's textual landscape, scientifically measured by Humboldt and dramatically retold by Prescott, now belonged in large part to the Americans, especially those in New Mexico and the Southwest. (Upper [Alta] California had passed to the United States, but there was popular sentiment for the annexation of Baja California and even the whole of Mexico as well.)

It is also ironic that when historian and statesman George Bancroft met Humboldt in France in 1848, he wrote ecstatically to President James Polk that the elder savant had given his "blessing" to American imperialism: "The amount of territory you demand, he deemed to be legitimately due to us. . . . His opinion is of value; for having been honoured with Mexican citizenship, the bias of his partialities is for Mexico."[39] A permanent American physical presence had moved in, propelled by the imagination that had once only dreamed of the Far West. Clavijero's literary successor could not deny this reality.

The second half of the nineteenth century, a time for assessing the territory gained in the Mexican War, was also a time of political and social consolidation. American historians now undertook the task of gathering texts and synthesizing them into an intelligible and consistent narrative for an English-speaking readership—just as Clavijero had done for his Spanish-speaking compatriots. A new monumental history of the West had to be written, incorporating all Spanish and other foreign-language documents and translating them (and thus "conquering" them as well) for the benefit of the Anglo-American heirs of Manifest Destiny.

In San Francisco the book dealer Hubert Howe Bancroft began collecting as many original manuscripts and rare books as he could find. His specialty was Spanish American historiography. Between 1886 and 1890, Bancroft and his staff produced thirty-nine volumes on the history of the American West, Mexico, and Central America.[40] His list of sources for each volume covers many pages, and his work remains a valuable guide to rare documents. He sold his collection to the University of California, Berkeley, in 1905; the school's Bancroft Library is still an important archive for research on the Hispanic West.[41]

In Bancroft's history Clavijero's name is easily lost in the immense bibliography, but the author did devote generous praise to the Jesuit as the best of the historians before the nineteenth century: Clavijero was, he noted, "perhaps the most clear-sighted writer on Mexico. . . . Indeed, no previous work in this field can at all compare with [his *History*] for comprehensiveness and correctness, depth of thought and clearness of expression."[42]

Other writers attempted their own syntheses of Hispanic chronicles of the New World with varying success, among them Justin Winsor, who produced the tedious *Aboriginal America* in 1889. Clavijero as a literary voice, however, was increasingly relegated to the footnotes of other authors' monumental (and increasingly hefty) histories. He had helped to found the literary West that had once stirred the imagination to seek and explore its spaces, but in the late nineteenth century, Clavijero was becoming more obscure as histories of the West became more turgid.

In 1937, Clavijero's *History of California* was translated for the first time into English and published by Stanford University Press. This book, which, as noted earlier, originally appeared in an Italian edition in 1789, had been largely ignored by the writers of California. Although Bancroft had admired the work and summarized it in his multivolume history, the release of the Jesuit's book in English reintroduced readers of the literary West to Clavijero and to his intimate portrait of the region as it was beginning to be explored and settled by the Spaniards. His creative voice was heard once again among the Anglo-American heirs of the West. Of those who responded to this voice with enthusiasm and a renewed sense of adventure, the novelist John Steinbeck (1902–1968) stands out.

In 1940, Steinbeck and a friend set out from Monterey on a sardine boat, the *Western Flyer,* to explore the Sea of Cortez and Baja California. Though Steinbeck stated that they had "no urge toward adventure," their voyage was indeed an adventure of discovery, one suggested to them (and guided) by a book—Clavijero's *History of California.*[43] In fact, the Jesuit occupied the pages of Steinbeck's *Log from the Sea of Cortez* from start to finish. Apparently the author was so impressed by the Jesuit's intimate prose that he did not realize that the exile had never been to California: "Clavigero, a Jesuit of the eighteenth century, had seen more than most and reported what he saw with more accuracy than most."[44] Clavijero's "sight" had enflamed the author's imagination; he could picture what Clavijero described so well in the text, and now he would see it for himself.

In the boat of the two twentieth-century explorers, Clavijero was affectionately dubbed "the old monk" by Steinbeck, and his book was deemed more vividly detailed and reliable than any map or coastal guide they could find: "[In] Clavigero . . . we found more visual warnings in his accounts of ships broken up and scattered, of wrecks and wayward currents; of fifty miles of sea more dreaded than any other."[45] Clavijero was their textual beacon, leading them safely past imagined perils. He helped the novelist see the way to the coast, and so, too, did he help Steinbeck show us the way as well—by first capturing our imagination as it tossed on the waves. In *Log from the Sea of Cortez,* Clavijero was the ultimate authority on all things California. Steinbeck cited the Mexican's fanciful conjectures on the origin of the word "California," and he returned to Clavijero several times, quoting him on the Seri Indians and on the names of islands off the coast.

The Jesuit exile continues to speak to us even today, his voice still disputing with and correcting those who have never visited his homeland. As we read the text, we cannot help but see John Steinbeck on his California fishing boat as he scribbles in his journal, a copy of Clavijero's history never out of reach. In the literary West of a later, more distant time, Steinbeck, like many authors before him, encountered a kindred spirit—another who made the landfall first in a book and then beckoned his readers to follow.

Notes

1. The Mexican's surname may be spelled "Clavijero" or "Clavigero." Most historians prefer the latter, as that is the way it is spelled on the title pages of his histories. However, Clavijero himself alternated spellings in his correspondence.

2. For the best study of Clavijero's childhood, see Charles E. Ronan, S. J., *Francisco Javier Clavigero, S. J. (1731–1787), Figure of the Mexican Enlightenment: His Life and Works* (Chicago: Loyola University Press, 1977).

3. Ibid., 63.

4. Anthony Pagden, *Spanish Imperialism and the Political Imagination* (New Haven: Yale University Press, 1990), 98.

5. Gilbert L. Lycan, *Alexander Hamilton and American Foreign Policy: A Design for Greatness* (Norman: University of Oklahoma Press, 1970), 30.

6. Francisco Javier Clavigero, *The History of Mexico,* trans. Charles Cullen (1787; reprint, New York: Garland Publishing, 1979), v.

7. See Antonello Gerbi, *The Dispute of the New World: The History of a Polemic, 1750–1900,* trans. Jeremy Moyle (Pittsburgh: University of Pittsburgh Press, 1973).

8. Buffon quoted in ibid., 5.

9. Buffon quoted in ibid., 6.

10. See Ronan, *Francisco Javier Clavigero,* 245–96, for an insightful discussion of the various "armchair critics" of the Americas to whom Clavijero responded.

11. Clavigero, *History of Mexico,* v.

12. Pagden, *Spanish Imperialism,* 99.

13. Clavigero, *History of Mexico,* 53.

14. Ibid., 12–13.

15. Francisco Javier Clavigero, *The History of [Lower] California,* trans. Sara E. Lake and A. A. Gray (Stanford: Stanford University Press, 1937), 66.

16. Ronan, *Francisco Javier Clavigero,* 32.

17. Copies of these manuscripts can be found in Mariano Cuevas, S. J., ed., *Tesoros documentales de Mexico, siglo XVIII—Priego, Zelis, Clavigero* (Mexico City: Editorial Galatea, 1944). However, Cuevas did not accurately transcribe the Clavijero manuscripts. For example, he rearranged the "Apuntes geográficos," or "Geographical Notes," but failed to note Clavijero's alternate use of Spanish and Italian, thus possibly concealing clues to these pages' true identity. They could be the outline of the exiled Jesuit's unrealized or "lost" history of the landscape of Mexico.

18. Thomas Jefferson, *Notes on the State of Virginia,* ed. William Peden (Chapel Hill: University of North Carolina Press, 1982), 54.

19. Ibid., 264.

20. Ibid., 265.

21. Thomas Jefferson, *Writings* (New York: Library Classics, 1984), 948.

22. Jefferson, *Notes,* 267–68.

23. Anthony F. Wallace, *Jefferson and the Indians* (Cambridge, MA: Harvard University Press, 1999), 243–45.

24. Russell F. Weigley, *Philadelphia: A 300 Year History* (New York: W. W. Norton, 1982), 241–42; Ronan, *Francisco Javier Clavigero,* 146.

25. Raymond Darwin Burroughs, ed., *The Natural History of the Lewis and Clark Expedition* (East Lansing: Michigan State University Press, 1995), 292–93.

26. Donald Jackson, ed., *Letters of the Lewis and Clark Expedition with Related Documents, 1783–1984* (Urbana: University of Illinois Press, 1962), 276.

27. Clavigero, *History of Mexico,* opposite p. 66.

28. Ibid., 58.

29. L. Kellner, *Alexander von Humboldt* (London: Oxford University Press, 1963), 99.

30. José Miranda, *Humboldt y México* (Mexico City: UNAM, 1962), 123, 153.

31. Alexander de Humboldt, *Political Essay of the Kingdom of New Spain,* 2 vols., trans. John Black (London: Longman, Hurst, Rees, Orme, and Brown, 1822), 1:91, 2:301.

32. Karl Bruhns, ed., *Life of Alexander von Humboldt,* vol. 1 (London: Longmans and Green, 1873), 352–53.

33. Donald G. Darnell, *William Hickling Prescott* (Boston: Twayne Publishing, 1975), 73.

34. Roger D. Wolcott, *The Correspondence of William Hickling Prescott, 1833–1847* (Boston: Houghton Mifflin, 1925), 29–30.

35. William H. Prescott, *History of the Conquest of Mexico* (New York: Modern Library, 1998), 14.

36. Ibid., 46–47.

37. Robert W. Johannsen, *To the Halls of the Montezumas: The Mexican War in the American Imagination* (New York: Oxford University Press, 1985), 245.

38. Ibid., 150.

39. Halina Nelken, ed., *Humboldtiana at Harvard* (Cambridge, MA: Widener Library, Harvard University, 1976), 68.

40. David J. Weber, ed., *New Spain's Far Northern Frontier: Essays on the American West, 1540–1821* (Albuquerque: University of New Mexico Press, 1979), XI.

41. Ibid., XII.

42. Hubert Howe Bancroft, *Works,* vol. 9 (San Francisco: A. L. Bancroft, 1883), 700.

43. John Steinbeck, *The Log from the Sea of Cortez* (New York: Viking Press, 1951), 6.

44. Ibid., 5.

45. Ibid., 6.

Suggested Readings

Ambrose, Stephen E. *Undaunted Courage: Meriwether Lewis, Thomas Jefferson, and the Opening of the American West.* New York: Simon and Schuster, 1996.

Gerbi, Antonello. *The Dispute of the New World: The History of a Polemic, 1750–1900.* Trans. Jeremy Moyle. Pittsburgh: University of Pittsburgh Press, 1973.

Johannsen, Robert W. *To the Halls of the Montezumas: The Mexican War in the American Imagination.* New York: Oxford University Press, 1985.

Kellner, L. *Alexander von Humboldt.* London: Oxford University Press, 1963.

Leckie, Robert. *From Sea to Shining Sea: From the War of 1812 to the Mexican War—The Saga of America's Expansion.* New York: Harper, 1993.

Lynch, John. *The Spanish American Revolutions, 1808–1826.* 2d ed. New York: W. W. Norton, 1986.

Pagden, Anthony. *Spanish Imperialism and the Political Imagination.* New Haven: Yale University Press, 1990.

Ronan, Charles E., S. J. *Francisco Javier Clavigero, S. J. (1731–1787), Figure of the Mexican Enlightenment: His Life and Works.* Chicago: Loyola University Press, 1977.

2

Eliza Hart Spalding
The Missionary Legacy of a Forgotten Feminist

Laurie Winn Carlson

Eliza Hart Spalding (1807–1851) was one of the first white women to cross the Rockies and settle in Oregon country. Part of the wave of missionary pioneers on the Overland Trail who were intent on "improving" the lot of Native Americans, she, along with Narcissa Whitman, opened up a new part of the West for women. Her travails demonstrated her strong sense of independence, her stamina, and her foresight—unusual qualities in a white woman in antebellum Euramerican society.

Finding her calling as a young adult, Eliza Hart married Henry Spalding, and in the 1830s, the couple traveled west as missionaries. They eventually settled among the Nez Perce Indians in what is now Idaho, and Hart began teaching the Native Americans, adults and children alike, everything from reading to domestic manufacturing. Filled with toil, her life was hardly romantic, but through her work in the family, classroom, and church, she left an indelible mark on both the Nez Perce and the Oregon frontier as she attempted, with the best of intentions, to supplant Indian tradition and religion with Euramerican culture.

In the essay that follows, we see that "frontiering" can at times be liberating for women. Eliza Spalding's story demonstrates how social, economic, and political power can evolve as boundaries of work, culture, and religion shift. The essay also reminds us that gender and race can reinforce oppression for people on one side of the cultural divide even as they intersect to offer opportunity for those on the other.

Laurie Winn Carlson has written fourteen books, including *On Sidesaddles to Heaven: The Women of the Rocky Mountain Mission* (1998), which examines the lives of Narcissa Whitman, Eliza Spalding, and four other New England women who went to the West in the 1830s. She occasionally teaches courses at Eastern Washington University in Cheney, Washington.

In 1836 two New England women—Eliza Spalding and Narcissa Whitman—made a trip that warrants a mention in every history book written about the American West. Their appearance on the frontier has been given monumental significance over the ensuing years, and their encounters with the fur trappers and Native Americans are seen as a turning point in western history. Indeed, Narcissa Whitman has become an icon of western mythology because of her death at the hands of Indian dissidents. It is unfortunate, however, that the tragic event has obscured Whitman's real accomplishments—and largely eclipsed the story of her counterpart, Eliza Hart Spalding.[1] It is also regrettable that in describing these two women, historians have often framed their depictions in a sexist manner, noting, for example, Narcissa's appealing hair and plump figure and describing Eliza Spalding, if she is described at all, as simply "tall and thin" (in Alvin Josephy's words) or "guilt-ridden" (to quote Bernard DeVoto). As historian Deborah Lynn Dawson observed, "Most of the works dealing with Pacific Northwest history are very clear about how Eliza Spalding and Narcissa Whitman looked and what they were to the men around them, but rarely do these works explore what exactly these women, particularly Eliza, actually *did*."[2]

Eliza Hart Spalding was born in 1807 in Berlin, Connecticut, and grew up in newly established Holland Patent, New York. Girls raised in that era benefited from improved educational opportunities, and they typically held higher aspirations than their mothers had at a similar age. The religious movement that grew into the Second Great Awakening was also sweeping across New York State at the time. These two movements—educational and evangelical—would later extend out of rural New York to the rest of the country, but as Eliza was maturing, she was in the center of both currents. School and church would crystallize the dreams and ambitions of many young women; Eliza's cohort was the first in the Protestant women's missionary field that can be described as North America's original feminist movement.[3]

Female academies sprang up in New York State, fueled by the desire to spread education to young women. Girls attended lectures and heard discussions of new ideas and world travels. However, this education would not help them move up the economic or social scale, for the prescriptive "cult of true womanhood" in the nineteenth century conceived of women as paragons of virtue, suited only for domesticity. Yet women did find ways to create and expand a "sphere" for themselves. They sought self-fulfillment through their domestic and religious roles, arguing that the disorderly public world needed nurturing and civilizing.[4]

The missionary movement, particularly during the Second Great Awakening of the early nineteenth century, glittered with opportunity for women. The idea that they could, through religion, change U.S. society and even the world was gripping. Women were learning about the outside world, and they wanted to be involved. The global effort to civilize the

No images or photos exist of Eliza Hart Spalding, but from descriptions of those who knew her, this portrait of her youngest child, Amelia Lorene Spalding Brown (b. December 12, 1846, Lapwai, Idaho; d. November 25, 1889, Brownsville, Oregon), looks much like her. From Eliza Spalding Warren, *Memoirs of the West* (Portland, OR: Marsh Printing Company, 1917), 145. WSU Libraries, neg. 92-168. *Courtesy of Manuscripts, Archives, and Special Collections, Washington State University Libraries, Pullman, Washington*

"dark" countries held exciting appeal and offered an opportunity to boost their self-confidence and esteem. Theirs was the age of expansion and settlement, and even housewives in tiny New England villages wanted to take part. Women enthusiastically supported mission efforts in the cities—called home missions—and around the globe. They donated cash, jewelry, and spare time, and missionary societies flourished. Eliza wrote in her diary, "When I reflect upon the wretched condition of those benighted souls who are sitting in the gloom and shadow of death, I actually long to depart and be with them, to tell them the story of a Saviour's dying love."[5]

In the 1830s the ethnocentric mission movement was focused on improving the lot of women and children around the world. Letters and diaries written by female missionaries never mentioned a domestic sphere or role that limited women; they seemed more interested in making changes in society than reinforcing the status quo as it affected women and children. That meant wiping out cultural practices they viewed as harmful: polygamy, slavery, animism, and nomadism. For women to raise children properly, they needed food and shelter; therefore, settling tribal peoples into houses and farming was considered imperative. Practices such as binding the feet of little girls in China and burning widows on their husbands' funeral pyres in India were cited as examples of non-Christian practices that had to be eliminated if women were to assume their rightful place in the world. When reports arrived in the East about the Pacific Northwest Indians who bound their infants' heads to boards in order to "flatten" them, the missionary zeal was ignited. However, trying to "save" the Indians was never a popular idea among Americans at large. Missionaries who had fought efforts by the state of Georgia, backed by President Andrew Jackson, to evict Native Americans from their property and send them west beyond the Mississippi River met with frustration; individuals who tried to prevent this relocation were jailed.

Living only ten miles from Utica, New York—a city open to new sociopolitical currents—Eliza Hart was aware of all these events. After graduation from a female academy, she took up teaching, and in August 1826, at the age of eighteen, she joined the Presbyterian Church on her own (her family was not particularly religious). During the same summer, Charles Finney, a famous evangelist, appeared in her town; no writings indicate he was the reason for her baptism, but it is likely his appearance had an effect. Finney's sermons were full of hellfire yet dignified, with more intellectual appeal than charisma—characteristics that could be applied to Eliza as well. She wanted to become a missionary, but that was impossible for an unmarried woman. By marrying a minister who obtained a mission

Eliza Hart Spalding's travel diary, written in 1836. *Courtesy of Northwest and Whitman College Archives, Penrose Memorial Library, Whitman College, Walla Walla, Washington* assignment, however, a woman could be officially designated "assistant missionary" by the American Board of Commissioners for Foreign Missions (ABCFM), which represented a combined Congregational and Presbyterian effort. Marriage, therefore, was more than a joining of two lives: it was also a way to forge a career.

In 1830, Eliza was a twenty-three-year-old schoolteacher when a female friend put her in touch with Henry Spalding, a twenty-seven-year-old university student who was looking for a "pious young lady" with whom to correspond. That contact marked the beginning of a friendship that blossomed into love and eventually marriage between two like-minded souls. Eliza's family evidently approved of the match so completely that they allowed their daughter to go to Cincinnati, Ohio, with Henry while he finished his last year of school at Lane Seminary. Once in Ohio the couple decided to marry in a small ceremony, embarking on life as student newlyweds. Eliza cleaned and cooked for boarders and tutored a few pupils on the side, and Henry worked for a printer and did odd jobs. Eliza was allowed to study alongside Henry because of her marital status, and she attended Lyman Beecher's lectures on Saturdays. Beecher and Calvin Stowe were on the faculty at Lane. Henry's classmates included Charles and Henry Ward Beecher, two of Lyman's sons.[6] Eliza certainly would have met them and their sisters—Harriet, who would author *Uncle Tom's Cabin,* and Catharine, a leader in women's education. In the two years the young couple lived in Cincinnati, Eliza studied Greek and Hebrew and belonged to a prayer group, a sewing club, and a female missionary society.

When Henry received his theological degree, they immediately applied to the ABCFM for a position. Although Henry's professor Artemis Bullard wrote only a lukewarm letter on his behalf, he recommended Eliza as "very highly respected and beloved by a large circle of friends on Walnut Hills in Cincinnati. She is one of the best women for a missionary's wife with whom I am acquainted."[7] Later, in the mission field, William Gray would also write about Eliza, calling her "a first-rate woman," with no "starch" in her. She had "good common sense," did not put on "any frills," and would "do first-rate to teach the Indians."[8]

The course of Eliza's life undoubtedly was influenced by Henry Spalding's personal history. An illegitimate child, he evidently was reared in a foster home. In 1825, after being baptized into the Presbyterian Church, he enrolled at Franklin Academy and began to put himself through school at the age of twenty-two. Despite his lack of education, ambivalent class background, poverty, and painful shyness, he applied himself. Hoping to become a foreign missionary, he enrolled as a ministerial student (which qualified him for free tuition). Now all he needed was a wife, for the ABCFM required missionaries to be married before going into the field; organization leaders believed that Christian marriage was a vital model for the "heathen," and they were also eager to enlist married women as teachers.[9] Henry therefore proposed to Narcissa Prentiss, a young woman in his hometown who wanted to go into the mission field, but she refused him. He later proposed to another young church member. She accepted, but after being stricken with tuberculosis, she encouraged Henry to find a wife who could help him with his vocation. That was when he put out the word that he wanted to correspond with a "pious young woman" and began writing to Eliza.

Eliza was confident in herself as a woman and as a missionary, and her choice of a spouse was a well-considered decision. Henry's poverty and illegitimacy were outweighed by his willingness to work hard for his goals and his devotion to evangelical work. Both traits suited Eliza just fine. Among the many couples who married in order to enter the mission field at this time, the Spaldings appear to be one of the very few who genuinely cared for each other and for whom marriage was more than a way to promote personal agendas. When Henry's assignment letter arrived from the ABCFM, they were elated. They would be going to the Osage Mission in present-day Missouri. But there was one minor problem: it was August 1835, and Eliza was about to have a baby and could not travel with childbirth pending. Hence, they declined the long-sought post.

Twenty-eight-year-old Eliza had a difficult delivery, and the baby died at birth. Eliza was bedridden for weeks with a sickness that "was protracted & severe"; in fact, illness would continue to haunt her during several pregnancies and miscarriages in the years to come.[10] Like other Christians of their era the Spaldings believed the Lord had taken their child as punishment for human failing or sin, so they renewed their vow to obtain another mission appointment. One did come through, and by late winter 1835, they were at last headed west to the Osage Mission.

As they traveled to their Osage appointment, another hopeful missionary heard of their plans and stopped them along the way. Marcus Whitman, an unmarried country doctor, had just returned from a trip exploring the Rocky Mountains and was eager to return to the West as part of a mission. He asked the Spaldings if they would go to the Rocky Mountains with him instead. The Nez Perce Indians, living west of the Rockies, were even more desperate for Christian teachers than the Osage, Whitman emphasized, and the Osage already had a mission, but the Nez Perce did not.

The decision was not an easy one. Henry and Eliza soon discovered that Whitman's wife-to-be, who agreed to marry him if he obtained a mission appointment, was none other than Narcissa Prentiss, the woman whom Henry had proposed to years before. How this affected the Spaldings is not clear from their writings, but Henry left the decision up to his wife. Eliza secluded herself in a room at the inn they were staying at to pray for guidance. They had but "a short time to decide the question, whether to change . . . course or not," Eliza realized. She soon reappeared, announcing to the two men, "I have made up my mind to go." To Eliza "[Christian] duty seemed to require it," and she seemed determined to be optimistic about what was to come. "We are now with joyful hearts looking for our place of destination west of the Rocky Mountains," she told herself.[11]

The Spaldings also met with George Catlin, an artist who had just returned from painting the West, especially Native Americans. He was adamantly against Eliza going westward, warning that the journey would be too physically difficult and that "the enthusiastic desire to see a white woman everywhere prevailing among the distant tribes, may terminate in unrestrained passion consequently in her ruin and the ruin of the establishment." Undaunted, Eliza replied that she "would trust in God and go forward without fear."[12]

The Spaldings, Whitmans, and William Gray, a handyman hired to work for the mission, departed together from Saint Louis, first taking a steamboat up the Missouri River and then beginning the overland trek on horseback. For Eliza and Narcissa, that meant riding sidesaddle, a liberating innovation for female travelers in the 1830s. The leaping horn had been added to the sidesaddle just a few years before by a French riding master, enabling women riders to press against the leather-covered hook with their left knee and right thigh in order to maintain their position in the saddle. In earlier days, a woman would slide forward or back off a horse when it went up or down steep trails, but with the advent of the leaping horn, female riders could keep up with men. In fact, Eliza and Narcissa usually rode ahead of their husbands on the trail, as the men hung behind to push along a little herd of dairy cattle and extra horses.

Eliza was sick at first, probably from drinking muddy water or eating too much fresh red meat. Within a short time, though, she wrote in her diary that "camping out at night has not been so disagreeable and uncomfortable as I anticipated. Traveling on horseback has appeared to benefit my health."[13] As they rode across the plains, Eliza noted that they met with few Indians, and she reasoned that "the natives who once roamed over these vast and delightful plains are fast fading away, as is the Buffalo and the other game which once in vast herds ranged throughout this country."[14] Her words—which echoed other women travelers' observations—reveal how desperate she thought the plight of the Indians was in advance of American settlement. The 1830s was a period of intense pressure for land, and Indian removal to territory farther west was a national policy—one she no doubt had read about in missionary tracts. Her words were shaped by that context. On her way west, Eliza actually saw few Indians until meeting the tribes gathered at a fur trade rendezvous.[15]

Eliza and Narcissa's experience was markedly different from that of the women who followed what became the Oregon Trail. They had very little responsibility on the trek, having no children or wagonloads of goods to contend with en route. The men did nearly all the labor, took care of the animals, and did much of the cooking.[16] Apparently, sex typing in the assignment of tasks did not occur in this group. The women spent spare moments mending, doing laundry, taking care of personal grooming, and writing in their travel journals or, in Eliza's case, trying to make a language dictionary to use with the Nez Perce. However, the going was not easy. While passing along the Snake River country in what is now southern Idaho, for example, Eliza's horse tripped on a hornet's nest, jumped aside, and threw her from the saddle. Her booted foot "remained a moment in the stirrup," and her "body was dragged some distance" until the frightened horse could be stopped. She "received no serious injury," but after being dragged over rough sand, lava rocks, and sagebrush, she was lucky to be alive.[17] After Whitman's medical ministrations, she was even more fortunate. Heroic medicine of the day meant using the lancet to bleed a patient until the body's inner balance could be "equalized." Whitman stopped long enough to bleed her extensively before they got back in the saddle and moved on. In a matter-of-fact tone, Eliza wrote about the incident the next day: "[I] suffered but little inconvenience in riding today in consequence of being thrown from my horse yesterday." Although there really was no way to turn back now, she vowed she would continue on "this adventurous journey."[18]

The Whitmans settled among the Cayuse people along the Walla Walla River at Waiilatpu (now Walla Walla, Washington). The Spaldings went about 120 miles northeast, to the Nez Perce homeland, settling along the Clearwater River in what is now Idaho. The location was known as Lapwai, "place of the butterflies." Eliza wrote in her diary, "Yesterday reached this desirable spot, where we expect to dwell the remainder of our earthly pilgrimage."[19] They lived in an Indian lodge while the Nez Perce eagerly assisted them with establishing and building their station. Eliza noted that "[the Indians] appear to be delighted with the idea of having us locate in their country, that they may be taught about God and the habits of civilized life."[20]

Eliza launched her plans for educating the Indians as quickly as possible. She confidently believed they were "perishing for the lack of knowledge" but felt they showed an "increasing interest in instruction." She prepared some watercolor paintings to illustrate events in Scriptures and began communicating visually. She had made up her own simple dictionary in Nez Perce and was determined to learn the language as quickly as possible. Her focus was on the children, who were interested in learning to read; "several are beginning to read in the Testament" she noted after three months. "We hope to come into circumstances soon to do more to benefit the children, for they are our hope of the nation," she wrote after six months at Lapwai.[21]

To teach the children, Eliza printed small pages by hand, then stitched them together with needle and thread. She taught Nez Perce to do the same and soon had small booklets to use in the classroom. She relied on rote memorization in her classes, but was an innovator in other respects. Cutting-edge teachers in that era were leaving behind the old ways based on pure drill and were focusing on the hands-on learning promoted by Johann Pestalozzi, a Swiss educational reformer. According to his method, learning was to be concrete first and abstract second. Students were grouped by abilities and taught at their development levels. Eliza's classroom was influenced heavily by Pestalozzi; she taught weaving, knitting, and baking, along with singing, arts and crafts, and reading. Henry described one of Eliza's classes as composed of "eleven adults, chiefs and principally men."[22] She divided up the duties in the classroom (she reportedly had as many as two hundred students at a time), giving headmen and leaders the task of teaching smaller groups. Eliza would teach a few students some verses, then they proceeded to teach others, and the entire group recited in unison.

Henry claimed that the Nez Perce were intensely involved in learning to read in their own language: "They come early in the morning and without waiting to be called into school, commence teaching one another, and often continue until after dark."[23] Eliza enlisted one of the chiefs to open the school and conduct the lessons while she was "taken up very much in printing" the little books.[24] She made pencil marks on paper for students to trace until they were proficient enough to copy pages of text for the booklets. Nine students made up a knitting class; three were spinning and weaving twenty-four yards of woolen cloth to make clothing.

Eliza's efforts to teach the Indian women domestic manufacturing skills such as knitting and baking might seem unimportant to us today, but in the early nineteenth century, mastering these skills was a means to increased economic power and outside income for women. By teaching girls and women to spin and weave as well as read, Eliza was preparing them to participate in the economy of rural America.

As the Nez Perce women became more acculturated, many of the young men in the tribe found they had no place in the new Americanized mission society. On the one hand the Indian women could have their grain ground into flour at the stone mill Henry Spalding built, they could obtain sheep to raise for woolen cloth, and they could trade moccasins and other handmade items to the Americans. On the other hand, although some Indian men were successful in raising cattle to trade with immigrants who later arrived on the Oregon Trail, many of the young men of the tribe were left out of the new female-driven economy. Henry Spalding lamented the young men of the tribe who refused to work and gambled incessantly. He seemed to give up on efforts to do anything with them, turning instead to the older men, whom he called the "principal" men, while Eliza worked with the women and children.[25] The angry young men retaliated, tearing down the mill dams, destroying fences, and killing the milk cows. Their actions were difficult to interpret. Did they want a place at the missionaries' "table"? Or did they simply want to return to the old ways, which meant the declining fur trade economy? Perhaps their actions stemmed from intratribal rivalry and conflict. Whatever the cause, the Spaldings seemed unperturbed by these events and felt they had substantial support from the Nez Perce community to remain at the mission.

Working by candlelight at night and in the classroom by day, in addition to fulfilling the ordinary duties of packing water and cooking in a fireplace, Eliza was a busy woman. After her daughter was born in November 1837, she wrote simply in her diary: "Through the astonishing mercy of God, I am now enjoying comfortable health. On the 15th day of last month I was made the joyful mother of a daughter."[26] She and Henry named the baby Eliza, and the pleased Nez Perce gave the tiny infant a pony, which the girl would ride for years.

Narcissa and Eliza both had infant daughters. Both also tried to replicate the maternal associations that existed back home. These groups were extremely popular at the time because they enabled women to participate in social, cultural, and political activities in an organized effort that valued their religious and domestic roles. Living quite a distance apart in far-off Oregon country, the two mothers decided to establish a chapter of their own and agreed to silently pray for their children each morning at the same time. This simple act was an almost metaphysical effort to bridge the miles between them. In 1838, when four other female missionaries arrived with their husbands, the women founded the Columbia Maternal Association, and Eliza was elected as president. The women wrote letters and articles and sent them round-robin fashion between the mission stations—four were eventually built—and corresponded with other maternal associations in New York, the Sandwich Islands (Hawai`i), south Africa, and Asia. Through such means, Eliza and the other female missionaries felt a bond with women around the world. The groups met on the second and fourth Wednesday of every month, and women who could not attend the meetings found time to meditate a few minutes, knowing that they were joined by thousands of other women across the globe. Thus, there was a vast network of women who gained strength from one another, although their bonds were largely unnoticed by the men.

Eliza's efforts at teaching the Nez Perce to read paid off, and clearly the Spaldings' mission was a success compared to the Whitmans' progress among the Cayuse at their mission at Waiilatpu. As Marcus Whitman wrote to the mission board in 1843, the Whitman school was less successful than that at Lapwai, "where Mrs. Spalding has taught a considerable number of people & children to read & write in their own language."[27] The training in household skills that Eliza offered had been a way to introduce Indian women to Christian domestic life and move them away from their traditional practices, and she had "succeeded very well in teaching several girls to spin & weave knit & sew some." She had them making patchwork quilts and knit leggings, too. Using natural dyes, they colored yarn black, yellow, red, and white. Once the fabric was woven, the girls were also helped to make dresses to replace their hide clothing; Eliza thought the new dresses were "much more comfortable and respectable."[28]

Unlike the Whitmans and the Methodist missionaries in the Willamette Valley, the Spaldings did not encourage Americans to emigrate to their area. In fact, one of their greatest fears was that a wave of white immigration would occur and alter the lives of the Indians in destructive ways. Yet they knew migration was inevitable, and so they tried to teach the Indians to acculturate as quickly as possible, believing that would strengthen them in the face of the white migration. "If the missionary does not help the Indian, no one will," Henry Spalding wrote to the mission board.[29] The Spaldings' attitudes were more similar to those of the Jesuit missionaries who arrived in the Pacific Northwest shortly after them, seeking to create self-sufficient Catholic Indian enclaves at their missions.

At times the Spaldings' efforts to teach literacy and agriculture seemed to overtake any efforts to teach Christianity. Because the Nez Perce learned domestic and agricultural skills so quickly, along with reading, other missionaries in the Oregon Mission project became jealous, even to the point of writing to the mission board to demand that the Spaldings be recalled. They complained that Eliza and Henry were moving too quickly and had allowed too many Indians to join the church. As far as the other missionaries were concerned, *no* Indians were actually ready for church membership.

The Nez Perce had respect and admiration for Eliza. When a man insulted her, the tribe favored hanging him, but she suggested he be allowed to live so he could repent his sin and improve in the future. Eliza was tolerant of Indian cultural ways, and she actually liked the Nez Perce. She bore four children at Lapwai and always allowed the Indians to visit and even tend her children. The Spalding children spoke the Nez Perce language from early ages and were totally bilingual. Eliza also never lost patience with the Indians. In a letter to her parents, she wrote that the Nez Perce "[are so] determined to take [infant Eliza] into their own arms, that they sometimes almost rend her from mine, and frequently when I am busy about my work, take her from the cradle and not infrequently I have the mortification to pick a flea or a louse from her clothes . . . these are little things and I will say no more about them." Within months of arriving at Lapwai, Eliza had taken in eight Indian children, not as household help but "into their family" as foster children. Indeed, the Indians were so enamored of her character that Chief Timothy was reported to have blessed his meals with the words "In the name of Jesus Christ and Mrs. Spalding."[30] As Eliza's biographer, Deborah Dawson, noted, "The Nez Perces had a respect for her that they had for few other whites. And it was this mutual affection that would help Eliza in bridging the immense gap between her culture and theirs."[31]

The winter of 1846 was harsh. Both Indians and whites lost livestock, food was difficult to find, and sickness and hunger prevailed. Given the strains of these conditions, past dissensions were magnified, and some angry Nez Perce accused the Spaldings of being insincere because they had taught the Indians to read not in English but in Nez Perce. The critics contended that if they had really wanted to help the Indians, they would have instructed them in English, since that language would have enabled people to secure a livelihood and appreciate the teachings of Christianity. Ironically the Indians' acculturation led to their hostility toward the Spaldings. They now felt they had been held back by not being proficient in English, and for this, they blamed the Spaldings—or at least they found the Spaldings an easy target for other animosities. Morale was low on both sides. Vandalism of mission property and discord were prevalent.

Soon after the Spaldings' eight-year-old daughter Eliza arrived at Waiilatpu to attend the Whitmans' school in November 1847, a Cayuse faction murdered the Whitmans and several other emigrants and took the remaining mission residents hostage. The measles epidemic that raged at the time is considered the final straw that led to the Cayuse attack on the mission at Waiilatpu. At Lapwai, Eliza was alerted to the danger and found shelter with Nez Perce friends, who protected her and her other three children as an angry mob looted and destroyed the mission home and grounds. Henry would arrive later, returning from a trek to Waiilatpu on foot, all the while fearing for his own life and worrying about the fate of his daughter.

The Hudson's Bay Company at Fort Vancouver negotiated the ransom of the captives for $400 worth of goods, and the remaining missionary families were ordered removed to lower Oregon. The Spaldings were reunited with their daughter, who was "too weak to stand, a mere skeleton, and her mind much impaired as her health," according to her father.[32]

The displaced Spalding family boarded around, staying with various settlers and at one point living in a tent before finally moving into a house with no windows or doors. Eliza's health declined quickly. Soon, she was too weak with tuberculosis to even stand in a classroom. As she wrote to Mary Walker, one of the mission wives, "I have lost my home, my employment, and my people . . . while in that field of labor I felt contented and happy."[33] To another friend, she wrote, "We have not felt that interest in any undertaking here which we used to feel while laboring for the Indians. Our hearts seem constantly inclined to return to the Indians."[34]

Less than three years later the California gold rush hit Oregon, and when the wealth began coming home, the atmosphere changed. Sudden wealth resulted in extravagance and ostentation, which Eliza could not accept. The mission and her hometown in New York had been worlds of frugality, where intellectual and spiritual life were considered more important than entertainment. The new "extravagance in dress," she said, was "disgusting," and the women who now settled in Oregon were not like those she had befriended in New York schools, in Cincinnati colleges, or in the mission field. She told her sister that her new neighbors were "western" and that, although they were kind and friendly, she had nothing in common with them. "It makes me feel very lonely to live amongst people & feel that I have no society," she wrote.[35] Life seemed to have lost its meaning. Not long thereafter, in 1851, Eliza Hart Spalding died quietly at the age of forty-three, leaving four children under twelve. In 1913 her remains were moved to Spalding, Idaho, and buried next to her husband a short distance from their mission home.

The work that she and Henry pursued as missionaries in Oregon country must be viewed in context. Although the Spaldings' impact on the Nez Perce was imperfect, they were not evil people. Their efforts were intended only to mediate between forces they could not control. They were part of a culture that they knew bore ill for the Indians, but they could not overcome or subvert those power relations. As Deborah Dawson put it, "Far more devastating to Indian culture would have been a history without the missionaries to prepare them for the onslaught of white immigration and settlement."[36] Literacy, Christianity, agriculture—all were adopted by most Nez Perce, and perhaps that accommodationist strategy explains why their tribe remained above the fray in white-Indian relations in the West. They did not go to war with non-Indians in the 1850s when the rest of the plateau region was rife with bloodshed; nor did they did fight in the 1870s. Instead, they held on to their homeland along the Clearwater River, and, by and large, they have survived with their dignity intact.

Unfortunately the dignity of the missionaries, particularly Eliza Spalding, is still little appreciated, for a female missionary who concentrated on teaching women goes largely unnoticed in a culture that prizes aggression, violence, and domination in its historical narrative. Certainly, Eliza Spalding did not cut as wide a swath through western history as other dominant (and mostly male) figures. Her efforts primarily impacted Nez Perce women, whose experiences were neither written down nor saved in other ways. Several years after the Spaldings had left Lapwai, Oregon Trail emigrants in the Blue Mountains were surprised to meet a Nez Perce woman who tried to trade them items she had *knitted*—the result of Eliza's efforts to teach the commercial skills of the era.[37] More than a century later, in 1988, Dawson interviewed a Nez Perce woman named Mylie Lawyer who said that her people continue to sing many of the hymns Eliza had taught their forebears some 150 years before.

Eliza Spalding's contribution to the Oregon Mission, the Nez Perce people, and her own society was an unceasing attempt to break down the barriers between the races and to bring two different cultures closer together. An intelligent woman, she wanted to be useful to society, and in the early nineteenth century, that meant working through family, classroom, and church. In her own way, she challenged the boundaries of the domestic ideal of "true womanhood."

Notes

1. In November 1847 a group of Cayuse dissidents and ex–fur trappers killed the Whitmans and several other Americans in what has become known as the Whitman Massacre; the incident resulted in the curtailment of the mission effort and led to the Plateau Indian wars of the 1850s. See Laurie Winn Carlson, *On Sidesaddles to Heaven: The Women of the Rocky Mountain Mission* (Caldwell, ID: Caxton Press, 1998), 219–41. For a description of the trial of five Cayuse men for the murders, held in Oregon City in 1850, see Ronald B. Lansing, *Juggernaut: The Whitman Massacre Trial, 1850* (Portland, OR: Ninth Judicial Circuit Historical Society, 1993).

2. Deborah Lynn Dawson, "Laboring in My Savior's Vineyard: The Mission of Eliza Hart Spalding" (Ph.D. diss., Bowling Green State University, 1988), 2.

3. R. Pierce Beaver, *American Protestant Women in World Mission: History of the First Feminist Movement in North America* (Grand Rapids, MI: William R. Eerdmans, 1980).

4. Catharine Beecher's efforts to open education as a field for women teachers was just beginning; Eliza would have known Catharine in Cincinnati, where the Beecher family was involved in the ministry and education. See Kathryn Kish Sklar, "Catharine Beecher: Transforming the Teaching Profession," in *Women's America: Refocusing the Past,* ed. Linda K. Kerber and Jane DeHart Mathews (New York: Oxford University Press, 1982), 140–48.

5. Eliza H. Spaulding quoted in Clifford Merrill Drury, *Henry Harmon Spalding* (Caldwell, ID: Caxton Printers, 1936), 59.

6. Lyman Beecher was "probably the most celebrated minister of the Republic" in 1826. He was a leader in forming benevolent missionary societies and fought for many moral reforms. His eleven children went on to seek larger reforms in abolitionism, women's rights, and education.

7. Artemis Bullard quoted in Drury, *Henry Harmon Spalding,* 64.

8. William Gray quoted in Bernard DeVoto, *Across the Wide Missouri* (Boston: Houghton Mifflin, 1947), 255.

9. Julie Roy Jeffrey, *Converting the West: A Biography of Narcissa Whitman* (Norman: University of Oklahoma Press, 1991), 37.

10. Clifford Merrill Drury, *First White Women over the Rockies,* 3 vols. (Glendale, CA: Arthur H. Clark, 1963), 1:180.

11. Eliza Spalding Warren, *Memoirs of the West: The Spaldings* (Portland, OR: Marsh Printing, 1917), 55.

12. Dawson, "Laboring in My Savior's Vineyard," 39.

13. Warren, *Memoirs,* 61.

14. Ibid., 62.

15. Until going down the Columbia River, Eliza had retained her eastern perceptions of Indians as "noble savages"—perceptions based on her limited acquaintance with the plains and plateau horse culture.

16. Jeffrey, *Converting the West,* 78.

17. Warren, *Memoirs,* 65.

18. Ibid.

19. Ibid., 68.

20. Ibid.

21. Ibid., 69.

22. Ibid., 73.
23. Ibid.
24. Ibid.
25. Ibid.
26. Ibid., 69.
27. Marcus Whitman quoted in Jeffrey, *Converting the West,* 161.
28. Dawson, "Laboring in My Savior's Vineyard," 75.
29. Henry Spalding quoted in ibid.
30. Warren, *Memoirs,* 35.
31. Dawson, "Laboring in My Savior's Vineyard," 81.
32. Drury, *Henry Harmon Spalding,* 345.
33. Dawson, "Laboring in My Savior's Vineyard," 172.
34. Ibid., 173.
35. Eliza H. Spalding quoted in ibid., 174.
36. Ibid., 101.
37. Ibid., 71.

Suggested Readings

Carlson, Laurie Winn. *On Sidesaddles to Heaven: The Women of the Rocky Mountain Mission.* Caldwell, ID: Caxton Press, 1998.

Drury, Clifford Merrill. *First White Women over the Rockies.* 3 vols. Glendale, CA: Arthur H. Clark, 1963–1966. Reprinted as *Where Wagons Could Go.* Lincoln: University of Nebraska Press, 1998.

Jeffrey, Julie Roy. *Converting the West: A Biography of Narcissa Whitman.* Norman: University of Oklahoma Press, 1991.

Riley, Glenda. *Women and Indians on the Frontier: 1825–1915.* Albuquerque: University of New Mexico Press, 1984.

Whitman, Narcissa Prentiss. *The Letters of Narcissa Whitman.* Fairfield, WA: Ye Galleon Press, 1986.

3

María Amparo Ruiz Burton and The Squatter and the Don

Rosamaría Tanghetti

María Amparo Ruiz Burton (1832–1895) is best known for her 1885 novel, *The Squatter and the Don.* Her life, relived vicariously through the characters in her novel, was one of great adventure. As a young girl, she witnessed the conquest of her homeland, Baja California, during the Mexican War (1846–1848). At the conclusion of the war, as the United States took control of those parts of today's Far West that Mexico had held, she emigrated to Monterey, California, where she married a U.S. Army officer who had been part of the force that occupied her native town, La Paz.

Ruiz Burton drew on her own experiences with invasion, the politics of capitalism, squatters, contested land claims, and marriage to an Anglo-American to create the cross-cultural themes she wove into the fabric of *The Squatter and the Don.* Her own story, like that in the novel, involved personal and ethnic dilemmas fostered by class status and racial background. Hers was a borderlands life lived in a time of enormous transition; like many other Hispanic people, she was caught in the turmoil of nationalism and the power of myopic images of peoples of color. In the following essay on this remarkable woman's life, Tanghetti illustrates the effectiveness of an interdisciplinary approach that combines literary analysis and historical evidence—one of the innovative ways in which scholars now study the U.S. West.

Rosamaría Tanghetti is a doctoral candidate in U.S. history at the University of California, Davis. Her interests include the histories of colonial Mexico, the borderlands, and the family.

Long before María Amparo Ruiz Burton became a published author, she prophetically informed her good friend José Matías Moreno that she would someday gain public recognition. In a letter written to him in 1859, when she was in her mid twenties, she confidently stated, "One day my countrymen will know me better, perhaps when I am thousands of leagues

This essay is based on an earlier paper, "Re-covering California History: A Return to Romance," submitted to the University of California, Davis, Graduate Latin American History Seminar, 1994, and presented at a Cross-Cultural Women's History Group conference, 1995.

away or covered by the cold earth."[1] Indeed, her yearning for acknowledgment was matched by her ability to prophesy, for just as she predicted, María Amparo Ruiz Burton was catapulted out of oblivion in 1992 when scholars recovering the Hispanic literary heritage of the United States published the novel she had written more than a century earlier, *The Squatter and the Don.*

Her life and novel provide a unique point of entry into California's past. Ruiz Burton experienced firsthand the major events of the nineteenth century—the Mexican War, the American Civil War (1861–1865), the decline of California's pastoral economy, and the concomitant capitalist transformation of the western states. After leaving Baja California and marrying an American soldier, she traveled to the East and resided there with her husband for most of the 1860s. Later, back in California, she was caught in a tangled web of protracted land-claim litigation as she battled on two fronts—against the United States and against Mexico—for her properties in southern and Baja California. Like many other southern California property owners of the 1870s, her fortunes were linked to the extension of the southern route of the transcontinental railroad. However, unlike some of her contemporaries who also wrote about California, such as Helen Hunt Jackson and Bret Harte, Ruiz Burton wrote from the perspective of an elite member of a conquered minority.

In *The Squatter and the Don,* she tapped her own experiences to spin a tale of land invasion and transcendent romantic love, of corporate power and dispossession: indeed, the issues so closely imbricated in the story of the fictional Alamar family were the very themes that defined Ruiz Burton's own life. Through her novel, she affirmed her desire for social recognition and bore witness to the social dislocations of her time. Her life story was similar to that of her fellow elite, landowning Mexican compatriots whose privileged social position was threatened and eventually undermined by the political and economic transformations of late-nineteenth-century California.

In telling a decidedly personal story, Ruiz Burton also contributed to two closely related literary genres of her time. *The Squatter and the Don* stands as yet one more example of California fiction from the late 1800s that romanticized the state's "Spanish" past. At the same time, her work also represents a variation on what historian Nina Silber has dubbed "the literature of reunion"—a body of work that spoke primarily to the nation's need for sectional reconciliation during the Gilded Age. Considered together, then, Ruiz Burton's life and novel aptly chronicle the political, economic, cultural, and social currents of the late nineteenth century.

A nineteenth-century California rancho house. While ranchos such as this one came to symbolize California's romanticized pastoral economy, they also served as focal points for the fierce struggle over land that ensued after the Mexican War. From Donald R. Hannaford and Revel Edwards, *Spanish Colonial or Adobe Architecture of California, 1800–1850* (Stamford, CT: Architectural Book Publishing Co., Inc., 1931 [reprinted 1990]), 77. *Courtesy of Architectural Book Publishing Co.*

The circumstances surrounding Ruiz Burton's birth on July 3, 1832, are somewhat mysterious. Because many local church records in Baja California were destroyed by natural disasters and the region's turbulent politics, the exact location of her birthplace has not been established. She was born either in La Paz or Loreto, and her mother, Isabel Ruiz, was the daughter of a distinguished officer of the Spanish royal army who served as governor of Baja California during the early years of the newly independent Mexican republic. José Manuel Ruiz's long military career and his ownership of a large land tract secured his place within the social and political elite of Baja California. Virtually no evidence remains regarding the identity of María Amparo's father. The fact that she used her mother's surname as her own suggests, at the very least, that her father probably was not a significant figure in her life. She derived personal identity from her mother's family and social position from her maternal grandfather, from whom she eventually inherited property in Baja California.

Her first experience with territorial invasion came when a U.S. Army regiment occupied La Paz on July 21, 1847, during the Mexican War. For a little over a year, soldiers from the First Regiment of the New York Volunteers, under the command of Lt. Col. Henry S. Burton, alternately battled Mexican patriotic insurgents and socialized with sympathetic La Paz residents. As a fifteen-year-old girl, María Amparo attended social events where U.S. Army officers and soldiers mingled with and were entertained by some of the local elite. Perhaps she was also privy to the political discussions that ensued as her relatives anxiously considered the merits of Baja California's possible annexation to the United States.

Decades of civil strife, economic crises, and disrupted trade lines in the years following Mexico's independence from Spain in 1821 had inhibited the development of strong nationalist loyalties among some residents of Baja California and other regions of Mexico's northern frontier. Feeling neglected by their national government, a number of these people harbored ambitions of achieving political autonomy through secession or, alternatively, union with other sovereign nations. During the Mexican War, Baja California residents who had pledged loyalty to the United States found themselves precariously situated when, in the course of peace negotiations, their territory was not included in the ceded lands. Fear of political retribution prompted these "traitors," as they were called by their loyalist Mexican compatriots, to press for political asylum. Over 350 *Bajacalifornios*—those who had sworn allegiance to the United States—departed La Paz on September 1, 1848. María Amparo Ruiz, her mother, and other family members were among the war refugees who sailed for Monterey in Alta California.

The historical record offers no direct clues concerning the fifteen-year-old girl's thoughts on territorial invasion and annexation. However, a letter written in 1875 to one of her long-time friends clearly demonstrates that as an adult, she linked desires for her own pecuniary gain with hopes for Baja California's annexation by the United States. At that time, María Amparo resided in San Diego, California, and owned land in Mexico less than one hundred miles south of the U.S. border, which she had inherited from her maternal grandfather. On December 4, 1875, she wrote to her well-connected friend George Davidson regarding her aspirations for her Mexican property:

> I have been trying to sell the half of the "All Saints Bay" tract to raise funds to start a Colony, but all in vain. There is not a man of means with brains enough to see what magnificent enterprise it would be to found a flourishing Colony which would open to the world the immense mineral wealth of that region. . . . Because the property is 85 miles South of San Diego *in Mexico!* no one has faith in it. . . . I wish you would find out & tell me whether there is any rumor in govt. circles of any probability of Lower California being annexed, . . . I would like to know it, not out of idle curiosity, but because it would be so important to my interests. . . . If nothing more is said this winter about acquisition of territory, I fear I shall have to sacrifice my property & it will be a great pity for it can be made *hundreds of millions*. Some of the mines assay . . . $200, and 400 to the ton of silver with $50 & 60 of gold.[2]

Like her good friend Mariano Guadalupe Vallejo, who had once supported Alta California's annexation, Ruiz Burton calculated that Baja California's incorporation by the United States would enhance her financial condition. In this instance, at least, she looked favorably on a possible U.S. acquisition of Mexican territory.

However, Baja California was not incorporated into the United States in the mid-1870s, and Ruiz Burton's land disputes did not secure her material well-being. Indeed, her struggle to retain ownership of her ranch in San Diego and to maintain title to her property in Mexico pitted her against squatters, the U.S. Land Commission, the U.S. Supreme Court, the Mexican government, and the International Company of Mexico. Her claim to her ranch in San Diego rested on tenuous ground. According to historian Kathleen Crawford, María Amparo and her husband, Henry Burton, homesteaded over half a million acres—Rancho Jamul—near San Diego in early 1854. This property had reverted to the public domain when the Burton family settled there, and its convoluted title history, involving the previous Mexican owners, contributed to María Amparo's difficulties in securing her hold on this land. When she returned to the ranch as a widow with two children after a ten-year hiatus from 1859 to 1869, she found her claim seriously hampered because her husband had died intestate. Further complications with a foreclosed mortgage, squatters, and challenges to her title by other claimants entangled Ruiz Burton in a web of litigation, which finally ended in 1889 with the California Supreme Court validating her homestead petition for less than one hundred acres of the original half-million-acre ranch.

Ruiz Burton's protracted battle to secure title to land in California typified the experiences of many of her fellow Mexican landowners. The Treaty of Guadalupe Hidalgo, which formally ended the Mexican War in 1848, promised to protect the property of inhabitants in the ceded territories, but the U.S. Land Act of 1851 and the Preemption Act passed by the California's state legislature in 1853 virtually overturned this pledge. The Land Act placed the burden of proof on landowners, who heavily mortgaged their properties to cover the costly legal fees incurred in their efforts to verify their claims before the U.S. Land Commission. Property owners also often found themselves besieged by squatters. The Preemption Act in effect sanctioned squatting when it opened for settlement public domain property that had not yet received official validation by the land court.

Ruiz Burton's own entanglement in California's land politics endowed her with an acute empathy for her landowning compatriots. However, the particular circumstances of her initial 1854 homestead made her situation unusual. Neither she nor members of her immediate family owned property in any of the ceded territories at the conclusion of the Mexican War. She had traveled to a ceded territory—California—as a war refugee after her family renounced their Mexican nationality. When she settled on Rancho Jamul in 1854, she did so as the young wife of a Yankee soldier, a veteran of the Mexican War. Indeed, she and her husband homesteaded the property after it had reverted to the public domain under the Land Act of 1851. In other words, they benefited, initially at least, from a law that made invalidated Mexican grants available to settlers; the very laws that worked against many of California's Mexican landowners (and eventually against María Amparo herself) enabled her and her husband to acquire property in 1854. Her long struggle to secure title to this land strongly suggests that she considered this form of land acquisition valid and saw herself as a legitimate owner.

María Amparo's efforts to retain her Mexican property—Rancho Ensenada de Todos Santos—pitted her against a powerful alliance between the Mexican regime of Porfirio Díaz and foreign capital. This gave her an altogether different appreciation for yet another kind of territorial invasion. Seeking to promote economic growth, President Porfirio Díaz and his Liberal regime delivered Mexico into the hands of U.S. investment capital with the enactment of the 1883 Mexican Law of Colonization, which permitted foreign-owned firms to purchase Mexican property. When a U.S.-owned development firm encroached on and attempted to sell portions of her Rancho Ensenada, María Amparo was once again thrown into a lengthy legal dispute, and in the end a Mexican court invalidated her claim to these lands. Her battle with the Mexican government was profoundly ironic. Ruiz Burton was a woman who had, at one point, desired U.S. annexation of Baja California, yet she battled a government that in effect transformed Mexico into an economic dependency of the United States. When foreign economic penetration threatened her own interests in Baja California, Ruiz Burton, quite justifiably, was ready to protest. There were, then, some forms of territorial appropriation that she would not abide.

María Amparo Ruiz Burton's engagement with land politics on two separate national fronts in the last three decades of the nineteenth century placed her squarely at the center of the major reconfiguration in land tenure that resulted from territorial conquest and the privileging of corporate capital over private, individual ownership. Over the course of her adult life, she had both benefited from and been adversely affected by these transformations. In response, she had developed, as suggested earlier, a rationale that justified some forms of territorial acquisition and condemned others.

The distinction between legitimate and spurious land invasion evident in Ruiz Burton's thoughts and actions found full expression in her *Squatter and the Don.* Specifically, the author conveyed this distinction through her portrayal and differentiation, based largely on class, of the Anglo-American settlers who take up residence on the Mexican-owned Alamar ranch. The novel chronicles the efforts of several families to remain financially solvent during a period of profound land redistribution and economic transformation in California. Set mostly at the fictional *Californio,* the aristocratic Alamar family's ranch near San Diego circa 1872, this work interweaves the stories of the Anglo-American settler families—the Holmans, Mechlins, and Darrells—with that of the Alamars.[3] As critics Rosaura Sánchez and Beatriz Pita have noted in their analysis of this work, Ruiz Burton drew a stark contrast between settlers and squatters by overlaying these categories with contrasting attributes—the settlers are depicted as legitimate, respectable, and middle-class, the squatters are illegitimate, vulgar, and lower-class.

The work begins with an introduction to the Darrell family as they discuss their anticipated settlement on the Alamar property. Mr. Darrell, who righteously justifies squatting, argues with his wife over the meaning of the words "settler" and "squatter." Mrs. Darrell, who represents the voice of reason and moral authority and vehemently opposes squatting, sternly informs her husband that "whenever you take up government land, yes, you are 'settlers,' but not when you locate claims on land belonging to anyone else. In that case, you must accept the epithet of '*Squatter.*' "[4] Undeterred by his wife's admonitions, Mr. Darrell moves his family onto the Alamar ranch, but unbeknown to him, his wife and his son, Clarence, secretly purchase their parcel. Only they and Don Mariano, the Alamar patriarch, are privy to this real estate transaction.

Throughout the novel, Ruiz Burton evoked sympathy for the settlers who appropriate land through proper channels. The fictional Anglo-American families—the Holmans and the Mechlins—are portrayed as legitimate settlers (they have purchased their property) and thus exist on the same social plane as the aristocratic, landowning Alamar family. As San Diego property owners, they share common economic interests. And the Mechlins and Alamars are also related through marriage. Through her positive characterization of these settlers, Ruiz Burton validated her and her Anglo-American husband's legitimate acquisition of Rancho Jamul—a former Mexican grant that had reverted to the public domain.

The novel also elicits disdain for the lowly, vile squatters who surreptitiously take advantage of the opportunities created by the 1851 Land Act and resort to criminality to acquire what they believe is theirs by "right of conquest." Ruiz Burton deployed her rhetorical skills to decry her own mistreatment and that suffered by other Mexican landowners at the hands of squatters, lawmakers, and unscrupulous lawyers. In this regard her novel denounces the laws that contributed to the near total dispossession of Mexican landowners in late-nineteenth-century California. In the years immediately following 1851, nearly half of the land held in Mexican grants was sold to defray the costs of title confirmation. As one of the novel's characters proclaims, squatters and lawmakers were determined to "drive the natives to poverty, and crowd them out of existence."[5]

Just as Ruiz Burton's experiences with territorial invasion deeply informed her portrayal of Anglo-American settlers, her elite caste and class status profoundly colored her depiction of California's Mexican landowners. Notwithstanding the Mexican republican ideal of democratizing the nation's citizens (which included indigenous peoples), Spanish and mestizo—mixed-race—*Bajacalifornios* continued to differentiate themselves according to a colonial hierarchy, based on caste and ethnic identity, that situated them above the Indian population. As the granddaughter of a prominent landowner and former provincial Mexican governor, María Amparo Ruiz stood at the pinnacle of this society in her early years in Baja California. In the United States her life, for the most part, was no less privileged. Her 1849 marriage to Henry Burton and their ten-year sojourn on the East Coast from 1859 to 1869 introduced her to elite military and political circles in Washington, DC, as well as to her husband's middle-class New England society. As the wife of then Brigadier General Burton, María Amparo attended social functions with the spouses of U.S. cabinet members and senators; her circle of acquaintances included both Mary Todd Lincoln and Varina Davis, the wife of former Confederate president Jefferson Davis.

In her sympathetic portrayal of the fictional Alamar family in *The Squatter and the Don,* Ruiz Burton embraced a fairly standard nineteenth-century American literary convention that racialized class differences within the Mexican population. According to Cecil Robinson, the dime novels that became popular during the Mexican War evinced North Americans' ambivalence toward the peoples of Mexico. These works racially distinguished upper-class landowners from ordinary Mexicans by juxtaposing genteel, cultivated, "Spanish" hacienda lords and swarthy, treacherous, and lazy Mexican "greasers." This dichotomy took firm hold in California, and as historian Antonia Castañeda has argued, the racialized class distinction extended to descriptions of California's Mexican women. Females from landowning families were characterized as Spanish and virtuous, whereas nonelite women (the vast majority of the population) were described as Mexican and immoral. Historian Hubert Howe Bancroft and authors Helen Hunt Jackson and Bret Harte adopted this convention in their historical and fictional accounts of nineteenth-century California. In fact, Jackson's immensely popular *Ramona,* published in 1884, and the works by Bancroft and Harte did much to ignite the myth of California's romantic Spanish past, contributing to the promotion of what Carey McWilliams identified as California's "Spanish fantasy heritage."

A contemporary of Jackson and Harte, María Amparo Ruiz Burton contributed to this largely Anglo-American literary movement through her portrayal of the Alamar family. However, unlike Jackson and Harte, who differentiated between the so-called Spanish and the Mexicans or, at the very least, emphasized the Spanish blood of Mexican land grantees, Ruiz Burton sidestepped this dichotomy altogether. Indeed, she foreshadowed authors such as Gertrude Atherton, who, according to critic Raymund Paredes, depicted her Spanish-speaking characters exclusively as "Castilian." In the *Squatter and the Don* the Alamar family possesses all the attributes of the most aristocratic of Spanish families. The patriarch, Don Mariano, epitomizes nobility of character, generosity, and refined gentility. His daughter, Mercedes, described as a "perfect picture of a 'sleeping beauty' " with golden curls that framed her blue eyes, could not be more virtuous or pure.[6] And as if to further underscore this family's racial pedigree, Ruiz Burton alluded to a possible Anglo-Saxon background in her depiction of two of Don Mariano's sons. One of these characters is said to look like an Englishman, and his brother, Victoriano, "is so light he looks more like a German."[7] Mexicans do not reside in Ruiz Burton's fictional California, and Indians, mentioned only briefly, appear as lazy and stupid ranch hands. By effacing Mexicans and Indians in her fictional narrative and racializing the upper-class landowners as Spanish, fair-haired, and blue-eyed, Ruiz Burton surpassed Jackson and Harte in fostering the illusion of California's Spanish heritage.

Ruiz Burton's portrayal of Mexican landowners did not merely reflect her elite point of view, and she clearly did not think of herself as Spanish. (Her private correspondence with Mariano Guadalupe Vallejo indicates that she harbored no delusions regarding her national origin, which, of course, was Mexican.) Rather, she used the literary device of racializing class differences to shore up her rhetorical denunciation of the U.S. land policies that threatened and eventually undermined her economic and social position. Much like Helen Hunt Jackson, who ennobled indigenous Californians through her romanticized characterization of Alessandro in the novel *Ramona* to underscore her critique of Manifest Destiny and the systematic removal of Indians from their lands, Ruiz Burton reimagined Mexican landowners as Spanish and aristocratic—in a manner that appealed to late-nineteenth-century readers—in order to elicit greater sympathy for herself and other Mexicans who faced dispossession. At the very least, it appears, she wanted readers to acknowledge that, as Mrs. Darrell says in the novel, "we [Americans] have treated the conquered Spaniards most cruelly, and our law-givers have been most unjust to them."[8]

Ruiz Burton's multilayered historical fiction stands as an embittered testimony to the economic and social dislocations suffered by California's Mexican landowners in the nineteenth century, and through its portrayal of the Alamar family as genteel Spanish aristocrats, this work holds its own in California's "Spanish fantasy" literary tradition. But *The Squatter and the Don* is also a romance novel. Drawing on her own marriage to a Yankee officer for inspiration, Ruiz Burton intertwined the fictional romance between Clarence Darrell, the Anglo-American settler, and Mercedes, the daughter of Don Mariano Alamar, with the narrative of dispossession. As a romance novel, *The Squatter and the Don* occupied a unique place within the broader context of the Gilded Age—the culture of conciliation so eloquently examined by historian Nina Silber in her work entitled *The Romance of Reunion.*

María Amparo's marriage to a member of the invading U.S. Army was not unique. After the conclusion of the war in 1848, a number of U.S. soldiers returned to Mexico or remained in the ceded territories and married women from the subjugated Mexican population. In southern California, for example, Col. Cave Johnson Couts, whose tour of duty had taken him through most of the Mexican northern frontier, settled in

San Diego and married Isidora Bandini, daughter of the socially prominent San Diegan Juan Bandini. However, although such marital alliances were accepted in some social circles, María Amparo and Henry Burton had to overcome religious impediments before they could wed. Unlike the Anglo-American men who had traveled to Mexican California before the war and converted to Catholicism in order to marry Mexican women, Burton, in the new political configuration of postconquest California, did not forgo his Protestant faith. Yet as a Roman Catholic, María Amparo was not allowed by her church to marry outside her religion. Undeterred by this obstacle the couple was married by a Protestant minister in a private ceremony. Eventually, as historian Hubert Howe Bancroft noted, they were also married in a Catholic ceremony—but only after negotiating the necessary dispensations.

Neither religious nor national differences pose a problem in the fictional romance between Clarence Darrell and Mercedes Alamar in *The Squatter and the Don.* Instead, the couple must reconcile a class difference before they can consummate their love in marriage. The proud, matriarchal Doña Alamar considers Clarence an undeserving, low-class squatter who must prove his worth before he can win her daughter's hand. Only after she discovers that he is really a legitimate settler who has purchased his land does she consent to the young couple's betrothal. Eventually, Clarence and Mercedes overcome a host of other obstacles and unite in blissful matrimony.

Clarence Darrell's marriage to Mercedes Alamar signifies much more than the happy resolution of a love quest. For Ruiz Burton, Clarence Darrell becomes a savior—the man who prevents the total dispossession of the Alamar family by purchasing their property with part of the fortune he has made through his mining investments. There is an implicit understanding that the aristocratic Mercedes's social position will not be compromised despite her father's financial ruin. Furthermore, Clarence's wealth and beneficence restore his brother-in-law, Gabriel—proletarianized during a stint as a hod carrier—to his middle-class position as a banker. In this novel, then, marriage serves as a metaphor both for the appropriation of formerly Mexican lands by Anglo-American capital (which typified California's incorporation into the nation) and for the unfettered union between an enterprising, energetic nation, symbolized by Clarence Darrell, and a conquered territory, reimagined as Spanish, aristocratic, and white through the character Mercedes Alamar.

To be sure, Ruiz Burton's romance narrative, with its resolution in the felicitous union between Clarence and Mercedes, works against her own denunciation of Mexican dispossession. Her novel is a work fraught with ambiguities, perhaps reflecting the author's own ambivalence toward territorial appropriation or the irony of her personal story. After all, she had been rescued from potentially dangerous La Paz by Lt. Col. Burton when her family sought refuge in the newly ceded U.S. territory only to find herself battling to maintain her economic and social position in California in later years. Nevertheless Ruiz Burton's deployment of the "Spanish fantasy" trope and her theme of marriage between an Anglo-American man and a supposedly Spanish woman bears a striking resemblance to other fictional narratives of the 1880s and 1890s that similarly romanticized another defeated territory; it also emphasized marriage as a gendered metaphor for regional incorporation. As Silber has noted, works such as *The Blue and the Gray* (1884), *Held by the Enemy* (1886), and *Shenandoah* (1888) featured idyllic southern plantation settings, military conflict, and romantic love between a northern man and a southern belle jeopardized, of course, by sectional tensions. These works glorified the previously vilified South by romanticizing it as a place inhabited by heroic, well-mannered men and gracious, proper ladies. Marriage between northern men and southern women in these literary works symbolized sectional reconciliation and served, as Silber has argued, to assuage the political tensions between the victorious North and the defeated South.

In part this literature of reunion served to mitigate sectional discord by evoking sympathy for the postwar economic plight of southern plantation owners. Quite often in these works an impoverished southern belle—a symbol of the prostrated South—secures financial recovery through the actions of a northern protagonist. We have seen how Ruiz Burton employed a variation of this literary theme in her story of Mexican California with the rescue of the Alamar family and, in particular, of Mercedes by the wealthy Anglo-American, Clarence Darrell. *The Squatter and the Don* lends no symbolic support to the reconstructed South per se, but Ruiz Burton nevertheless evinced compassion for the South through her discussion of a southern transcontinental railroad.

The Alamar and Mechlin families—heavily invested in San Diego real estate—stand to gain handsomely with the designation of San Diego as the terminus for the Texas Pacific Railroad. Thus, Ruiz Burton's characters are quite aware of the links between their economic prosperity and the financial health of the southern states. In particular, George Mechlin, a New York banker who is married to another of the Alamar daughters and who also has a personal stake in the railroad, keenly appreciates the connections between southern California and the South. In one of his more ardent moments, he exhorts: "There never can be any better arguments in favor of the Texas Pacific than are now plain to everybody. So, then, if in the face of all these powerful considerations Congress turns its back and will not hear the wail of the prostrate South, or the impassionate appeals of California, . . . is there any ground to expect any better in the uncertain future?"[9] The same Mechlin later informs his wife, Elvira, that "the construction of the Texas Pacific ought to be advocated by every honest man in the United States, for it is the thing that will help the exhausted South to get back its strength and vitality."[10]

Just as the narrative in *The Squatter and the Don* paralleled Ruiz Burton's life, so might her character's position on the South have reflected her astute understanding of the economic implications of a southern transcontinental railroad for the South, for southern California, and for herself. A well-informed woman, she closely followed railroad magnate Thomas A. Scott's plans to extend the Texas and Pacific Railroad from Louisiana to Texas and farther on to a Pacific terminus during the early 1870s. As a San Diego property owner, she had a rather large stake in the fate of the rail line, and, together with other property owners, she hoped that San Diego would be selected as its terminal point. She perceived the potential for personal and regional financial gain should San Diego become a transportation nexus for the United States and northern Mexico. However, she also understood railroad politics and the economic harm that would befall San Diego if Scott's efforts failed. In a letter to a friend, she asked, "And what do you think are the chances of the Texas Pacific? Is Tom Scott to succeed? Gov. Stanfor [*sic*] will do all he can to prevent it. . . . He has formed a plan in his brain for a certain R. Road system of his own & he will crush San Diego & all of us if he fancies we are in his way."[11]

Thomas Scott was outmaneuvered by the powerful Southern Pacific Railroad conglomerate, and San Diego was bypassed when the "Big Four" (Collis P. Huntington, Charles Crocker, Leland Stanford, and Mark Hopkins) extended their road from Los Angeles east to San Bernardino. Despite this setback, Ruiz Burton continued to pin her hopes for financial security on prospective railroad and property development ventures throughout the 1880s. Private correspondence reveals that she never ceased thinking of ways to profit from the many economic projects she undertook on Rancho Jamul.

When María Amparo Ruiz Burton died on August 12, 1895, in Chicago, she had already lost Rancho Ensenada de Todos Santos in Baja

California, and she was still deeply enmeshed in litigation over her San Diego property just before her death. During her life, however, she witnessed the major redrawing of political boundaries between Mexico and the United States. As a landowner on both sides of the reconfigured border, she struggled to secure her place within a shifting pattern in land tenure. In *The Squatter and the Don,* she inscribed her story onto the literary landscape and fixed her place alongside other observers of late-nineteenth-century California. Since the re-publication of her novel in 1992, her life and work have generated a great deal of interest. At last, María Amparo Ruiz Burton has achieved the recognition that she so desired more than 140 years earlier.

Notes

1. In Spanish, the letter reads, "Algún día me conocerán mis paisanos mejor, quizá cuando esté miles de leguas distante o con la tierra fría por cobija" (my translation). María Amparo Ruiz Burton to José Matías Moreno, February 27, 1859, Helen P. Long Collection, Henry E. Huntington Library, San Marino, California.

2. María Amparo Ruiz Burton to George Davidson, December 4, 1875, George Davidson Papers, Bancroft Library, University of California, Berkeley.

3. María Amparo Ruiz de Burton, *The Squatter and the Don,* with an introduction by Rosaura Sánchez and Beatriz Pita (Houston: Arte Público Press, 1992). "Californio" was the term used in the nineteenth century to denote a native-born Californian of Spanish or Mexican descent.

4. Ibid., 57.

5. Ibid., 146.

6. Ibid., 151, 159.

7. Ibid., 89.

8. Ibid., 255.

9. Ibid., 216.

10. Ibid., 296.

11. Ruiz Burton to George Davidson.

Suggested Readings

Aranda, José F., Jr. "Contradictory Impulses: María Amparo Ruiz de Burton, Resistance Theory, and the Politics of Chicano/a Studies." *American Literature* 70 (September 1998): 551–79.

Castañeda, Antonia I. "Gender, Race, and Culture: Spanish-Mexican Women in the Historiography of Frontier California." *Frontiers* 11, no. 1 (1990): 8–20.

Crawford, Kathleen. "Maria Amparo Ruiz Burton: The General's Lady." *The Journal of San Diego History* 30, no. 3 (Summer 1984):198–211.

Gutiérrez, Ramon, and Genaro Padilla, eds. *Recovering the U.S. Hispanic Literary Heritage.* Houston: Arte Público Press, 1993.

McWilliams, Carey. *North from Mexico: The Spanish-Speaking People of the United States.* 1948, reprint. New York: Praeger, 1990.

Paredes, Raymund A. "Mexican-American Literature: An Overview." In *Recovering the U.S. Hispanic Literary Heritage,* ed. Ramon Gutiérrez and Genaro Padilla, 31–51. Houston: Arte Público Press, 1993.

Robinson, Cecil. *Mexico and the Hispanic Southwest in American Literature,* rev. from *With the Ears of Strangers.* Tucson: University of Arizona Press, 1977.

Silber, Nina. *The Romance of Reunion: Northerners and the South, 1865–1900.* Chapel Hill: University of North Carolina Press, 1993.

4

Henry De Groot and the Mining West

Gerald Thompson

The exploits and writings of Henry De Groot (1815–1893) during the initial period of the 1862 La Paz gold rush in Arizona attest to the role played by journalists and cartographers in shaping the image of the region as the land of opportunity, the place of mobility and movement. The California gold rush that followed swiftly on the heels of the Mexican War in 1848 soon led to others throughout the interior West. From its humble beginnings as an individual enterprise, mining quickly became a consolidated, industrialized business.

In this award-winning essay, the late Gerald Thompson demonstrates that local Hispanics and American Indians interacted closely with the arriving wave of Euramerican miners, merchants, and speculators: either they provided food, shelter, or information to the newcomers or they competed with them for the shimmering riches buried in the earth. De Groot, for his part, objectively reported on this cultural interaction, which alternately reflected cooperation, duplicity, mythmaking, and conflict on both sides of the culture divide. The West's legendary associations with self-reliance and individual responsibility seem less credible in this light. Conquest may have been the overriding theme in the history of the region, but the opening of the West clearly included the participation of and even, at times, manipulation by nonwhites. It was also a story of human courage, hope, and understanding.

Gerald Thompson earned three degrees from the University of Arizona in Tucson. In 1977 and 1978, he served as assistant editor of *Arizona and the West,* and from 1984 to 1990, he was editor of *The Historian.* He joined the faculty of the University of Toledo in Ohio in the fall of 1979, where he remained until his untimely death in May 1998. During a professional career of over twenty years, he published two books and nearly two dozen articles and essays, mostly related to the American Southwest and historiography.

Henry De Groot began to take an interest in Arizona as accounts of fabulous wealth from gold placers on the Colorado River circulated in northern California during the late spring of 1862. A student of mining

Adapted from Gerald Thompson, "Henry De Groot and the Colorado River Gold Rush, 1862," *Journal of Arizona History* 37 (Summer 1996): 131–48. Reprinted by permission of the Arizona Historical Society and Margaret H. Thompson.

history, a prolific writer, and a man with considerable field experience, he was familiar both with Spanish mining activities as well as current attempts to open lode mines in southern Arizona and on the upper reaches of the Colorado River, fifty miles north of Beale's Crossing. He also knew that a stampede to the Gila City placers, a few miles east of Yuma Crossing, had occurred three years earlier. The general conclusion, however, seems to have been that Gila City's wealth was small in comparison to the attention the mines had received in the newspapers.[1]

According to De Groot, exaggerated tales of wealth that clung to the name "Arizona" were worse than failed mining rushes like Gila City, making educated miners and investors highly skeptical of any reports of mineral riches emanating from the region. In the 1850s, François X. Aubry originated the best known of these stories. Aubry claimed that during one of his rapid journeys across the Southwest in the 1850s, he had encountered Indians supplied with gold bullets. De Groot labeled Aubry a purveyor of tall tales.[2]

During more than a decade of reporting on mining, De Groot had established a reputation for honesty and impartiality. A graduate of prestigious Union College in Schenectady, New York, De Groot—with his wife, Eliza—was managing a finishing school for young ladies in Ossinning, New York, when word of a fabulous gold discovery in the Sierra Nevada foothills reached the East Coast in September of 1848. Horace Greeley of the *New York Tribune* decided to send a reporter to California and offered De Groot the assignment.[3]

Sailing into San Francisco Bay in late February of 1849, De Groot wasted little time in setting out for the gold strike. He reached Sutter's Mill and quickly interviewed the principals involved in the discovery—John A. Sutter, James Marshall, and others. His published letters were widely read throughout the East and encouraged the great immigration of 1849 and 1850. For himself, De Groot resolved to return to New York and bring his family to California, which he eventually did.[4]

De Groot soon became a recognized authority on technical developments and visited countless mining districts, often joining rushes to new locales as reports of gold and silver strikes reached San Francisco. During the 1850s, he visited Gold Bluff (1851), Kern River (1854), and Fraser River (1858). Always a prolific correspondent for newspapers, De Groot also worked occasionally as an in-house editor for several of the major San Francisco papers. Sometime during the decade, he found time to learn and practice the skills of cartographer and surveyor.[5]

Upon hearing of the great gold and silver discoveries on the eastern

Courtesy of The Bancroft Library, University of California, Berkeley

slope of the Sierra in 1859, he once again packed a bag and headed for the Washoe camps. The Comstock Lode caused such international excitement that De Groot's small book, *Sketches of the Washoe Silver Mines* (1860), went through several editions and was translated into French by a Swiss publisher. Even more important, *De Groot's Map of the Washoe Mines* (1860) was published in both San Francisco and Geneva, and ran through several printings. A practical guide accompanying the map served as an indispensable tool for anyone who wished to undertake the arduous journey to western Nevada.[6]

When stories of Colorado River gold began to make the rounds in San Francisco, the prestigious and knowledgeable *Mining and Scientific Press* judged that there was insufficient credible information to determine whether the discoveries at La Paz were legitimate. "Is there a gold field east of the Colorado?" the paper asked. This question was often asked, but it never received a satisfactory answer.[7]

By late May, newspapers in heavily populated northern California had run articles about the Colorado River placers abbreviated from the lengthy coverage of the *Los Angeles Star*. As time passed, stories from the Los Angeles newspapers carried to the Bay Area by coastal steamers were reprinted extensively in the newspapers of the northern part of the state.[8]

The West Coast's two leading newspapers decided to send special correspondents to Arizona to determine the true nature of the La Paz placers. The *San Francisco Bulletin* selected Henry De Groot as their representative. The rival *Alta California* dispatched J. H. Riley ("J. H. R."), a far better-known writer than De Groot and a man whose stiletto wit could deflate a mining bubble if the gold strike turned out to be a fraud.[9]

Few readers knew that Riley had already determined that the La Paz stories were grossly inflated and largely the work of mine speculators and merchants. He believed that economically depressed southern California was trying to tap into northern California's prosperity, recently enhanced by the Washoe discoveries.

De Groot and Riley decided to travel together to La Paz. Agreeing to pool information and resources, the two reporters departed San Francisco aboard the steamer *Senator* on June 3, 1862, disembarking two days later at San Pedro. Reaching Los Angeles, neither of them could detect the "Red River fever" that recently had been detailed in the pages of the *Star*. Before leaving for the Colorado River placers, Riley wrote, "The town or Pueblo de Los Angeles is very dull . . . I have only to say that if this is what they term 'excited,' I should as a matter of curiosity, like to see it while in a quiescent mood." In contrast to Riley's cynical, sardonic style, De Groot wrote in a manner that can best be described as moderate, scholarly, and objective. Unlike "J. H. R.," Henry De Groot rarely attempted humor in his accounts for the *Bulletin*. In workmanlike fashion, De Groot observed:

> I can learn nothing more at this place in regard to the mines on the Colorado than in San Francisco, and which has already appeared in the columns of the Bulletin. There is *very little said about them here, and as for excitement I can discover nothing of the kind. Of the American and foreign population very few have as yet left for them*—though a good many Californians and Sonorians have gone.

De Groot's reporting contained an important insight as he casually noted that a significant number of Mexicans had left southern California bound for Arizona.[10]

With clarity of observation, De Groot accurately described the nature of the early months of the Colorado River gold rush, which, during the late winter and spring of 1862, had been confined largely to the Hispanic population. Pauline Weaver, the old mountaineer recently turned prospector, had sparked the gold rush when he showed some La Paz gold dust to José María Redondo, a trader and miner at the Gila City diggings. Contemporary evidence indicates that Redondo, Felipe Amvisca, Antonio Contreras, and Jesús Contreras may have been the true discoverers of the La Paz placers. For several years, the Mexicans had been engaged in mining at Laguna on the east bank of the Colorado River a few miles above Fort Yuma. By February of 1862, word of the discovery had spread throughout the region, but intense interest existed primarily within the Hispanic community.[11]

During April and May the City of the Angels succumbed to the full ravages of the Colorado River fever as samples of Arizona gold reached the city. Juan Ferrar, a forty-eight-year-old Sonoran, had picked up one famous specimen, the size of a "hen's egg." Other Mexican miners shipped gold dust in quantities that varied from twenty to sixty ounces to their Los Angeles relatives. In accompanying letters, they urged friends and family members to abandon their current occupations and make haste for the Colorado River. All doubts vanished when George Hooper, the trader at Fort Yuma, showed up in Los Angeles with $8,000 in gold dust. "Even the most incredulous had to believe his own eyes and be convinced of the richness of the new mines," exclaimed an observer.[12]

De Groot discovered that the La Paz placers were located in a virtual terra incognito. Only a few published reports mentioned the region, and an adequate map of the area was nonexistent. The La Paz mines were more isolated than the east slope of the Sierra, and travel to the Colorado River was more difficult and dangerous than going to Washoe. The most frequented route to the mines went via Fort Yuma, then followed a trail north along the river. A few opted for the Mojave Trail, which ran to the northeast across the desert to Fort Mojave, and then from there followed the Colorado to La Paz, often rafting part of the way down the river. It was approximately 400 miles to the mines via Fort Yuma, while the longer Mojave Road covered 450 miles.[13]

As De Groot and Riley were planning their imminent departure from San Bernardino, news reached them that William Bradshaw had opened a

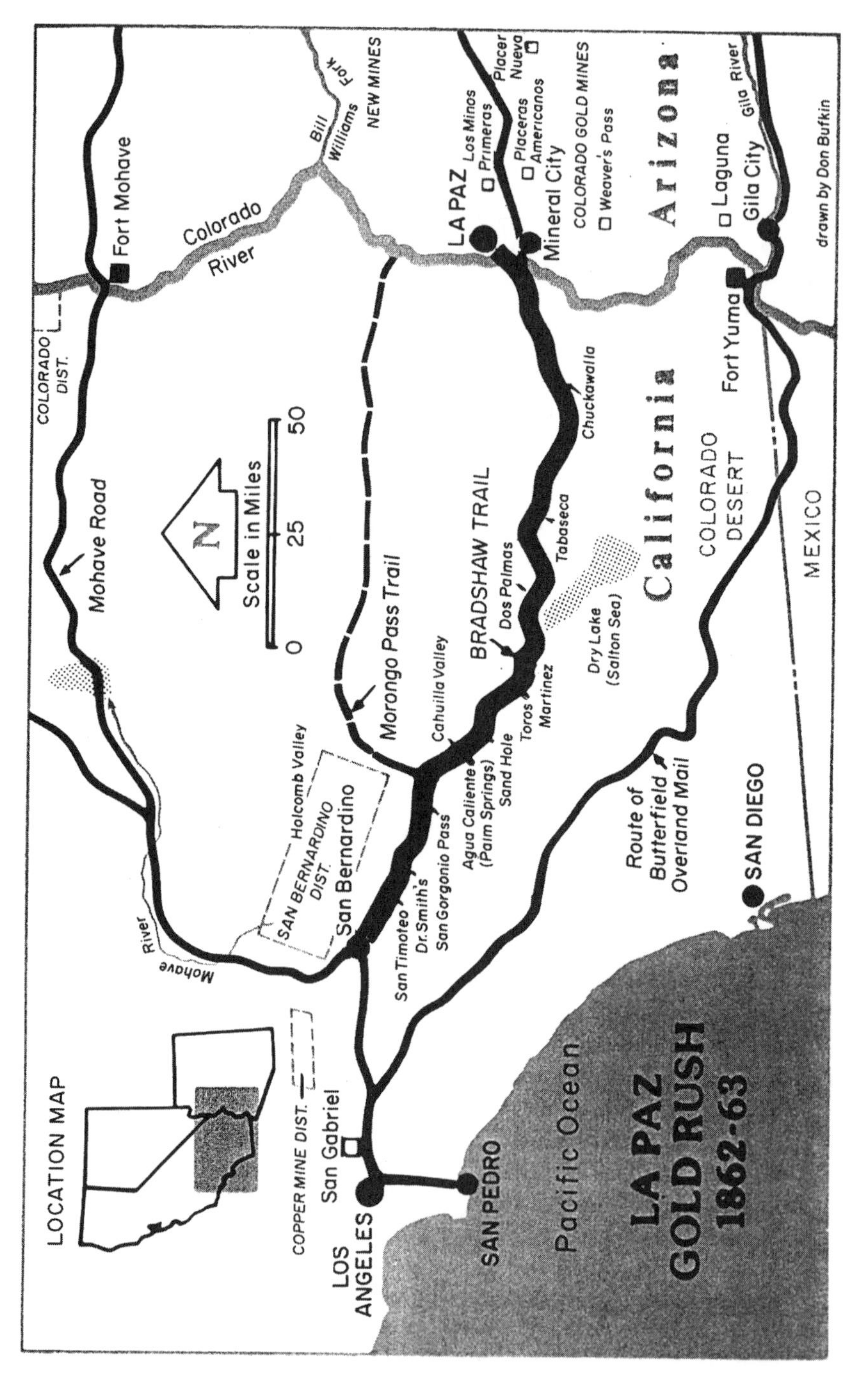

LA PAZ
GOLD RUSH
1862-63
LOCATION MAP
Pacific Ocean
LOS ANGELES
San Gabriel
SAN PEDRO
COPPER MINE DIST.
Mohave River
San Bernardino
SAN BERNARDINO DIST.
Holcomb Valley
San Timoteo
Dr. Smith's
San Gorgonio Pass
Agua Caliente (Palm Springs)
Sand Hole
Toros
Martinez
Cahuilla Valley
Morongo Pass Trail
BRADSHAW TRAIL
Dos Palmas
Tabaseca
Chuckawalla
Dry Lake (Salton Sea)
Mohave Road
Scale in Miles
0 25 50
N
COLORADO DIST.
Fort Mohave
Colorado River
Bill Williams Fork
NEW MINES
LA PAZ
Los Minos Primeras
Placeras Americanos
Placer Nueva
Mineral City
COLORADO GOLD MINES
Weaver's Pass
Arizona
California
COLORADO DESERT
Route of Butterfield Overland Mail
SAN DIEGO
Fort Yuma
Laguna
Gila City
Gila River
MEXICO
drawn by Don Bufkin

new, shorter route to the mines. Bradshaw was acquainted with Cabezon, the most prominent leader of the Cahuillas. It seems likely that the chief brought him together with a Maricopa Indian familiar with a trail that ran from Palm Springs to the Pima Villages, crossing the Colorado near La Paz. The Maricopa provided Bradshaw with a crude map to the mines, and soon Bradshaw asserted that the new route would save 200 miles and ten days of travel.[14]

Although Bradshaw declared himself the discoverer of a new road to the Colorado mines, James Grant claimed to have pioneered the identical route. Grant's report in a letter to the *Los Angeles Southern News* was less detailed than Bradshaw's, however. Consequently, Bradshaw's name eventually stuck as the trail designation, and most travelers to the mines immediately opted to take that new trail.[15]

De Groot's party left San Bernardino on June 13, and soon joined up with several other groups bound for La Paz. Thirty men, some on foot, others on horseback, made up the party, which was accompanied by three wagons. Myron Angel, a friend of De Groot, who was actively engaged in mining and newspapers, attached an odometer to one of their wagon wheels to obtain exact distances. Based on their Washoe experiences, De Groot and Angel were probably thinking about the possibility of publishing a guide to the mines, should the diggings prove worthwhile.[16]

De Groot and Riley followed the well-traveled road to San Gorgonio Pass, where the reporters spent the first night at the residence of J. R. Frink, owner of a large stock ranch at San Timoteo Creek. Frink, who had been employed by Col. Henry Washington during the desert surveys of the mid-1850s, contended that Washington's party had used the new wagon road several years prior to its "discovery" by Bradshaw. The rancher provided De Groot and Riley with a detailed and highly accurate map of the route.[17]

The differing work habits of De Groot and Riley emerged as the men and wagons moved east. While De Groot took notes on geography, distances, water holes, and fodder—the practical concerns of any traveler—Riley wrote copious stories in a small diary. Deeply cynical and assuming he was on another wild goose chase, Riley diligently collected tales that illustrated man's gullibility and deceitfulness. With more practical mining experience, De Groot sensed that something important might have happened in Arizona, and he wanted to see the mines for himself. He may already have begun work on his elaborate map of southern California and western Arizona that would prove valuable even if the La Paz placers should dissolve like a desert mirage.

After spending the night of June 14 in San Gorgonio Pass, the party pushed on and encamped at San Jacinto Creek. Beyond the pass, the trail descended and they began to experience the desert heat. On June 16, they reached Agua Caliente (modern Palm Springs) about twenty-five miles east of Chapin's ranch. The prospectors decided to rest there for the remainder of the day, permitting the animals to gather strength for the difficult stretches ahead. Only a few Indians were in residence; most of the villagers had fled to the surrounding countryside in the aftermath of the murder of San Bernardino County deputy sheriff Rush Dickey.

De Groot learned that, a few days earlier, Euroamericans had attempted to arrest Dickey's killer, Omos, an Agua Caliente who, with a couple of followers, was preying upon travelers and residents. With speculations rife about an Indian war, the principal chiefs of the Cahuillas, Juan Antonio and Cabezon, promised to apprehend Omos. They also expressed their strong desire for continued good relations and trade with the Americans. Travelers across the desert had come to depend upon the Indian villages to supply feed for their livestock. The De Groot party coaxed several Indians out of a nearby canyon and bargained with them to purchase grain.[18]

De Groot and Riley also negotiated for a night's shelter. The hut's Indian owner asked the two men many questions about their length of stay and departure time, revealing that he had had previous contact with Americans. Eventually, he agreed to rent his abode for seventy-five cents. Riley noted in his diary: "The Doctor [De Groot] drily remarked that I had better have a written lease."[19]

De Groot, Riley, and companions departed at two o'clock the next morning, avoiding the intense afternoon heat that could prove lethal to man and beast. Around 8:00 A.M., they came across a guidepost placed by James Grant, who had traveled ahead of the main party in his wagon, marking the road and watering spots. The fingerboard indicated that there was water in a sand hole 150 yards to the trail's left. Hence, for a short period of time, anyone venturing over the road was familiar with a place named Sand Hole. Seeking shade, De Groot lay down under a mesquite bush and awaited the arrival of Joe Fountain's team, carrying the supplies. It was too hot that afternoon to travel through the barren desert. Men and animals dealt with sun, heat, and thirst as best they could. "Not a breath of air; too hot to lie still; too hot to go on," complained Riley.[20]

In the twilight around 8:00 P.M., the men moved forward, making for the Toros Indian village some twenty-five miles past Agua Caliente. The road did not run in a straight line to Toros but hugged the western mountain slopes. In places, the heavily loaded wagons negotiated stretches of soft sand with great difficulty. It took eight hours to reach Ranchería de los Toros.

Shortly after arriving at Toros, De Groot learned that several men had perished in the desert from lack of water and exposure to the sun. Once more, Indians saw that the party was well supplied with life's necessities. Early in the evening of June 19, the Colorado River argonauts again moved east, stopping briefly at Martínez village and at Lone Palm (Soda Springs) at two o'clock the next morning. Eighteen miles east of Toros, the sandy road proved especially difficult for loaded wagons. Because Soda Springs was heavily impregnated with sulfur and alkali, the group pressed on another seven miles to Dos Palmas, which afforded potable water. One man died from exposure.[21]

That night, the thirty remaining members of De Groot's party started on a northeastern course for springs known as "Water in the Canyon," located in Brown's Pass twelve miles distant. The next morning, June 21, the travelers reached the springs. After a few hours of rest, the party set out for Tabaseca Spring, eight miles to the east.[22]

After Tabaseca Spring, the road improved considerably and the wagons made good time to Chuckwalla Springs, where the party arrived just before noon on Sunday. The many travelers headed for the La Paz diggings had drained the desolate water holes; blankets had been draped over the pits to prevent evaporation, while armed guards permitted only one tin cup of water per person. The De Groot party moved up the arroyo and dug their own water hole, which filled so slowly that it took an entire day to obtain enough liquid for the animals. Some members of the group began calling the unpleasant spot "Choke for Water." Nevertheless, even at this remote place, deep in the Colorado Desert, native inhabitants came forward to trade and bargain, supplying the mules and horses with grass.[23]

The next morning, the San Francisco correspondents encountered their first returnees from the Colorado mines. All looked exhausted. A few spoke favorably of the mines, but the majority felt the claims were fraudulent or already played out. They unanimously agreed that the daytime heat was so intense that hard physical labor was impossible. Riley, who had suffered during the desert crossing, decided that he had the evidence he needed to proclaim the La Paz rush a humbug. Several men, similarly discouraged by their desert travails, held a council to debate the pros and cons of continuing. They had no desire to experience the worst stretch of the Bradshaw Trail, thirty-five miles without water from Chuckwalla to the Colorado River. On the morning of June 24, Riley bid a hasty good-bye to Henry De Groot and returned to Los Angeles. De Groot, meanwhile, chose to push forward and see the mines for himself. Despite his small stature and slight build, De Groot was physically stronger than most men and never seemed to mind the hardships on the trail.[24]

On the previous evening, De Groot had written a long letter for the *Bulletin.* The paper published the correspondence under the headline: "A Terrible Narrative—Heat, Thirst, Exhaustion, Death." In it, De Groot wrote: "The mines are a failure, the gold being scarce, while the heat and drouth [*sic*] are such that no man can endure them." Several murders had occurred over water—a commodity, De Groot said, that required armed guards. He concluded his piece with a warning that he had heard so many stories of suffering and death, that any man who had considered going to the Colorado mines should abandon the thought or "at least wait until some more favorable account shall reach us from that quarter."[25]

Within forty-eight hours of leaving Chuckwalla Springs, a refreshed De Groot was at Laguna de la Paz, writing a lengthy description of his travels, the community, and the mines. He began with an apology to readers, stating that prior to reaching La Paz everything he had written about Colorado mines had been based on rumors and statements picked up along the route. Then, in his methodical manner, De Groot related what he had learned of the mines.

In sum, he reported that the gold deposits were uneven; a man might unearth several ounces in one day and find nothing during the next week. The individuals who profited the most had arrived first and had taken out considerable quantities of gold but "if you inquire of them, they will tell you that they have no dust and affect the extreme of poverty, yet are always able to produce a small quantity when wishing to make a purchase." De Groot felt that the Hispanic population had deliberately downplayed the richness of the mines to discourage Americans from usurping their claims. He observed that Yaqui Indians, experts at gold-washing, had "been making good and often large wages here for three or four months past." What about the hardships involved in getting to the mines? De Groot replied that "the reported cases of suffering and death, as well as of violence and outrage, of which I made mention in a former letter . . . appear to have been much exaggerated." Moreover, individuals who were physically unfit for the rigorous journey, or who relied upon misleading persons, often brought problems on themselves.[26]

De Groot estimated that some 500 persons resided in the area. He broke down the figure as "200 Sonoranians, and others of Spanish origin; 200 Indians—Yumas, Pi-Utes and Mojaves, and 100 Americans." An additional 100 Americans had left the mines during the previous week with virtually nothing to show for their trip to La Paz. A combination of factors had led to their failure: the intense heat, lack of water in the mines, shortage of kegs for hauling water, and unfamiliarity with the technique of dry washing. Moreover, some of the returnees were not miners at all, but ranchmen and city dwellers who had hoped to make quick and easy money.[27]

From the dates of his La Paz letters, Henry De Groot evidently spent a week at the river community and in the nearby mines. He wrote three letters from La Paz (a total of thirty-two pages of typescript), which provided San Francisco miners and businesspeople with the first definitive, objective account of the La Paz placers and mining prospects in west-central Arizona. His methodical and careful approach confirmed that gold existed in the region and the mining craze had not been a fraud as J. H. Riley insisted. Yet, De Groot pointed out, the strike was not of such a large scale to warrant a sizable emigration. What he observed was simply a beginning. It would take years to fully explore and develop the region's mineral resources. La Paz showed Arizona's potential, but it was not yet a rival to the Comstock Lode or the days of Forty-nine.

De Groot noticed that La Paz needed a steamboat landing in order to supply the interior. Unfortunately, the community of Laguna de la Paz was situated on a shallow slough—a difficult location to serve as a principal depot for the mines. A new town was likely to be developed a few miles down the river where the water ran deeper. In this latter prediction, De Groot may have been influenced by his friend and trail companion Myron Angel, who would soon lay out the town of Olivia. In 1866, the river changed course, leaving the slough a dry channel and La Paz landlocked.[28]

The *Mining and Scientific Press* praised De Groot for his objectivity and perseverance. In later years, some miners recalled that De Groot's letters in the *San Francisco Bulletin* had inspired them to go to western Arizona in 1862. Thus, Henry De Groot's trek across the deserts of southern California to the La Paz diggings helped Arizona's fledgling mining industry emerge from behind a facade of stories about lost Spanish mines and Indians supplied with golden bullets.[29]

Other aspects of De Groot's visit, however, were just as important. He made careful notes while on the trail and visiting the mines. These notes were the basis for a sixteen-page pamphlet, entitled *Guide to the Colorado Mines,* published in early 1863 by H. H. Bancroft. Like so many who were employed by Bancroft, De Groot was not credited with the authorship of the valuable guide, but internal evidence confirms it as De Groot's work. Even more important was the map that accompanied the guidebook.

Entitled *Bancroft's Map of the California Mines,* it was the first detailed survey of southern California and the lower Colorado River region. The *Los Angeles Star* of April 4, 1863, praised the guide and map as "an indispensable companion" for anyone who planned to visit the mines of Coso or Slate Range or those near the Colorado River. "Much of this topography and many of the names on this map were never before published on any map," observed the *Star*'s editor.[30]

Fortunately, either Bancroft or De Groot kept the original hand-drawn map that served as the basis for the Colorado mines plate. The margin of the carefully drawn original carries the phrase, apparently in De Groot's handwriting, "Compiled by Dr. Degroot." But unlike his widely distributed *De Groot's Map of the Washoe Mines and Vicinity,* which highlighted his name in the title, the Colorado mines map, an important contribution to the cartographic history of the Far Southwest, does not acknowledge De Groot. He seems to have anticipated that publisher Bancroft would not give him credit, for—on the north slope of the San Gabriel Mountains—one finds a small, unimportant stream with a tiny name: "Degroot's Creek." There is no indication that such a creek ever existed. It may have been Henry De Groot's way of signing his work to ensure that his contribution to cartography would not be lost.[31]

Following his trek to Arizona, De Groot generally divided his time between Nevada and California. He started several mining camp newspapers in Nevada, while continuing to write extensively on mining subjects for various San Francisco papers. De Groot also produced mining prospects for numerous clients and served as secretary for the California Hydraulic Mining Association. During these years, he regularly contributed articles to *Overland Monthly* on topics that ranged from the tragedy of the Donner party to the growth of the dairy industry in California. At the time of his death in 1893, De Groot was planning to resume his position as assistant geologist for the California State Mining Bureau, a job he had held for a number of years. Although there is no record that De Groot returned to Arizona after 1862, his son, Henry De Groot, Jr., served a term as secretary of the Pioneer Mining District in 1878.[32]

When histories of Arizona were subsequently written, Henry De Groot's role was forgotten. It is not surprising that he was overlooked. Regional history often concentrates on those male settlers who take up permanent residence in an area and become the Founding Fathers of local legend. But it cannot be denied that De Groot played a critical role during a key event in Arizona's history. His judicious reporting of the La Paz Rush of 1862 convinced many miners and businessmen that the unexplored regions of Arizona offered opportunities for prospectors, wage earners, and capitalists. In addition, De Groot's meticulous notes and sketches served as the basis of his 1863 map of southern California and western Arizona, adding hundreds of place names to the geographer's lexicon, while at the same time making travel in the region significantly safer. If La Paz was the "Gateway to Territorial Arizona," as one author has observed, Henry De Groot's cartographic efforts and reporter's skills surely qualify him as an individual who helped to open that gateway.[33]

Notes

1. The earliest newspaper accounts of the Colorado River placers appeared in the *Los Angeles Star* in March 1862. Gila River stories had been especially prevalent in the *Los Angeles Star, San Francisco Alta California,* and *San Francisco Herald* during the fall of 1858 and throughout 1859.

2. *San Francisco Bulletin,* July 22, 1862. For Aubry's journal, see *Cincinnati Railroad Record,* March 25, 1856. Entry of August 27, 1853, quoted in Gerald Thompson, "Is There a Gold Field East of the Colorado?—The La Paz Rush of 1862," *Southern California Quarterly* 67 (Winter 1985): 346.

3. Frederick E. Birge, "Henry De Groot," *Overland Monthly,* 2d ser., vol. 11 (September 1893): 261; Henry De Groot Alumni File, Union College, Schenectady, New York; Henry De Groot, M.D. (Pioneer Card), Biographical Files, California State Library, Sacramento. Henry and Eliza Mead De Groot had four children—three (Cornelia, Henry Jr., and Isabel) survived into adulthood. Donald A. Keefer to Gerald Thompson, February 22 and April 4, 1995, author's files.

4. Birge, "Henry De Groot," 261–62; Henry De Groot, Pioneer Card, California State Library.

5. John F. Pinkham and W. P. Harrington, "In Memoriam: Doctor Henry De Groot," Obituary Records, vol. 3, 12–17, Society of California Pioneers, San Francisco. De Groot's numerous obituaries amply illustrate the prominent spot he occupied in mining circles. See *San Francisco Chronicle,* March 29, 1893; *San Francisco Examiner,* March 29, 1893. Henry De Groot, *British Columbia: Its Condition and Prospects, Soil, Climate, and Mineral Resources, Considered* (San Francisco: Alta Job Office, 1859), is based on De Groot's Fraser River experiences.

6. John W. Reps, *Cities of the American West: A History of Frontier Urban Planning* (Princeton: Princeton University Press, 1979), 227; Henry De Groot, *Sketches of the Washoe Silver Mines, with a Description of the Soil, Climate, and Mineral Resources of the Country East of the Sierra* (San Francisco: Hutchings and Rosenfield, 1860); *Californie, Description physique de l'Utah accidental et dernières découvertes métallurigiques dans cet état* (Geneva: Imp. de J. G. Fick, 1860); *De Groot's Map of the Washoe Mines* (San Francisco: Hutchings and Rosenfield, 1860); *Carte de la region des mines de Washoe (Californie)* (Geneva: Imp. Koegel, 1860).

7. *San Francisco Mining and Scientific Press,* June 21, 1862.

8. *San Francisco Bulletin,* May 25, 1862; *Alta California,* May 27, 28, 1862; *Marysville Appeal,* May 24, 1862.

9. De Groot's unsigned articles appear in the *San Francisco Bulletin,* June 10, 18, July 9, 14, 17, 19, 21, August 1, 6, and September 22, 1862. For Riley's articles, see *Alta California,* June 11, 18, 26, July 14, 17, 21, 30, and August 2, 1862.

10. Riley's quote in *Alta California,* June 11, 1862; De Groot's quote in *San Francisco Bulletin,* June 10, 1862.

11. Thompson, "La Paz Rush of 1862," 349–50; Frank Love, *Mining Camps and Ghost Towns: A History of Mining in Arizona and California along the Lower Colorado* (Los Angeles: Westernlore Press, 1974), 29–38; Jim Byrkit and Bruce Hooper, *The Story of Pauline Weaver—Arizona's Foremost Mountain Man, Trapper, Gold-seeker, Scout, Pioneer* (Flagstaff: Sierra Azul Publications, 1993), 32–33.

12. Thompson, "La Paz Rush of 1862," 50; *Alta California,* May 17, July 30, 1862; *Los Angeles Star,* May 17, 1862.

13. *Mining and Scientific Press,* June 14, 1862, relates the journey of a Holcomb Valley miner named Griffis, who traveled to La Paz via Fort Mojave.

14. Bradshaw's report is printed in the *Los Angeles Star,* June 14, 1862, and reprinted in the *Alta California,* June 18, 1862.

15. *San Francisco Bulletin,* July 4, 1862. Grant's letter is in *Los Angeles Southern News,* June 13, 1862.

16. *Alta California,* July 17, 1862.

17. Ibid., July 14, 17, 1862.

18. Ibid., July 17, 1862.

19. Ibid.

20. Ibid.

21. Ibid., July 17, 21, 1862; *Guide to the Colorado Mines* (San Francisco: H. H. Bancroft, 1863), 13–14.

22. Tabaseca is the modern spelling. De Groot used the spelling "Tabasaca," and Riley "Taba-Saca." "Tabasacca" was preferred by Bancroft's *Guide to the Colorado Mines,* 14–15. Delmer G. Ross, *Gold Road to La Paz: An Interpretive Guide to the Bradshaw Trail* (Essex, Calif.: Tales of the Mojave Road Publishing, 1992), 101.

23. *Alta California,* July 30, 1862. Modern spelling is Chuckwalla. De Groot used "Chu-cu-le-walla," "Chucu-le-walla," and "Chu-cu-le-wallah." His multiple syllables may come closer to the Indian pronunciation of the spring than anglicized Chuckwalla.

24. *Alta California,* July 30, 1862; David W. Hassler, "Charles O. Cunningham: California Arizona Pioneer, 1852–65," *Arizona and the West* 27 (Autumn 1985): 253–68; David Thompson, "Introduction," in Henry De Groot, *The Comstock Papers* (Reno: Grance Dangberg Foundation, 1985), v–vii.

25. *Bulletin,* July 9, 1862.

26. Ibid., July 19, 1862.

27. Ibid.

28. Ibid., July 19, August 28, 1862; Byrd H. Granger, comp., *Will G. Barnes' Arizona Place Names* (Tucson: University of Arizona Press, 1960), 382.

29. Mahlon D. Fairchild, prominent in California and Nevada mining history, recalled in his later years that it was Henry De Groot's published letters that caused him to abandon hydraulic mining in northern California and go to the Colorado River. Mahlon Dickerson Fairchild, "A Trip to the Colorado Mines in 1862," *California Historical Society Quarterly* 12 (March 1933): 11–17.

30. The *Guide to the Colorado Mines* is a rare document found in only a few libraries. In several copies, the map has been removed, but the California State Library's copy is intact. De Groot was also known to have worked extensively on Bancroft's multivolume *History of the Pacific States of North America. Los Angeles Star,* April 4, 1863.

31. The original [Map 12 (s) 1863 C] in the Bancroft Library bears the inscription "Colorado River Region and the routes to it compiled by Dr. Degroot 1863." The writing appears to be the same as the signature on De Groot's membership application in the records of the Society of California Pioneers.

32. Birge, "Henry De Groot," 162–63; "Bibliography of Henry De Groot," 1–3, author's file. Information on Henry De Groot, Jr. is in B. Sacks Collection, Arizona Historical Foundation, Tempe.

33. Pamela Renner, "La Paz: Gateway to Territorial Arizona," *Journal of Arizona History,* 24 (Summer 1983): 123–24.

Suggested Readings

Johnson, Susan Lee. *Roaring Camp: The Social World of the California Gold Rush.* New York: W.W. Norton, 2000.

Love, Frank. *Mining Camps and Ghost Towns: A History of Mining in Arizona and California along the Lower Colorado.* Los Angeles: Westernlore Press, 1974.

Paul, Rodman W. *Mining Frontiers of the Far West, 1848–1880.* New York: Holt, Rinehart and Winston, 1963.

Sheridan, Thomas E. *Arizona: A History.* Tucson: University of Arizona Press, 1995.

Thompson, Gerald. "Is There a Gold Field East of the Colorado?—The La Paz Rush of 1862," *Southern California Quarterly* 67 (Winter 1985): 345–63.

5

William Jefferson Hardin
Wyoming's Nineteenth-Century Black Legislator

Roger D. Hardaway

William Jefferson Hardin (ca. 1830–1889) was both typical and atypical of the mass of Americans who went west after the Civil War. Like many others, he tried his hand at numerous endeavors and moved to several locales. Unlike most, however, he achieved a high degree of personal success. His achievements were all the more remarkable because he was an African American and lived in a time when, outside of Texas and Oklahoma, the black population in the West was small (as it would be until after World War II). The son of a free black mother, the light-complected Hardin possessed unique advantages that served him well. As one of only two African Americans in state or territorial legislatures outside the South in 1879, he championed racial equality and women's rights in an era when neither was a popular issue.

Hardin's success in Wyoming must be evaluated in the context of time and place. Territorial voting patterns in the late nineteenth century, as explored in this essay, reflected the general failure of ethnocultural politics and partisanship to take firm root in the West; instead, westerners tended to respond to charismatic leaders more than to ethnicity or political parties. Hardin's public career attested to the fluidity of the sociopolitical structure on the frontier. Politics in the West during the 1800s were distinctive; women's suffrage became a reality far more quickly there than in the East, and the region led the way in adopting Progressive reforms of direct democracy (such as the initiative, referendum, and recall). Nonetheless racial borders were never too far in the background, especially considering the fact that Asian Americans, American Indians, and Mexican immigrants were either denied citizenship or chose not to acquire it.

Roger D. Hardaway is an associate professor of history at Northwestern Oklahoma State University, Alva, Oklahoma. He is the coeditor of *African Americans on the Western Frontier* (1998) and the author of several other works on African Americans in the American West.

Adapted from Roger D. Hardaway, "William Jefferson Hardin: Wyoming's Nineteenth-Century Black Legislator," *Annals of Wyoming* 63 (Winter 1991): 2–13. Reprinted by permission of the *Annals of Wyoming* and Roger D. Hardaway.

Several thousand African Americans went west during the late nineteenth century as a small but vital part of the westward movement. Like their white counterparts, blacks on the frontier were trappers and traders, soldiers, cowboys, miners, farmers, and entrepreneurs. After the Civil War, most blacks who left the South in search of a better life went north, and only a comparative few turned west. Consequently, until recently, the contributions blacks made to the western frontier have been ignored. During the past several decades, however, historians have attempted, to some degree, to chronicle the achievements of blacks in the American West.[1] This article is an effort to contribute to that endeavor by focusing on William Jefferson Hardin, an African American who was twice elected to the Wyoming Territorial Legislature in an era and from a place where whites greatly outnumbered blacks and often subjected them to discriminatory treatment.

Hardin took an erratic route from his native South to the Rocky Mountain West. Born in Kentucky around 1830, Hardin lived in that state until he reached adulthood. He was never a slave because his mother was a free black and his father was white. Hardin's free status allowed him to receive an education, and he subsequently became a school teacher for a brief period in the Kentucky city of Bowling Green. With the advent of the gold rush to California, Hardin decided sometime after 1850 to seek his fortune there. He spent the next several years as a wanderer, living in Canada, Wisconsin, Iowa, and Nebraska before settling in Denver, Colorado, in 1863.[2]

Hardin lived in Denver for a decade, and became a leader in the city's black community. A dynamic speaker, he soon became known as the "Colored Orator of Denver." He advocated integrated public schools and led the fight for black suffrage against formidable white opposition. Then, when Congress granted the franchise to black men in all of the territories in 1867, Hardin became an important asset to the local Republican Party. He helped deliver the African American vote for the GOP, and party leaders rewarded him for his efforts. In 1872 he was a delegate to the Republican National Convention that nominated President Ulysses S. Grant for a second term. A more lucrative recompense was the job party officials obtained for him at the Denver branch of the U.S. Mint in 1873.[3]

In the latter year, however, Hardin left Denver with his reputation and career in shambles. First, he married Nellie Davidson, a white woman from New York who worked as a milliner in the Colorado capital. Soon thereafter, a black woman calling herself Caroline Hardin came to town with

Courtesy of the Wyoming Division of Cultural Resources

proof that she had married Hardin in Kentucky in 1850, and claiming that this marriage had produced a daughter. Moreover, she charged that Hardin had moved from Omaha to Denver in 1863 only to avoid being drafted into the Union army. Hardin admitted that he had dodged the draft, that he had participated in a marriage ceremony with the woman, and that he was the father of the daughter. He argued, however, that the marriage to Caroline was illegal and therefore void when it was made because he had been a minor and she a slave at the time. Hardin was never charged with bigamy or any other crime, and he continued to live with Nellie for years after his purported marriage to Caroline became public knowledge. This episode nevertheless prompted the director of the mint to fire him, and Hardin decided to leave Denver, where his future looked bleak, and move north to Wyoming in late 1873.[4]

Hardin settled in Cheyenne and opened a barbershop. The typical late-nineteenth-century barber was black, and undoubtedly Hardin became well known to Cheyenne's white male leaders in part because so many of them frequented his establishment. By the end of the decade of the 1870s, Hardin was known and respected by most people in the territory's small capital city. The scandal that had forced him out of Denver apparently did not in any way limit his acceptance into Cheyenne social and political life.[5]

One interesting aspect of Hardin's makeup that bears noting was his physical appearance. The *Cheyenne Daily Sun* described him as being "of slim and slender build, five feet ten inches high, weighs 140 pounds . . . ; has black curly hair with moustache and elfin whiskers of the same color and black eyes. Has sharp well cut features, thin lips and small mouth, long sharp nose and an orange complexion." His mother had one white parent, and, thus, Hardin was only one-fourth black. He was very light-skinned, and the newspaper portrayed him as having "no resemblance in his features to the African race." Moreover, the paper concluded, "he looks more like an Italian or a Frenchman than a colored man." In the late nineteenth century, African Americans who did not have pronounced Negroid characteristics were usually more acceptable to whites and more likely to progress in a white-dominated society. One Colorado historian has argued that most of the successful blacks in Denver in the late nineteenth century, including Hardin, were of mixed blood. Another has noted that a Denver newspaper editor attributed Hardin's intelligence and leadership abilities to the "white" blood that he possessed.[6] Presumably, his light skin was an asset to him in Wyoming as well as in Colorado.

Two attributes that were definitely advantageous to Hardin's political success were his oratorical ability and his outgoing personality. Perhaps his journey to the Wyoming legislature began in March 1878 when he addressed the membership of a local Presbyterian church on the evils of alcohol. The *Daily Sun* reported that it was only the second public speech Hardin had made since moving to Wyoming. His effort, the paper reported, was "frequently interrupted by applause." By the following year, Hardin was so well known that he was often called on to address public meetings.[7]

Hardin's ability to make friends is evident in examining the manner in which he came to be nominated and then elected to the Wyoming House of Representatives in 1879. Laramie County, where Cheyenne was (and is) located, was the most populous county and was entitled to four delegates in the Council, the upper chamber, and nine members in the House.[8] Each party was to nominate candidates at a county convention for the general election to be held on September 2, 1879. On August 7 the *Cheyenne Daily Leader,* the other newspaper in the capital city, proposed the creation of a fusion or union ticket made up of both Democrats and Republicans. This fusion would, in effect, allow the delegates to the two county conventions, rather than the voters, to choose the people who would represent Laramie County in the legislature. Party leaders assented to the plan, and each party agreed to nominate at county conventions two of its members for the Council and four for the House. A drawing was held for the ninth House seat, and the Republicans won that position.[9]

The parties held their conventions at the Cheyenne city hall at the same time so that party leaders could keep up with the proceedings of the other body. The Republicans quickly settled on two Council and four House nominees. A struggle ensued, however, when the delegates sought to choose their fifth House candidate. Three people were being considered for the ballot position, including Hardin who was a delegate to the convention. At this point in the proceedings, several Democrats, whose convention had adjourned, came into the Republican meeting hall. When the Democrats learned that Hardin was in the running for the last position on the bipartisan slate, they "electioneered openly for him" among Republican delegates. After two ballots, both of which Hardin led, Republican leader Francis E. Warren moved that Hardin be declared nominated. "The motion was carried," the *Daily Leader* observed, "amid loud cheering." Hardin's acceptance speech was applauded by members of both parties, and "brought down the house."[10] The *Daily Sun*'s editorial praised the selection of Hardin as "one of the best nominations made" by the two conventions. "Although classed with our colored brethren," the newspaper noted, "he has broken down race prejudice . . . by pre-eminent manifestations of ability and upright conduct."[11]

Hardin, like all other candidates on the fusion ticket, believed that his nomination assured him of election. That, however, was not to be the case.

Some people in Cheyenne began to complain about the manner in which the slate had been chosen. A convention of "workingmen" met at city hall on the Friday night before the Tuesday general election and nominated a second group of candidates for the legislature.[12]

Hardin was present at the workingmen's convention as a spectator. After the delegates chose their thirteen legislative nominees, they urged Hardin to make a speech prior to adjourning. The day after the convention met, four of the nominees who had not attended the gathering declined to run. The backers of the workingmen's movement rushed to fill those places on their ballot, and they offered one of the House positions to Hardin. Thus, he went into the election as a nominee on both tickets.[13]

Obviously, Hardin had support among all political factions in Cheyenne. Not surprisingly, blacks in the city were elated with his nomination and supported him wholeheartedly. They held a meeting and drafted a resolution that was published in the *Daily Sun* on the morning of the election. In the declaration, they praised Hardin and the white political leaders who had supported his nomination. "We believe him to be a good man," their statement said, "and one who is worthy of this position. . . . We rejoice to know that our white fellow-citizens were mindful enough of the colored race to give them one representative in Wyoming Territory."[14]

Hardin had many friends and acquaintances in Cheyenne and strong support among them is evident in an analysis of the election returns. For the House, each voter was allowed to vote for nine candidates, and the nine people with the most votes would be elected. Hardin won easily, finishing third among all candidates.[15] Hardin did much better in the city of Cheyenne than in the rural precincts of Laramie County. Sixteen candidates were running for the nine county House seats. These included the nine fusion candidates and seven additional workingmen's nominees. Hardin finished second among all candidates in Cheyenne, winning 903 votes from the 1,256 people who cast ballots there; thus, 79.1 percent of Cheyenne's voters gave one of their nine votes to Hardin. In the rural precincts, however, only 29.1 percent of the electorate supported him. There, he received eighty-five votes from 292 voters and finished fifteenth among the candidates. Thus, he did very well among his fellow city dwellers, but not well at all among rural voters who surely did not know him as well as did Cheyenneites.[16]

Another obvious observation is that most Cheyenne voters exhibited no racial prejudice. Certainly, some whites refused to vote for an African American, but the number was so small as to be insignificant. Rural voters, however, must have allowed race to affect their voting behavior to a great extent. The other House candidate endorsed by both factions finished first in both Cheyenne and the rural areas. One would expect Hardin, the only other candidate with a dual endorsement, to finish at least second in the rural precincts as he did in the city. Had he been as well known among rural voters as he was with city dwellers perhaps he would have received more rural votes. But the difference between his city and rural results is so great that racial prejudice is the only plausible explanation.[17]

Further evidence of the racial tolerance of Cheyenne's 1879 white voters is found in examining the demographics of Laramie County. This can best be done by studying the 1880 Wyoming census. In that year, only 194 (or 3 percent) of the 6,409 people counted by the census bureau in the county were black; most of them lived in Cheyenne. Just how many African Americans voted in 1879 is not known, but the number was obviously small—no more than 194. Hardin's margin of victory over the losing candidate with the most votes, the person who finished tenth, was 263 votes. Had every black person in Laramie County been eligible to vote in 1879 and had all voted for Hardin, he nevertheless had received enough support from white voters to be elected. Consequently, Hardin's election shows that, compared to other frontier areas and even rural Laramie County, the voters of Cheyenne were remarkably free of racial prejudice in 1879. The *Daily Leader* agreed, calling Hardin's election "a moral triumph for the people." Moreover, the paper added, "what other territory or northern state can boast of such liberality?"[18]

Wyoming's Sixth Legislative Assembly met in Cheyenne for forty days, from November 4 to December 13, 1879. Hardin was appointed to only one of the sixteen standing committees of the House, the relatively minor one of Indian and Military Affairs. He was also the House's representative on a two-man Joint Standing Committee on Printing which was likewise not a choice assignment. That Hardin did not receive better committee appointments is puzzling since Republicans held sixteen of the twenty-seven House seats, and the speaker of the House and Hardin were friends. Perhaps Hardin was appointed to the committees on which he wished to serve, or perhaps the House leadership was reluctant to assign a black legislator to more significant committees.[19]

Hardin lived up to his reputation as a distinguished orator during the 1879 session of the Wyoming legislature. When, on opening day, the members of the House selected H. L. Myrick as speaker, they chose Hardin to make the speech introducing the new leader to the representatives. On at least one occasion he was called upon to sit in the speaker's chair to preside over the House when it met as a committee of the whole. Perhaps the two most memorable speeches of the session were Hardin's opposing the move of the capital from Cheyenne to the city of Laramie and resisting a reapportionment bill that would have cost Laramie County seats in the legislature. On both occasions, the gallery of the House was packed with local citizens who applauded loudly their representative's stirring words.[20]

Hardin introduced six bills during the Sixth Legislative Assembly. The subjects of those measures ranged from building fences and killing chicken hawks to setting salaries of county officials. Of the six, two of Hardin's proposed laws were enacted. One, "to protect dairymen," is impossible to track through the 1879 session laws under that title or subject matter. This is not surprising when one realizes that Hardin's other successful bill, "to protect poultry," was renamed "an act for the destruction of hawks and eagles" before its final enactment. The contents of this latter law suggests to some degree what was important to the residents of a sparsely populated frontier territory in the late nineteenth century.[21]

One of the more significant bills passed by the Sixth Legislative Assembly changed the meeting dates of future territorial legislatures. Instead of convening in November of odd-numbered years, legislatures would assemble in January of even-numbered years beginning with 1882. Although the law was silent on the dates of election, future territorial assemblies were chosen at the regular general elections held in November of even-numbered years. Thus, the Seventh Legislative Assembly was elected in November 1880, but did not meet until January 1882. This fourteen-month space between elections and meetings continued for the remaining legislatures of the territorial period, which ended in 1890.[22]

Hardin was the only House member of the Sixth Legislative Assembly to serve in the House during the seventh session. One Laramie County representative, B. F. Deitrick, lost his re-election bid; another, W. C. Irvine, successfully ran for the Council as did Representative W. A. Hocker of Uinta County. Most members, however, retired after their one term was completed. A possible reason for this is that service in the legislature was less an honor than a civic duty. With only 20,789 people in the territory in 1880, Wyoming's population was equivalent to that of many small towns, and serving in the legislature was perhaps perceived as much like being a member of a city council. Surely, most members of the legislature were not there to launch political careers.[23]

At the 1880 Laramie County Republican Party convention, the first order of business was selecting four candidates for seats in the Council. Hardin was nominated, but finished fifth in the balloting. When convention delegates considered possible nominees for the House, Hardin's name was again placed before the convention. The legislator declined to run, however, and asked that his name be withdrawn. Nevertheless, he received the eighth-most votes, making him one of the party's nominees. Hardin again asked to be allowed to withdraw from consideration, but the conventioneers refused his request and declared him a nominee.[24]

Laramie County voters were allowed to elect only eight members of the House in 1880. Congress, which controlled many territorial affairs, had passed a law limiting the size of all territorial legislatures to twelve members in the upper house and twenty-four in the lower chamber. Thus, Wyoming's Seventh Legislative Assembly had three fewer House members than did the sixth assembly, and Laramie County's representation in the House decreased from nine to eight. Consequently, county voters in 1880 voted for eight House candidates, and the top eight vote-getters were elected.[25] The election was held on November 2, 1880. Unlike 1879, the Democrats and Republicans did not have a fusion ticket; however, a workingmen's slate was once again offered to the electorate. In the House races, the workingmen endorsed three Republicans (including Hardin), three Democrats, and two candidates who were not on the tickets of either major party. Thus, eighteen candidates were on the ballot—eight Republicans, eight Democrats, and two workingmen.[26]

Hardin barely won his second term in the Wyoming House of Representatives. He finished eighth among the candidates, receiving 1,277 votes, a mere fifty-eight ballots ahead of his closest rival. Hardin had the sixth-highest vote total in Cheyenne. However, once again he fared poorly in the outlying regions of the county, garnering only the fifteenth-most votes. Thus, as in 1879, he won his victory in the city and overcame racial prejudice but garnered few votes in the rural precincts.[27]

Moreover, support from the workingmen's organization helped Hardin win in 1880. He openly courted that support, speaking to a workingmen's rally a few days before the election. All three Republicans endorsed by the workingmen for seats in the House were victorious. Additionally, Hardin was aided by the fact that 1880 was a Republican year in Laramie County, as six of the eight House seats went to the GOP. Several possibilities explain why he did no better than he did after having made such an impressive showing the year before. For one thing, his reluctance to seek re-election might have given some voters the impression that he did not really want the seat again. Secondly, he undoubtedly made some enemies during his first term although published reports of his service were uniformly positive. Perhaps, too, the fact that most incumbents did not seek re-election to the House indicates that tradition generally limited legislators to one term in office, a practice that prevailed in some areas of the country in the late nineteenth century. Finally, the fact that—with no fusion ticket—the Democrats had a full slate of candidates to support in 1880 prevented some of Hardin's friends in that party from voting for him.[28]

The Seventh Legislative Assembly met from January to March 1882. Although the majority of the Laramie County delegation was from the Republican Party, the Democrats held more seats in the House of Representatives than did the GOP. This, of course, would presumably have affected adversely Hardin's ability to be effective. Nevertheless, as the only returning member, he was given a committee chairmanship, that of the relatively unimportant Engrossment Committee. Moreover, as in the 1879 session, he occasionally presided over the House when it met as a committee of the whole.[29]

Hardin introduced three bills in the 1882 legislative session. One, concerned with "running cattle with dogs," was defeated easily in the House. Another, having to do with amending the law that incorporated Cheyenne, apparently expanded the city's borders and became law. The third, which was also enacted, made it a misdemeanor to "exhibit any kind of fire arms, bowie knife, dirk, dagger, slung [*sic*] shot or other deadly weapon in a rude, angry or threatening manner," except in the defense of self, family, or property.[30]

One bill Hardin wanted passed was introduced by another member at his request in an attempt to avoid the appearance of a conflict of interest. This proposed law would have prohibited barbershops from opening on Sundays. This prompted Hardin's fellow barber, George P. Goldacker, who knew who the author of the bill was, to write an angry letter to the *Daily Leader* criticizing the measure. Goldacker argued that some people who were employed by the Union Pacific Railroad or on ranches had to work on other days and could visit their barbers only on Sundays. Furthermore, Goldacker declared, "If the gentleman [Hardin] has too much money, or his religion does not allow him to work on Sunday, he has the right to close up his place of business, the same as I have the right to open mine." Evidently, Goldacker's logic was persuasive because, although the bill easily passed the House, it died in the Council and did not become law.[31]

Perhaps the two most important laws passed during the seventh session of the territorial legislature won Hardin's support. One repealed a prohibition on interracial marriages and the other granted married women several rights. Both measures were significant actions for a territory that prided itself on treating everyone equally. Hardin, whose wife was white, delivered one of his patented moving speeches in support of removing the interracial marriage ban. The *Daily Leader* described his oration as "earnest and eloquent, bristling with facts." The law had been enacted in 1869 by the First Legislative Assembly, but apparently it was not uniformly enforced. Hardin was probably not in violation of the law since the statute made it a crime for an interracial couple to marry in the territory, but not to live in Wyoming while married. The Hardins had married, as previously mentioned, before moving to the territory.[32]

The statute concerning married women was designed to remove many restrictions that had been imposed upon Wyoming women under the Common Law. Wyoming's action was part of a trend by legislatures in the late nineteenth century to grant women some small measure of equality, and such a law was only fitting in Wyoming which had become in 1869 the first jurisdiction in the United States to provide for female suffrage. The law allowed a married woman to sell her property without obtaining her husband's permission, to sue and be sued without her spouse being made a party to the action, and to be a witness in any civil or criminal matter.[33]

Hardin did not run for a third term in the Wyoming House of Representatives. On the day the Republican county convention met in October 1882, the *Daily Leader* reported that Hardin's name was being suggested as a candidate once again. However, the account of that meeting in the newspaper's next edition does not mention him as having been in attendance.[34] Apparently, he convinced party leaders beforehand that he did not wish to run again. His term ended presumably in January 1884, when the Eighth Legislative Assembly was sworn in, but he apparently had no duties after the 1882 session adjourned in March of that year. Legislatures of that era did not have as they do now committees that met throughout the year, and the Seventh Legislative Assembly did not hold any special sessions after the regular term ended. Still, it is accurate to say that Hardin was a territorial representative from November 1879 to January 1884.

When Hardin's term in the Wyoming legislature ended, he and his wife left the territory. They sold their Cheyenne real estate in 1881 and 1882, perhaps in contemplation of leaving the city. A Cheyenne business directory dated "1884–85" does not list Hardin as one of the city's barbers, indicating that he had left town by 1884. Why the couple chose to relocate is unknown, but perhaps the wanderlust that had taken Hardin from Kentucky to the West some thirty years before caused him to move on once again.[35]

According to an obituary notice in a Park City, Utah, newspaper, Hardin and his wife moved from Cheyenne to the Mormon territory. They settled in Ogden where Hardin opened a barbershop. But this move—unlike the earlier ones to Colorado and Wyoming—led to disaster rather than success for the intrepid civic and political leader. First, Nellie Hardin left him, took the money they had realized from the sale of their Wyoming property, married another man, and moved to Seattle. Hardin then established a barbershop in Park City, but poor health forced him to quit the tonsorial trade. He tried to earn a living selling books but without success. Despondent over the loss of his wife, health, money, and professional skills, he committed suicide in Park City on September 13, 1889, by shooting himself through the heart.[36]

William Jefferson Hardin is a significant figure in the history of Wyoming and of African Americans in the West. After a successful career in Denver was ruined by scandal, Hardin relocated to an area with only a tiny number of blacks. Yet he became a well-liked and respected member of the entire Cheyenne community. And although he was a loyal Republican, he had many friends in the Democratic Party and in all political factions that existed in the frontier capital city. His two elections attest to his personality and speaking ability and to the liberal attitude of the white men and women whose votes were largely responsible for putting him in office.

Hardin's primary importance lies not in what he accomplished as a legislator, although some of his votes were significant ones. His support of women's rights and racial equality and his opposition to efforts to move Wyoming's capital from Cheyenne are all noteworthy. His tenure in the Wyoming legislature is principally significant, however, because it occurred when and where it did—in an area with few African Americans and in an era when blacks were generally not allowed to participate in political decision-making. Hardin and his fellow citizens broke down racial barriers when he ran and they twice elected him to represent their interests in the legislature.[37]

Undoubtedly, Hardin endured some discriminatory treatment in Cheyenne just as he had in Denver and elsewhere throughout his life. Some people did not vote for him because of his race. Cheyenne newspaper editors, while lauding his achievements, nevertheless felt compelled to refer to him as the "colored orator" and the "colored legislator."[38] But the majority of Cheyenne's voters viewed him simply as a community leader who just happened to be black. His political success, therefore, makes him a significant figure in Wyoming territorial history while it also serves as one dramatic example of the positive contributions African Americans made to the settlement and development of the American West in the late nineteenth century.

Notes

1. The best general survey of the subject is W. Sherman Savage, *Blacks in the West* (Westport, Connecticut: Greenwood Press, 1976). See also William Loren Katz, *The Black West,* rev. ed. (Garden City, New York: Doubleday, 1973), which is profusely illustrated. A pioneering historian in the field was Kenneth Wiggins Porter whose several articles on the topic are collected in *The Negro on the American Frontier* (New York: Arno Press and the New York Times, 1971). An early assessment of the work done by recent historians in this area is Lawrence B. de Graaf, "Recognition, Racism, and Reflections on the Writing of Western Black History," *Pacific Historical Review* 44 (February 1975): 22–51.

2. *Cheyenne Daily Sun,* November 9, 1879, 2; Eugene H. Berwanger, "William J. Hardin: Colorado Spokesman for Racial Justice, 1863–1873," *The Colorado Magazine* 52 (Winter 1975): 52, 62; Forbes Parkhill, *Mister Barney Ford: A Portrait in Bistre* (Denver: Sage Books, 1963), 127; *1880 Wyoming Census,* 316, copy in Historical Research and Publications, Division of Parks and Cultural Resources, Wyoming Department of Commerce (HR&P), Cheyenne. Berwanger places Hardin's year of birth at 1831 because he was thirty-nine when the 1870 Colorado census was taken. The 1880 Wyoming census, taken on June 4, 1880, lists Hardin as being fifty years old at that time. Hardin always claimed that his father was the brother of Kentucky Congressman Benjamin Hardin who is profiled in James L. Harrison, compiler, *Biographical Directory of the American Congress, 1774–1949* (Washington, DC: U.S. Government Printing Office, 1949), 1265.

3. Hardin's activities as a leader of the black community in Denver are detailed in Berwanger, "William J. Hardin," 52–65. See also Eugene H. Berwanger, "Hardin and Langston: Western Black Spokesmen of the Reconstruction Era," *The Journal of Negro History* 64 (Spring 1979): 101–15.

4. Berwanger, "William J. Hardin," 61–64; Parkhill, *Mister Barney Ford,* 159. Nellie Davidson Hardin's place of birth is found in *1880 Wyoming Census,* 316. Hardin's move to Wyoming, but not the reasons for it, is mentioned in the *Cheyenne Daily Sun,* November 9, 1879, 2.

5. *Cheyenne Daily Sun,* November 9, 1879, 2; January 29, 1878, 1; Berwanger, "William J. Hardin," 53. In *1880 Wyoming Census,* 316, Hardin is listed as being a barber. On blacks and the barbering profession, see Kenneth Wiggins Porter, "Foreword," to Elmer R. Rusco, *"Good Time Coming?": Black Nevadans in the Nineteenth Century* (Westport, Connecticut: Greenwood Press, 1975), XIII; Harmon Mothershead, "Negro Rights in Colorado Territory (1859–1867)," *The Colorado Magazine* 40 (July 1963), 213; Berwanger, "Hardin and Langston," 102.

6. *Cheyenne Daily Sun,* November 9, 1879, 2; Lyle W. Dorsett, *The Queen City: A History of Denver* (Boulder, Colorado: Pruett Publishing, 1977), 53; Robert G. Athearn, *The Coloradans* (Albuquerque: University of New Mexico Press, 1976), 80. Hardin may have had even less than one-fourth black blood. Berwanger, "William J. Hardin," p. 52, says that Hardin's mother was one-fourth black, making Hardin only one-eighth black. However, Berwanger's source for this statement appears to be the *Daily Sun* article cited above which states that Hardin, not his mother, was one-fourth black.

7. *Cheyenne Daily Sun,* March 19, 1878, 4.

8. T. A. Larson, *History of Wyoming,* 2d ed., rev. (Lincoln: University of Nebraska Press, 1978), 96; Marie H. Erwin, *Wyoming Historical Blue Book: A Legal and Political*

History of Wyoming, 1868–1943 (Denver: Bradford-Robinson Printing, 1946), 137; *Cheyenne Daily Leader,* December 14, 1879, 4.

9. *Cheyenne Daily Sun,* September 2, 1879, 4 (reprint of editorial that appeared in the *Cheyenne Daily Leader,* August 7, 1879); *Cheyenne Daily Leader,* August 19, 4, August 21, 4, August 30, 1879, 4.

10. *Cheyenne Daily Leader,* August 19, 4, August 21, 1879, 4. See also *Cheyenne Daily Sun,* August 21, 1879, 4.

11. *Cheyenne Daily Sun,* August 22, 1879, 4.

12. *Cheyenne Daily Sun,* August 30, 1879, 4; *Cheyenne Daily Leader,* September 1, 1879, 2; Larson, *History of Wyoming,* 125.

13. *Cheyenne Daily Leader,* August 30, 4, August 31, 1879, 4.

14. *Cheyenne Daily Sun,* September 2, 1879, 4.

15. Official election returns are reproduced in *Cheyenne Daily Leader,* September 14, 1879, 4; and in Erwin, *Wyoming Historical Blue Book,* 224–25. Hardin received 988 votes from 1,548 voters; 63.8 percent of the electorate voted for him.

16. *Cheyenne Daily Leader,* September 14, 1879, 4; Erwin, *Wyoming Historical Blue Book,* 224–25. Three other people who had been nominated on the workingmen's ticket but later withdrew received a few scattered votes from the rural precincts probably because the ballots sent to those polling places were printed before they announced their withdrawals.

17. *Cheyenne Daily Leader,* September 14, 1879, 4; Erwin, *Wyoming Historical Blue Book,* 224–25.

18. *Cheyenne Daily Leader,* September 4, 4, September 14, 1879, 4; Erwin, *Wyoming Historical Blue Book,* 224–25; and *Compendium of the Tenth Census (June 1, 1880), Compiled Pursuant to an Act of Congress Approved August 7, 1882,* Part I (Washington, DC: U.S. Government Printing Office, 1883), 379. Ironically, the *1880 Wyoming Census,* 316, incorrectly listed Hardin as being white. The only other black person elected to a state or territorial legislature outside the South in 1879 was George Washington Williams of Ohio. Letter to author from Gary J. Arnold, Ohio Historical Society, May 23, 1990.

19. *Cheyenne Daily Leader,* December 14, 1879, 4–5; Erwin, *Wyoming Historical Blue Book,* 162.

20. *Cheyenne Daily Sun,* November 5, 1879, 4; *Cheyenne Daily Leader,* December 4, 1879, 4; *Laramie Sentinel,* December 20, 1879, 2; C. G. Coutant, "History of Wyoming, Written by C. G. Coutant, Pioneer Historian, and Heretofore Unpublished, Chapter XXII," *Annals of Wyoming* 14 (April 1942), 151.

21. *Cheyenne Daily Leader,* December 12, 1879, 4–5, December 14, 1879, 4–5; *House Journal 1879,* 94, 124, 132; *Session Laws of Wyoming Territory, Passed by the Sixth Legislative Assembly, Convened at Cheyenne, November 4, 1879* (Cheyenne: Leader Steam Book and Job Printing, 1879), chapter 35, 74–87, chapter 46, 101–2.

22. *Session Laws of Wyoming Territory . . . 1879,* chapter 52, 109; Erwin, *Wyoming Historical Blue Book,* 138–39; Larson, *History of Wyoming,* p. 136.

23. Erwin, *Wyoming Historical Blue Book,* 162–63; *Compendium of the Tenth Census,* Part I, 2. Hardin himself remarked in a speech at the 1879 Laramie County Republican convention that it was difficult to convince qualified people to run for the legislature. See *Cheyenne Daily Leader,* August 21, 1879, 4.

24. *Cheyenne Daily Leader,* October 13, 1880, 4. Hardin was also elected to a two-year term on the county Republican Party executive committee.

25. Erwin, *Wyoming Historical Blue Book,* 138; *Cheyenne Daily Leader,* October 13, 1880, 4.

26. *Cheyenne Daily Leader,* October 30, 1880, p. 1 of supplement.

27. *Cheyenne Daily Leader,* November 6, 4, November 14, 1880, 4; Erwin, *Wyoming Historical Blue Book,* 231.

28. Erwin, *Wyoming Historical Blue Book,* 231; *Cheyenne Daily Leader,* October 31, 4, November 14, 1880, 4.

29. Erwin, *Wyoming Historical Blue Book,* 139; *Cheyenne Daily Leader,* January 18, 4, February 17, 4, March 9, 1882, 1; *Cheyenne Daily Sun,* February 17, 1, March 9, 1882, 1; Larson, *History of Wyoming,* 138.

30. *Cheyenne Daily Leader,* January 26, 4, February 10, 1882, 1; *House Journal of the Seventh Legislative Assembly of the Territory of Wyoming, Convened at Cheyenne, January 10, 1882* (Cheyenne: Sun Steam Book and Job Printing, 1882), 40, 45, 63, 67, 71; *Session Laws, Wyoming Territory, Passed by the Seventh Legislative Assembly, Convened at Cheyenne, January 10, 1882* (Cheyenne: Sun Steam Book and Job Printing, 1882), chapter 81, 174; *Cheyenne Daily Sun,* March 11, 1882, 1.

31. *House Journal of the Seventh Legislative Assembly,* 102, 134–35; *Cheyenne Daily Leader,* March 4, 1, February 25, 1882, 4.

32. *Cheyenne Daily Leader,* February 18, 1882, 1; *Session Laws, Wyoming Territory . . . 1882,* chapter 54, 134; *House Journal of the Seventh Legislative Assembly,* 93. For a detailed examination of Wyoming's 1869 interracial marriage law and a second one enacted in 1913, see Roger D. Hardaway, "Prohibiting Interracial Marriage: Miscegenation Laws in Wyoming," *Annals of Wyoming* 52 (Spring 1980): 55–60.

33. Homer H. Clark, Jr., *The Law of Domestic Relations in the United States* (St. Paul, Minnesota: West Publishing Co., 1968), 219–22; *Session Laws, Wyoming Territory . . . 1882,* chapter 68, 154–55; *House Journal of the Seventh Legislative Assembly,* 148.

34. *Cheyenne Daily Leader,* October 14, 3, October 15, 1882, 3.

35. *Deed Record, Laramie County, Wyoming,* Deed Book 5, 270–72, Deed Book 15, 110–12; A. R. Johnson, compiler, *1884–1885 Residence and Business Directory of Cheyenne* (Cheyenne: Leader Printing, 1884–1885), 114.

36. *The Park Record,* September 14, 1889, 2–3.

37. Hardin's legislative career has been examined briefly in Rick Ewig, "Wyoming's First Black Legislator," which appeared in several Wyoming newspapers including the *Laramie Boomerang,* March 2, 1986.

38. See, for example, *Cheyenne Daily Sun,* August 30, 1879, 4; *Cheyenne Daily Leader,* December 16, 1879, 4.

Suggested Readings

Berwanger, Eugene H. "Hardin and Langston: Western Black Spokesmen of the Reconstruction Era." *Journal of Negro History* 64 (Spring 1979): 101–15.

———. "William J. Hardin: Colorado Spokesman for Racial Justice, 1863–1873." *The Colorado Magazine* 52 (Winter 1975): 52–65.

Billington, Monroe Lee, and Roger D. Hardaway, ed. *African Americans on the Western Frontier.* Niwot: University Press of Colorado, 1998.

Guenther, Todd R. "At Home on the Range: A History of Blacks in Wyoming, 1850–1950." Master's thesis, University of Wyoming, 1988.

Hardaway, Roger D. *A Narrative Bibliography of the African-American Frontier: Blacks in the Rocky Mountain West, 1535–1912.* Lewiston, N.Y.: Edwin Mellen Press, 1995.

Savage, W. Sherman. *Blacks in the West.* Westport, Conn.: Greenwood Press, 1976.

Taylor, Quintard. *In Search of the Racial Frontier: African Americans in the American West, 1528–1990.* New York: W. W. Norton, 1998.

6

Henry Ossian Flipper
African American Western Pioneer

Theodore D. Harris

The deeds—and misdeeds—of Henry Ossian Flipper (1856–1940) have often been forgotten in the Euramerican canon of the past. Though he was born into slavery in Georgia, his family's urban ties and mulatto background offered him an entrée into the white-dominated society. His father's success in business in post–Civil War Atlanta made it possible for Henry to receive a formal education and enter West Point at age seventeen. Though rejected by his peers because of his race and class status, he served his country gallantly on the southwestern frontier during the Indian wars of the late 1870s and 1880s. After a controversial dismissal from the army, Flipper went on to a successful career in engineering and eventually became the first African American editor of a white-owned newspaper in U.S. history.

Flipper was a multitalented individual, and his life demonstrates that, in spite of racism, some African Americans in the West found both social and economic mobility (though not necessarily more than those in the East). The movement to and through the West as experienced by African Americans transformed their lives dramatically; as they intermingled with other peoples, the old culture changed and values were reshaped. As he advanced from slave to capitalist, Flipper's vicissitudes in life reflected the confluence of migration, a powerful central government, contested lands, and an extraction-based economy—all of which marked the uniqueness of the West in relation to other regions of the republic.

Theodore D. Harris is a pioneer historian of African Americans in the U.S. West. A military historian as well, he has also published articles and reviews in that field. In 1963 he edited Henry O. Flipper's western memoirs. They were republished in 1997, with newly discovered material, as *Black Frontiersman.* Harris taught at the University of Minnesota, Minneapolis-Saint Paul, and the University of Texas, El Paso.

Henry Ossian Flipper began his career in the American West in a highly official manner on New Year's Day 1878. On that holiday the twenty-one–year-old second lieutenant of cavalry from Georgia reported for duty at Fort Sill in the Indian Territory, a racially turbulent frontier region that would have to wait for twenty-nine more years to become the state of Oklahoma in 1907. What marked the otherwise routine arrival at a frontier military outpost as historically significant was the fact that on June 4, 1877, Lt. Henry O. Flipper had become the first black graduate of the U.S. Military Academy at West Point and the regular army's first black commissioned officer. His arrival at Fort Sill inaugurated a forty-one-year military and civilian saga of adventure and achievement in the American West, from 1878 to 1919. His exploits and accomplishments were unmatched by any other black person on the American frontier before his era, and he blazed a trail for the African Americans who would follow.

Henry Flipper's parents were slaves, and he was born a slave on March 21, 1856, in Thomasville, Georgia. However, his father's background and the environment of Henry's early years provided opportunities denied to most victims of slavery, and they built the foundation for his remarkable achievements. In 1859 the Flipper family left behind life on the plantation and became urban slaves in Atlanta, Georgia. They were members of a somewhat more privileged mulatto caste of American slavery. Henry's father, Festus Flipper, became highly skilled at carriage construction and repair and was permitted by his owner to retain a large portion of his earnings in that field. After the Civil War, during Henry's early teenage years, Festus became a successful mulatto entrepreneur. A prominent bootmaker in Atlanta, he had white as well as black clients.

Parents with middle-class values and an ardent ambition for upward mobility naturally placed strong emphasis on formal education for their children. Henry's younger brother, Joseph Simeon Flipper, responded to such motivation by attaining notable success within the limits of racially segregated southern society. He became president of a black college and a bishop of the African Methodist Episcopal Church. Yet it was Henry Flipper, the eldest son, who dared to strive for distinction in the competitive mainstream white society of the nineteenth century.[1]

Henry's early education strengthened the values he had learned from his parents. His formal schooling took place in Reconstruction-era Atlanta at Storr's School, followed by one year at Atlanta University. These academies for black youth were founded and administered by the American Missionary Society of New England. Their dedicated white, northern faculty members taught and preached the Puritan virtues of industriousness, self-reliance, and worldly success. Such views found fertile soil in the mind of the academically gifted young Henry Flipper, where similar seeds had already been sown by his family. His outstanding intellectual talents and interests would be fostered by his love of learning and bear fruit throughout a long lifetime.

Henry Flipper in 1896, the year he published *Did a Negro Discover Arizona and New Mexico?* From the Arizona Historical Society, Tucson

His potential and his family's respectability prompted James Crawford Freeman, a white Republican member of Congress from Georgia, to grant the young black man an appointment to West Point. This appointment provoked a storm of protest from those Georgia newspapers still controlled by white supremacists, and Flipper was even offered a $5,000 bribe to reject it. Despite all this opposition, however, Henry O. Flipper became a cadet at the U.S. Military Academy in 1873. He was only seventeen years old at the time.[2]

At West Point, Flipper endured four years of social ostracism by the white cadets.[3] Such isolation was no doubt a factor in the pervasive sense of solitude that characterized Flipper's personality throughout the remainder of his life. Nonetheless, he remained steadfast in the pursuit of his goal. He graduated from West Point in the class of 1877, was commissioned a second lieutenant in the regular army, and was assigned to the cavalry—the first African American to win such distinction. Unforeseen by him at the time, his West Point education was to prove even more valuable to his future civilian career in the American West than it was to his military duties. In addition to an emphasis on civil engineering, the Academy required study of the Spanish language and both constitutional and international law. After his service in the army was completed, his knowledge in these fields would help propel Flipper to many landmark achievements on the frontier.

During the long periods of loneliness at West Point, he made notes of his experiences and recorded his reflections on them. In the early months of his frontier service at Fort Sill, the young black cavalry lieutenant combined his Academy material with facts about his earlier years to craft an autobiography. It was published that same year, 1878, by Homer Lee and Company of New York City, under the title *The Colored Cadet at West Point: Autobiography of Lieut. Henry Ossian Flipper, U.S.A., First Graduate of Color from the U.S. Military Academy.* Flipper's book was an important intellectual and historical accomplishment, especially for an author only twenty-two years of age. *The Colored Cadet at West Point* was also one of the earliest authentic African American autobiographies, and in its pages, Flipper formulated a gradualist philosophy for racial progress that was a generation ahead of similar theories popularized later by Booker T. Washington. Furthermore, his book provided the most detailed account available of West Point during the 1870s.

Henry Flipper's active military career lasted only from 1878 to 1882, but all of it was spent on the southwestern frontier during the Indian wars, including an Apache uprising. He was stationed at several army posts that played historical roles in the often violent settlement of the American Southwest. In addition to Fort Sill in the Indian Territory (Oklahoma), he saw field service at Fort Elliott in the Texas Panhandle, Forts Concho and Davis in west Texas, and Fort Quitman along the Mexican border. He served in the Tenth Cavalry Regiment, one of four regiments organized after the Civil War composed entirely of black enlisted personnel, with white commissioned officers, and designated the Ninth and Tenth Cavalries and the Twenty-fourth and Twenty-fifth Infantries. Flipper was the only black commissioned officer in the entire army. The four black regiments compiled distinguished combat records throughout the Indian wars, which did not end officially until 1891. Several African American soldiers received the Medal of Honor.[4]

Indian warriors paid their respects to the black cavalry regiments by calling them the "Buffalo Soldiers." To the Indians the texture of the black trooper's hair resembled the wooly hair of the bison, an animal they considered sacred and knew to be ferocious if cornered. The troopers proudly accepted the title. Flipper's regiment could boast of several distinguished officers during its frontier service. World War I's Gen. John J. Pershing, for instance, had won his renowned nickname, "Black Jack," while serving with the black Tenth Cavalry. During Flipper's time his regiment was commanded by Col. Benjamin F. Grierson, a Civil War cavalry hero. Flipper also served with Lt. Richard R. Pratt, founder of the Carlisle Indian School in Pennsylvania. Carlisle became the model for preparing Indian youth for life in white-dominated America.

The army in the West, like most sectors of American culture, was racially segregated. However, though a conservative institution, the army provided advantages to black men that were unmatched in civilian society until well into the twentieth century. Unlike civilian black men, black soldiers received the same pay and did the same work as their white counterparts, and their opportunities for promotion were equivalent. In civilian America, by contrast, the growing labor union movement was closed to black workers. The army also provided free medical and dental care, benefits unavailable to anyone in civilian society, and black career soldiers earned retirement benefits, a rarity for civilian workers of either race. Furthermore, the army offered black troops in the West educational opportunities not provided for white soldiers. Each black regiment was assigned a chaplain who provided basic education instruction as well as religious guidance. White troops were served only by post chaplains who were assigned to major installations and who had no educational responsibilities.[5]

Until the Spanish-American War in 1898, soldiers of the four black units spent their entire service west of the Mississippi. Over the years, some of them, including Henry Flipper, chose to settle in the West as civilians after leaving the army. They became a part of the African American population of the American West that has only recently claimed the attention of historians.

Young Lieutenant Flipper soon found adventure and mortal danger in the Far West. In 1880 the fierce Apache chieftain Victorio was leading his band of mounted raiders on a destructive rampage through the Texas frontier. The black Tenth Cavalry took the field against the marauding Apaches. Flipper was ordered to deliver dispatches to Colonel Grierson, who was ninety-eight miles away at Eagle Springs, Texas. Galloping through hostile Apache country, he made the journey in twenty-two hours, falling from his saddle in exhaustion as he reported to his colonel. A few days later, in a cavalry charge worthy of a twentieth-century Hollywood Western film, Lieutenant Flipper helped lead his Buffalo Soldiers against Chief Victorio's Apache warriors. The Indians were dispersed and fled into Mexico. After the battle, Flipper read the Episcopal service at the burial of the American casualties.

Even while in uniform, Flipper made contributions to Western development that were constructive and beneficial to civilian society as well as the military—specifically, in the field of civil engineering. Popular interest in the frontier army's Indian-fighting exploits have overshadowed its vital role in exploring, surveying, mapping, and constructing and maintaining internal improvements throughout the American West. On the frontier the army's West Point graduates were among the few professionally trained civil engineers.

Fort Sill had been plagued by malaria since its founding in 1869 by Civil War hero Gen. Philip H. Sheridan; indeed, the disease had caused many fatalities over the years. An attempt to devise a drainage system to eradicate concentrations of stagnant water, under the supervision of a white engineering officer trained at Germany's Heidelberg University, had failed. In 1879 young Lieutenant Flipper was assigned to the project. His design and construction of the system was so successful that malaria was permanently eliminated at Fort Sill. The drainage system, dubbed locally as "Flipper's Ditch," still serves to control floods and erosion in the area, and it won official recognition as a National Historic Landmark in 1977.[6] On two other engineering projects, Flipper was again selected as a "troubleshooter" when the white officers originally assigned proved incapable of accomplishing their missions. He expertly surveyed the route and supervised the construction of a road from Fort Sill to Gainesville, Texas, that met the standards for civilian commercial use as well as military transportation. Thirty-eight years later, in 1916, he could report that his road from Oklahoma to Texas was still in use. His third successful engineering rescue mission was the innovative building of an intricate telegraph line from Fort Elliott, Texas, to Fort Supply, Indian Territory, in 1879.

Flipper turned twenty-three at Fort Elliott in March 1879. His exacting duties there continued to prepare him for some of his later historic civilian roles. Established in 1874 in the Texas Panhandle, Fort Elliott sprawled over the prairie in an amorphous and most unorderly manner. Flipper conducted the first complete survey and scientific mapping of this extensive and confusing military facility. He also designed plans for additional buildings, including cavalry stables, and positioned and installed the post's sundial.[7]

Unfortunately Flipper's service in the U.S. Army ended with a scandal that would overshadow his significant accomplishments. In 1881, while stationed at Fort Davis in southwest Texas, he was serving as post commissary officer. That summer a shortage of $3,791.77 was discovered in his commissary account. After an investigation by the commanding officer, Col. (later Maj. Gen.) William Rufus "Pecos Bill" Shafter, Flipper was tried by court-martial on two charges: embezzlement of government funds and conduct unbecoming an officer and a gentleman. He was found innocent of embezzlement, for though he was shown to be grossly negligent in his handling of public funds, there was no proof of theft on his part. Lieutenant Flipper was, however, found guilty of conduct unbecoming an officer and a gentleman. Military law in 1881, specifically the Sixty-first Article of War, made dismissal from the service mandatory for any officer convicted of that charge. Accordingly, Henry Flipper was dismissed from the army as of June 30, 1882.

The guilty verdict on the second charge was based on proof that, prior to discovery of the shortage, Flipper had concealed it by submitting four official and signed reports falsely attesting that funds had been transmitted, as required, to higher headquarters in San Antonio, Texas. These four offenses had been compounded by a fifth. Hoping to cover some of the deficit after its discovery, Flipper had presented a personal check, proved to be knowingly fraudulent, for $1,440.43. He knew that he did not even have an account at the bank on which it was drawn.[8]

It was this fifth offense that must have sealed Flipper's fate as an officer. The code of honor by which army officers lived during that time maintained that "an officer's word is his bond." The intentional writing of a bad personal check was considered a heinous breach of that code and was held to reflect on the integrity of the entire officer corps, which alone could be cause for dismissal from the service. Such a culprit was a disgrace as an officer and, importantly, as a gentleman.

The story of Henry O. Flipper's military downfall is surrounded by controversy and unanswered questions to this day. Thus far, none of the historians who have written of his life have uncovered the complete truth. We do know that this remarkably self-disciplined young man became temporarily dysfunctional. This misjudgment could have been caused by the symbolic racial burden he had borne since his West Point admission nine years earlier. However, it is an oversimplification to blame his misconduct entirely on racism within an army that accepted black enlisted personnel but was skeptical about black commissioned officers. His guilt of dishonorable conduct is undeniable and his punishment understandable.

Flipper's dismissal did not constitute a dishonorable discharge according to military law in 1882; it simply meant that the army no longer desired his services. It entailed neither imprisonment nor monetary fine. Significantly for his subsequent career, the discharge also did not prohibit him from working as a civilian employee in the federal government. It is ironic that this deepest abyss of Flipper's life ultimately proved to be the turning point after which he rose to a continued succession of unique achievements that would help future African Americans overcome significant barriers.

When Henry Flipper involuntarily reentered civilian society in 1882, he made a decision that would mark his trail for the rest of his life: he decided to stay in the American West. It was a wise decision, for in a frontier environment a man's practical contributions to the developing society could sometimes surmount the hurdles of racial, ethnic, or national origins. He set out for the booming town of El Paso, Texas, on the Mexican border of the Rio Grande. On the ethnically diverse and more socially indulgent southwestern frontier, he was able, by his own talents and efforts, to carve out an extraordinary civilian career that would have been denied him elsewhere in America.

At age twenty-six, he began to put his expert engineering skills and competence in Spanish to highly productive use. Between 1883 and 1893, he worked as America's first African American professional surveyor, cartographer, and civil and mining engineer. As early as 1887, he made black history by establishing a private civil and mining engineering practice in the Mexican border community of Nogales, in Arizona Territory. He set another racial precedent by upgrading that pioneer practice in 1896 when he won official designation as a U.S. deputy mineral surveyor.[9]

Flipper crossed trails with many historical and flamboyant characters while pursuing his profession on the untamed Arizona frontier. Like Oklahoma, Arizona was still a territory, and it did not attain statehood until 1912. In 1886, while the campaign against the famous Apache leader Geronimo was raging in the vicinity, Flipper shared a camp for two weeks with physician Leonard Wood and grew to know him quite well. Wood went on to command Theodore Roosevelt's Rough Riders in the 1898 Spanish-American War, became military governor of Cuba and then the Philippines, was later the army's chief of staff, and almost won the

Republican presidential nomination in 1920. In 1891, near Yuma, Flipper permitted an impoverished southern white woman to do his camp washing and learned that she was a niece of former Confederate president Jefferson Davis. Two years later, in Nogales, Flipper and his friend Jesse Grant conspired to successfully defeat an arrogant white candidate in a local election with a hilarious scheme worthy of a Mark Twain tale of bizarre frontier politics. Grant, son of President Ulysses S. Grant, would go on to become a prominent businessman of early-twentieth-century San Diego, California, where he managed the well-known U.S. Grant Hotel.

During his frequent field trips across the Southwest frontier and in northern Mexico, Flipper often kept only hours ahead of hostile Indians, American outlaws, Mexican bandits, and, from 1910 to 1912, violent Mexican revolutionaries. On one surveying expedition, he fired an insubordinate white man he had hired as a camp foreman. Only later did he learn that the man was Zebina Nathaniel Streeter. Known as the "White Apache," Streeter was one of the borderland's most terrifying desperadoes and mass murderers, with a $5,000 price on his head.[10]

In 1893, Flipper won the admiration and gratitude of the citizens of Nogales when his meticulous research and expert testimony on Spanish land law upheld the validity of the Nogales land grant in a lawsuit that could have ruined the city. Though not a lawyer, he demonstrated a brilliant talent for legal analysis and scholarship, augmenting his exceptional technological and linguistic skills.[11]

James J. Chatham was an Arizona political figure and owner of the Nogales *Sunday Herald.* He felt confident in entrusting Flipper with the editorship of his newspaper for four months during the spring of 1895, while he was away on political business. Thus, Henry Flipper won the distinction of becoming the first African American editor of a white-owned newspaper in American history.[12]

Flipper's success in the Nogales land grant case led to his appointment as the only black special agent of the Justice Department's U.S. Court of Private Land Claims. He performed field investigations on land and mining disputes between American and Mexican claimants throughout west Texas, New Mexico, and Arizona. He became the principal consultant to the government attorneys in the preparation and trial of several important federal cases that saved the titles of many American claimants. Flipper's duties also involved translating and editing for publication valuable modern and historical works on Spanish and Mexican land and mineral law. By 1901 this black frontiersman, born a slave, was America's acknowledged expert on these complex subjects.[13]

In the late 1890s, capitalizing on his frontier experiences, he turned his ever productive mind to the field of practical invention. He qualified for a federal patent for an easily transported and assembled four-man tent made from a single piece of material. He thereby became one of the few African Americans to gain a registered patent prior to the twentieth century.[14] Also during the nineties Flipper's insatiable intellectual curiosity led him to an intensive study of southwestern and Spanish American history. His mastery of Spanish enabled him to pursue research in primary historical sources, and he possessed the additional advantage of personal field experience in many of the geographic regions he was studying historically and culturally. Henry Flipper soon became a pioneer scholar and authority on the history of the Spanish borderlands, a topic only beginning to attract the interest of white professional historians.

In 1896 his scholarly research bore significant fruit. He published a monograph in Nogales entitled *Did a Negro Discover Arizona and New Mexico?* It established the key historical role in the Southwest of the African guide Estevanico during the sixteenth-century Spanish expedition of Marcos de Niza. The book also included the first English translation of Pedro de Castañeda's account of that expedition. Flipper thus made a pioneering scholarly contribution to both Spanish American colonial history and African American history. It is a testament to his mental and physical vigor that he was able to do so while pursuing his other rugged and often dangerous frontier professions.

Throughout his life, he retained a deep sense of national loyalty despite the heartbreaking collapse of his army career. By February 1898 the Spanish-American War was approaching. From El Paso, Texas, he sent a telegram to Secretary of War Russell A. Alger. Though nearly forty-two years old, Flipper volunteered, as a West Point graduate, for wartime service. He was saddened when his telegram was not even acknowledged.

During frequent expeditions south of the border, Flipper became interested in the famous legend of the lost Spanish silver mine of Tayopa in Sonora, Mexico. He made his own explorations and became an authority on the tale, thereby adding folklore to the impressive list of his areas of expertise. In later years, he felt that with more time in Mexico, he might have discovered the fabled Tayopa mine.

In 1901 the Court of Private Land Claims completed its mission and was deactivated by the U.S. Justice Department, leaving Flipper at liberty. His reputation as a Tayopa expert brought him to the attention of Col. William Cornell Greene. In 1901, Greene engaged him as an engineer for one of his mining companies in northern Mexico, making him the first

African American to be so employed. Bill Greene was one of the American Southwest's most spectacular promoters and speculators: some called him "the Cecil Rhodes of America." The romantic tale of hidden wealth at Tayopa captivated the flamboyant Greene. In partnership with another buccaneering Western tycoon, William Randolph Hearst, Greene sent Flipper all the way to Spain to search Spanish archives for clues to the mine's location. Reluctantly, Flipper had to report that his research netted little relevant information.[15]

Colonel Greene, nevertheless, was impressed by Flipper's technological and intellectual abilities and frontier-bred resourcefulness. He promoted him to positions of major responsibility as a field manager at mines in his vast mineral enterprises in northern Mexico. Once again, Flipper was breaking new professional ground for an African American in the first decade of the twentieth century. It was while employed as a mine manager that he renewed his acquaintance with Albert Fall, whose patronage was to be a central factor in the now middle-aged black pioneer's strenuous life from 1908 to 1923. Flipper had met Fall in the Southwest while serving with the Court of Private Land Claims from 1893 to 1901.

Albert Bacon Fall was as fabulous a frontier Croesus as Bill Greene, having accumulated large holdings in mineral, cattle, and petroleum-rich land in the Southwest and in Mexico. He became a powerful Republican senator from New Mexico after it attained statehood in 1912, the same year as Arizona. He later became secretary of the interior in the ill-fated Harding administration. However, Fall's colorful career collapsed in disgrace in the mid-1920s. Convicted of complicity in the infamous Wyoming Teapot Dome oil-lease scandal, he was sentenced to prison.

Sixteen years earlier, Albert Fall had been Bill Greene's attorney and business partner, as well as general manager of Greene's extensive mining operations in Chihuahua, Mexico. He respected Flipper's professional abilities and decided to utilize them in his own enterprises. In 1908, he engaged him as legal and mining consultant for his Sierra Mining Company. It was another milestone for a black American. Senator Fall later recalled that during those years, "Mr. Flipper was my right hand man and adviser."[16] In 1912, with Americans fleeing the violence of the Mexican Revolution, Fall stationed Flipper in El Paso, Texas.

Under the tutelage of the wily and ambitious Fall, Flipper's adventurous life was now to be spiced with the element of international intrigue. In El Paso, right on the Mexican border, his duties were expanded to include an assignment as personal intelligence agent for his employer. In 1913, Albert Fall was in Washington, DC, serving as a

Republican senator from New Mexico and chairing a Senate committee investigating the Mexican Revolution's impact on American economic and political interests. He retained sizable financial interests in Mexico, which were threatened by the revolution. Fall relied on Flipper to gather and analyze military and political information from Mexico to help him influence American policy and protect his investments. By 1913, Flipper was dispatching detailed intelligence reports to the senator in Washington. Many of them proved highly valuable to the Senate committee, irrespective of their value to Fall personally.

During his El Paso years, from 1912 to 1919, Flipper did not limit his professional activities to his duties for Senator Fall. He continued his scholarly research and writing on regional history. In 1914 he published a groundbreaking article entitled "Early History of El Paso," in *Old Santa Fe,* the forerunner of the *New Mexico Historical Review.* Its editor ranked Flipper as the preeminent authority on the Spanish and Mexican history of the borderlands.[17]

An even more historically significant work was written in El Paso in 1916 by the now sixty-year-old black frontiersman. He wrote a manuscript detailing many of his remarkable military and civilian experiences in the American Southwest and Mexico from 1878 to 1916. The manuscript was not published until 1963, twenty-three years after his death. Amazingly, Flipper's narrative remains the only authenticated Western frontier memoir written by a black American to be discovered thus far. It was republished in 1997 with additional selections from his writings, including the 1896 *Did a Negro Discover Arizona and New Mexico?* under the title *Black Frontiersman* (see Suggested Readings).

The El Paso years also saw the birth of a melodramatic legend concerning Flipper's alleged collaboration with the highly publicized Mexican insurgent leader Gen. Francisco "Pancho" Villa. For several years, articles occasionally appeared in newspapers around the country claiming that Henry Flipper was serving with Villa's forces and even that he was the famous Mexican general's chief military adviser. Despite Flipper's angry public denials and vehement denunciations of Villa and the Villista revolutionary movement, the romantic myth outlived both men.

The investigations undertaken by Fall's Senate committee on Mexican affairs grew increasingly complex. He required an outstanding expert on his staff. In 1919, he summoned Flipper to Washington, DC, appointing him consultant, translator, and interpreter for the Senate committee. The appointment was a notable distinction for a black American in 1919. Two years later the newly elected president, Warren G. Harding, named Albert

Fall to his cabinet as secretary of the interior. Flipper had performed so competently for the Senate committee that Fall promoted him to assistant to the secretary of the interior, an unusually high federal post for an African American in that era, and Fall won praise from black leaders. Appropriately, Flipper became involved with America's last frontier when his Interior Department duties included professional tasks for the Alaskan Engineer Commission in Washington, DC.

When Fall resigned from the cabinet in 1923 amid rumors about Teapot Dome, Flipper submitted his own resignation. From 1923 to 1930, he served as the expert in South American mineral law for an American petroleum company in Venezuela.[18] However, the economic crash of 1929 cost him his employment and wiped out his financial assets. He realized that the time had finally arrived to bring his arduous adventures to a halt.

In 1931, at age seventy-five, Henry Flipper returned to his roots in Atlanta, Georgia. There, he resided at the home of his brother, Bishop Joseph Simeon Flipper, for the remaining nine years of his life. Echoes from the American West still haunted him. Because of his long association with Albert B. Fall, coupled with dim recollections of his court-martial in the West, a tale spread that Henry O. Flipper had been the secret mastermind behind Wyoming's sensational Teapot Dome scandal. He chose to ignore this latest outrageous fantasy.

Flipper's last years were solitary ones. Throughout his life, he had remained, in Western jargon, a loner and had very few confirmed romantic relationships with women. At age thirty-five, in 1891, he did venture into a common-law arrangement with a woman of Mexican descent in Nogales, Arizona Territory, but the union could not be recognized as a legal marriage because of territorial antimiscegenation laws. The relationship ended in less than seven months, and Flipper declared that he could never bring himself to marry any woman, whatever her race, on the Southwest frontier.[19]

On the morning of May 3, 1940, the old soldier and frontiersman was found in his bedroom, dead of heart failure at the age of eighty-four. The story of Henry Flipper's contributions to Western and African American history passed with him until told by historians of a later era. Death did not, however, end the Flipper saga. The great frustration of his life was the futile forty-year struggle he waged to reverse his court-martial conviction and win army reinstatement. From 1884 to 1924, he had nine unsuccessful bills introduced in Congress to petition for those goals. In 1922, while Flipper was serving on his staff, Secretary of the Interior Fall used his influence with Secretary of War John W. Weeks in a fruitless effort to aid

Flipper's cause. In his rejection of Fall's personal appeal, Secretary Weeks echoed the army's official position on Flipper's 1882 dismissal and reflected the general climate of opinion prevailing in the America of 1922.[20]

Half a century later, social and political attitudes in America had changed. In 1976, after a campaign by civil rights advocates led by Ray O. McColl, a white schoolteacher from Georgia, Flipper won partial posthumous vindication. The Army Board for Corrections of Military Records declared that it lacked authority to reverse Flipper's conviction, but by a vote of four to one, board members did convert his separation record to a certificate of honorable discharge. In 1978 Henry Flipper's remains were removed from Atlanta to his birthplace of Thomasville, Georgia, and reinterred with full military honors. His final resting place was beside his parents and near the actual scene of his birth in 1856, the site of the old slave quarters.[21]

Continued advocacy on his behalf by Flipper's descendants was instrumental in his achieving a final unique historical accomplishment. On February 19, 1999, President Bill Clinton granted Henry Flipper a presidential pardon. It was the first posthumous presidential pardon ever granted to anyone in the history of the United States.

Flipper was the type of individual characterized by modern sociologists as a "marginal man." He felt embarrassed in black society because his intellect and cosmopolitan experiences were deemed—by prevailing white standards—to make him culturally superior. However, he could never feel at ease in white society because he was conscious of belonging to a race that was patronized and even despised by the white majority, regardless of his own individual achievements. Secretary Fall described Flipper's lifelong social dilemma perfectly in a letter to a colleague: "His life is a most pathetic one. By education, by experience and because of his natural high intellectual characteristics, he can find no pleasure in association with many of his own race, and because of his color he was and is precluded in this country from enjoying the society of those whom he would be mentally and otherwise best fitted to associate with."[22]

It was also Flipper's misfortune that, during a long and productive life, he was always ahead of his time. His achievements were unique for a black person in American society, but they occurred before the mainstream of that society was prepared to accept and respect black citizens on a basis of freedom and equality. Nonetheless, it is clear that Henry Ossian Flipper was a cultural trailblazer—a true man of the West, who genuinely earned the title of "Black Frontiersman."

Notes

1. Theodore D. Harris, comp. and ed., *Black Frontiersman: The Memoirs of Henry O. Flipper, First Black Graduate of West Point* (Fort Worth: Texas Christian University Press, 1997), 3–4.

2. Steve Wilson, " A Black Lieutenant in the Ranks," *American History Illustrated* 17 (December 1983): 32.

3. See Henry Ossian Flipper, *The Colored Cadet at West Point* (1878; reprint, Salem, NH: Ayer, 1991).

4. William H. Leckie, *The Buffalo Soldiers: A Narrative of the Negro Cavalry in the West* (Norman: University of Oklahoma Press, 1967), 208, 233, 244.

5. Ibid., 6.

6. Harris, *Black Frontiersman,* 5.

7. Ibid., 4–5, 72–73.

8. Charles M. Robinson III, *The Court-Martial of Lieutenant Henry Flipper* (El Paso: Texas Western Press, 1994), 53, 95–96.

9. Harris, *Black Frontiersman,* 167, n. 41.

10. Ibid., 45–46, 49–50, 166, nn. 35, 36.

11. Jane Eppinga, *Henry Ossian Flipper: West Point's First Black Graduate* (Plano: Republic of Texas Press, 1996), 147–76.

12. Harris, *Black Frontiersman,* 7, 9, 50–51.

13. Ibid., 9, 103–4.

14. Eppinga, *Henry Ossian Flipper,* 172.

15. J. Frank Dobie, *Apache Gold and Yaqui Silver* (Boston: Little, Brown, 1950), 203–9.

16. Letter from Secretary of the Interior Albert B. Fall to Senator James W. Wadsworth Jr., September 9, 1922, U.S. Department of the Interior Records, Washington, DC.

17. Eppinga, *Henry Ossian Flipper,* 196.

18. Ibid., 202, 205–13.

19. Harris, *Black Frontiersman,* 13–14.

20. Ibid., 14.

21. Robinson, *The Court-Martial of Lieutenant Henry Flipper,* 109–10.

22. Letter from Secretary of the Interior Fall to Senator Wadsworth.

Suggested Readings

Black, Lowell D., and Sara H. Black. *An Officer and a Gentleman: The Military Career of Lieutenant Henry O. Flipper.* Dayton, OH: Lora, 1985.

Cage, James C., and James M. Day. *The Court-Martial of Henry Ossian Flipper: West Point's First Black Graduate.* El Paso, TX: El Paso Corral of the Westerners, 1981.

Carroll, John M., ed. *The Black Military Experience in the American West.* New York: Liveright, 1971.

Eppinga, Jane. *Henry Ossian Flipper: West Point's First Black Graduate.* Plano: Republic of Texas Press, 1996.

Harris, Theodore D., comp. and ed. *Black Frontiersman: The Memoirs of Henry O. Flipper, First Black Graduate of West Point.* Fort Worth: Texas Christian University Press, 1997.

Leckie, William H. *The Buffalo Soldiers: A Narrative of the Negro Cavalry in the West.* Norman: University of Oklahoma Press, 1967.

Robinson, Charles M., III. *The Court-Martial of Lieutenant Henry Flipper.* El Paso: Texas Western Press, 1994.

7

Clara True and Female Moral Authority

Margaret D. Jacobs

Clara True's professional career speaks to the cross-cultural tensions that existed in Euramerican women's search for power in a time of masculine privilege and the sex-typed division of labor. The participation of women in waged labor and politics ran against the dictates of the prescriptive "true womanhood" and seemed to support the neo-Turnerian argument that the West was a place of cultural change and new departures. But women such as True also found themselves co-opted into the Victorian gender ideology; what was familiar in the East was replicated in the West. Their attempts to "uplift" Native American women and men—through industrial training, education, citizenship, and Christianization—became an exercise in maternalism that not only disparaged indigenous cultures but also sustained unequal power relations between men and women, non-Indians and Indians, guardians and wards. Ultimately the sway of Social Darwinism along with the demands of early-twentieth-century capitalism undermined the search for power, both for True and for the Native Americans.

In this essay, Margaret D. Jacobs, a scholar in the field of U.S. women's history, explores a familiar tale about the assimilation of the first peoples of North America at the turn of the twentieth century. Knitting together various markers of difference—race, class, gender, and ideology—Jacobs's essay shows us the contested nature of identities and fragile social relations.

Jacobs received her Ph.D. in history from the University of California, Davis. She is currently an assistant professor at New Mexico State University, Las Cruces, where she specializes in cross-cultural relations between women. Her publications include *Engendered Encounters: Feminism and Pueblo Cultures, 1879–1934,* published in 1999, and several journal articles.

Clara True spent more than fifty years of her life working as a reformer on behalf of Native Americans. Born in Kentucky in the late 1800s and college-educated in Missouri, she became involved in Indian reform work in the 1890s when she was stationed as a teacher by the Bureau of Indian Affairs (BIA) at the Lower Brule Agency on the Sioux Reservation in South Dakota. There, she eventually served as principal of the boarding school for six years.[1] From 1902 to 1907, True worked as the teacher in the day school at Santa Clara Pueblo in New Mexico, and from 1908 to 1910, she served as the superintendent of the Malki Indian Agency at the Morongo Indian Reservation near Banning in southern California. In 1910, she returned to New Mexico to settle in the Española Valley, close to Santa Clara Pueblo, where she owned and managed a series of ranches. From 1910 until the 1940s, although True no longer worked for the BIA, she involved herself intensely in both its administration and the affairs of Santa Clara Pueblo.[2]

True's career spanned a crucial era in Indian-white relations, from the days of the assimilation policy to the period of the so-called Indian New Deal. From approximately 1880 to 1930 the federal government promoted assimilation through allotment of communally held Indian land to Indian families and individuals, education in dominant American ideals in a network of day schools and boarding schools, and severe restrictions on Native American religious practices. Designed to blot out all vestiges of indigenous cultures and to absorb Indians into white-dominated American society (at least as marginal, low-skilled, low-paid workers), the assimilation policy separated family members, reduced Indian lands still further, and threatened centuries-old cultural practices.[3] True's life illustrates the crucial role that white women played in promoting and carrying out the policy of assimilation and the ways in which their work empowered white women, creating new sources of employment, status, and self-confidence in a society that still did not grant them basic citizenship rights. Yet white women's empowerment often came at the expense of the Native Americans they targeted in their assimilation efforts. Assured by their own upbringing that they knew what was best for the Indian, True and other white women often carried out policies that had tragic and painful consequences for Native Americans.[4]

True's work to assimilate Native Americans did pay off for a time, for she gained a following of Pueblo Indians who seemed to support assimilation. Through her work with Native Americans, she also realized her desire to gain greater authority as a woman. Yet both of True's successes proved to be short lived. By the 1920s, as Indians resisted or turned assimilation to their own purposes and as a new generation of white reformers who espoused cultural relativism took up their cause, True and other assimilationist women fell increasingly out of step with their times. Additionally, the notion of women's moral authority had lost its cultural power; True and other female moral reformers found themselves marginalized from the political arena. Ironically, just as True denied the possibility of self-determination to Native Americans, the society in which she

From Harry Lawton, *Willie Boy: Desert Manhunt* (Balboa Island, CA: Paisano Press, 1960). *Courtesy of the University of California, Riverside*

lived refused to accord her and other women full control over their own lives as well.

Extensive interaction in the assimilation era between white women and Native Americans could have yielded a sense of common cause and mutual respect. Yet, rather than playing a sisterly role with Native Americans, True and other white women adopted what some historians call a "maternalist" position toward Indians. As Linda Gordon has formulated it, maternalism embodied three components: the view that motherhood and domesticity represented women's essential role in society; the belief that women's potential as mothers made them ideally suited to reform society; and, most important for this essay, a commitment on the part of white, middle-class women to mothering those they perceived as less fortunate than themselves.[5] As True's story reveals, most maternalist white women remained convinced of their cultural superiority and unable to imagine total equality between themselves and the people they professed to serve.

In the late nineteenth century, True was one of many women who found a new calling in reform work for Native Americans. During that period the BIA offered unprecedented opportunities for white women (and even some Native American women educated in boarding schools) to engage in paid work outside the home as teachers, nurses, field matrons, and other officials, often in locales that must have seemed exotic. According to David Wallace Adams, 312 out of 550 teachers in Indian schools between 1892 and 1900 were women. By 1900, 286 out of 347 such teachers were women, and more women than men served as principals in the Indian schools. Though outnumbered by men in the higher echelons of the BIA, some women, including True, even attained the rank of superintendent. Moreover the typical female teacher was single.[6] For an adventurous woman who did not wish to follow the more traditional path of marriage and motherhood, a career as a BIA schoolteacher, field matron, nurse, or other official may have offered economic independence, a satisfying career, and a degree of social and cultural authority.

Although schoolteaching had become a woman's occupation by the late nineteenth century, it seems curious that the BIA would have elected to assign women, many of whom were single, to remote locations on Indian reservations. After all, the BIA and other white Americans deemed Native Americans "savages" and often portrayed Native American men as lecherous would-be rapists who preyed on white women. As Lisa Emmerich has shown, however, women's reform organizations developed powerful maternalist justifications for white women's work among Indians and influenced the BIA to hire women as field matrons and schoolteachers. In the last decades of the nineteenth century, in fact, white women had led the way in calling for a reform of Indian policy. In 1879 a group of white, middle-class women formed the Women's National Indian Association (WNIA) to address injustices against Native Americans. Not until 1882 did white men establish their own reform organization, the Indian Rights Association (IRA), to address the same matters. At that point the WNIA forfeited what they regarded as the more "male" activity of lobbying for land issues and treaty rights to the IRA and instead turned to establishing schools and missions on Indian reservations, where educated, middle-class white women would help to "uplift" supposedly degraded Indian women.[7]

Such a sentiment grew out of nineteenth-century ideals regarding women's proper sphere. In the early 1800s, in part as a way to distinguish itself as a class, the emerging middle class had developed a new set of gender norms that focused on women's subordinate and separate role in the supposedly private sphere of the home. Prescriptive literature stipulated that women could enjoy an elevated status by carefully adhering to the tenets of "true womanhood": submissiveness, purity, piety, and domesticity. Yet middle-class women often parlayed their association with purity and piety into public activism, believing it their moral duty to rectify social wrongs in order to maintain pure lives and homes. Gradually white, middle-class women became involved in a greater number of social issues, from temperance and Sabbatarianism to abolitionism and women's rights and eventually Indian reform.[8]

In the process, women formed political networks and personal bonds with one another that sometimes lasted a lifetime. During her work at Morongo, True met Mary Bryan, whom she described as a "woman of wealth and position." Bryan served as treasurer of the Redlands Indian Association and later as financial clerk for True at Morongo. Mary Bryan "was so closely connected with all of my work," True declared, "that we slept, ate and camped as well as worked together. At the close of my official life, she elected to keep up the intimacy."[9] When True left Morongo to return to New Mexico, Bryan accompanied her, living out her days with True on her ranch in the Española Valley. True and Bryan's arrangement, whether involving a sexual component or not, was not unusual in the nineteenth and early twentieth centuries for white women involved in social reform. Women found sustenance, comfort, and companionship with other like-minded women, enabling them to carry out their reform work.[10]

By the late nineteenth century middle-class women reformers identified as their primary goal the so-called uplifting of other women who, reformers believed, did not enjoy the privileges and status of white, middle-class women. Reformers organized homes for prostitutes, wayward girls, and unwed mothers. They sent women missionaries out to convert Chinese and Arab women to Protestantism. Through the WNIA, they became interested in uplifting Native American women. According to Amelia Stone Quinton, the president of the WNIA, "patriotic Christian women" could hear the "cry of suffering, undefended, ever-endangered Indian women" and their "pleas . . . for the sacred shield of law." Partly influenced by the labor of the WNIA and the IRA, the federal government enshrined the WNIA's notion of women's work for women into its new assimilation policy.[11]

Early in her career, True benefited from the BIA's newfound, if limited, interest in white women employees. The heyday of her career occurred from 1908 to 1910 during her tenure as superintendent of the Malki Agency on the Morongo Reservation in southern California. Commissioner of Indian Affairs Francis E. Leupp passed over many men to elevate True to the position, deciding that "the very man" to help the ailing agency was a woman. "I gave her a man's work," Leupp declared, "and she has done it better than any man who has been in there for thirty years." Leupp also recognized other white women's accomplishments in the BIA, referring to the female employees under his direction as his "Amazonian corps." He remarked that "the part that women play in the education of the backward races I do not think has ever been sufficiently emphasized."[12]

Like Leupp and many other BIA officials, True believed Indians were backward and often compared them to children. Arguing for the prohibition of alcohol to Native Americans, she asserted that "we do not intend to permit [the Indian] to injure himself with something he does not know the danger of, any more than we would permit a baby to crawl into a pretty fire."[13] Because she believed most Native Americans were comparable to children, True did not regard them as competent to look after their own affairs. Instead she deemed herself their caretaker. "I can protect the Indians and put them on their feet I think a little better than most others, because I know the Indians so well and they all know me," True wrote to the IRA.[14]

Underneath her maternalistic tone, True concealed a deeper contempt for Native American cultures and individuals. As she embarked on her work at Morongo, she wrote, "Few of the [Indian] people I am to spend time with seem more interesting or spiritual than a brickbat, yet they are said to have souls. I'll see if they can be made conscious that they have. To begin, I'll see if I can get enough of them sober at once to experiment with." As for Indian women, True wrote that they were "being sold at ten dollars per head within sound of the church bells. If they stayed sold it would not be so bad; but they are not worth ten dollars, and the men soon regret the purchase."[15]

True's disrespectful attitudes had grave consequences for the Native Americans with whom she worked. Within a few months of her arrival at Santa Clara Pueblo in 1902, a diphtheria epidemic struck. According to True one group in the pueblo was "reluctant to openly give up their last tribal custom—that of 'making medicine' "; they refused to cooperate and instead hid their sick children from True and the doctor. Only the children's burials announced their fate. Rather than being sympathetic to their loss and grief, True simply dismissed those Santa Clarans who tried to keep faith in their religion, describing one older woman who resisted treatment as an "old hag."[16] As the scope of the epidemic increased, True found herself unable to enforce an effective quarantine. Desperate for help, she believed that only armed federal troops could alleviate the situation in Santa Clara. True, indeed, confronted enormous difficulties. Yet it was not inevitable that the Santa Clarans would refuse her treatments. In other similar epidemics white field matrons who respected indigenous medical practices had greater success in persuading Native Americans to accept western therapies. True's lack of regard for Indian religions and their curing and healing ceremonies only made the Santa Clarans more resistant to the lifesaving medicines she offered.[17]

The influence of nineteenth-century women's reform ideology on True is evident in her initial concentration on the uplift of young Indian women. While stationed at Morongo, she claimed credit for rescuing Indian girls in southern California from a life of vice: "I robbed the Los Angeles Red Light and got back the girls, many of them Sherman Institute educated but gone wrong from a bad start. . . . I made Southern California pretty safe for Indians." Her friend Marah Ellis Ryan agreed that True "did stop the sale of slave [Indian] girls at $10 each—formerly a habitual traffic across the [U.S.-Mexican] border." True then continued her "rescue" of Indian women in an informal capacity in New Mexico. In 1924 she rented rooms and ran a free employment agency in Santa Fe, primarily for Indian girls who left school after the eighth grade.[18] Up to this point in her life, she saw herself as a motherly figure who could shield Indian women from male exploitation and degradation.

Sometime in the 1920s, however, True became much more involved with Native American men and their political and economic affairs within the pueblos than with the moral uplift of Native American women. Rather than maintaining her view that all Native American men sought to degrade

Native American women, True came to make distinctions between the "bad" Indian males who clung to their traditional ways and the "good" ones who renounced their tribal customs.[19] True and many BIA officials championed a group of Indians they called Progressives—returned boarding-school students who had "broken away from the old tribal customs," sent their children to schools, improved their homes, and displayed good citizenship. Yet, according to True, they were "practically given no share in the government of the pueblo."[20] To undermine the traditional governing and cultural practices of Santa Clara and other pueblos, Clara True set about promoting the Progressive Party, and in the process, she fostered some of the factionalism in the pueblos. She also sought to help individual Indians who alleged that tribal leaders took away their land as punishment for refusing to dance in the pueblo's religious ceremonies.[21]

Some Native Americans may have genuinely appreciated True's efforts on their behalf. "What are we going to do when Miss True dies?" Joseph Tafoya, president of the Progressive Party, lamented to the IRA, "I want to get our affairs in good shape while she is still with us." Other Pueblo Indians objected to the Progressives' and True's characterization of them as persecuted victims. In a statement released to the major newspaper of northern New Mexico, the *Santa Fe New Mexican,* governors of several pueblos and the chairman of the All-Pueblo Council addressed the so-called Progressives: "It is a proven fact that you are only a few persons, a bunch of [dis]gruntled fellows who refuse to do your share of work in your own Pueblo which is for your own good. . . . If you were progressive you wouldn't try to destroy your people's unity." The writers also referred to an American woman, undoubtedly True, as the "cause your Santa Clara people can't get together."[22]

True took full credit for any successes the Progressives had in gaining power within their pueblos. "I keep them thinking they did it all and they are quite cocky about their ability," she wrote to the IRA. In another revealing letter to the president of the Progressive Pueblo Indian Council, she reminisced about her role in shaping the lives of the young Indians:

> If I have steered you past the rocks until your boat is in smooth water, I am glad to have been of help to my old boys of the little day school in Santa Clara where I carried some of you on my back when you were too little to walk to a school picnic. . . . It seems but yesterday since I ran the clippers over your hair by order of the Indian Bureau. I have spanked a good many of you. As you grew up, we were companions in hunting and fishing and gardening and "busting" broncos. Later on in life, most of you worked for me on my ranch. We have been almost like the same family for nearly thirty years. . . . You are always my "boys." Don't forget that, whatever happens.[23]

True's letter to the Progressives reveals how much more she identified with the activities of men—hunting, fishing, and busting broncos—than she did with those of women. She seems to have lost interest in the moral uplift of "her girls."[24] Perhaps she became more involved in the public world of the Indian because she was more interested in village politics and economics—the province of Pueblo men—than in the home lives of Pueblo women. At the same time, her continual reference to the Native American men as "boys" exposes her sense of power and authority over them. True lamented her lack of power in relation to white men, but she clearly believed she could exert dominance and authority over Native American men. One of her friends once claimed that "Miss True's ambition is to have a large following among the Indians; . . . evidently she loves power more than money."[25]

Unlike many of her female colleagues, True also became very interested in land issues, a province usually reserved for white male reformers. At the Morongo Reservation, she worked tirelessly to challenge attempts by non-Indians to take over Indian land. According to Marah Ellis Ryan, "She kept going for the man 'higher up' in certain land and water abuses against the Indians, until she got up against the So[uthern] Pacific R[ail] R[oad] and there was a cabinet meeting on her case in Washington. She was going further than any Agent had dared to go, and had to be halted for political reasons." True resigned in 1910 rather than contend with the politicians and returned to the Rio Grande Valley to run her own business.[26] Curiously, however, when a conflict erupted in the early 1920s over protecting Pueblo land from squatters, True sided against the Pueblos. Sen. Holm Bursum of New Mexico had introduced a bill in the Senate to settle title disputes to land claims within the borders of territory claimed by the Pueblos. If the claimant could prove he or she had held the land for at least ten years prior to 1912, he or she would be given legal title to the land. The Bursum bill (1922) elicited a firestorm of protest from a coalition of Pueblo Indians as well as the IRA and a newly radicalized group of white Americans—including a young New York City reformer named John Collier—who had taken up the cause of Native Americans. True, however, supported the bill. During the controversy, she portrayed herself as acting in the best interests of the Pueblos and characterized other Anglo reformers as either corrupt individuals who sought to swindle the Indians or misguided fools.[27]

There is evidence, however, that True was looking out for her own interests, having in fact taken over land that belonged to Santa Clara Pueblo. "My own ranch I am amazed to discover," she wrote to a colleague in the IRA, "is within a *Spanish* purchase and at the end of the present suit I will likely find myself a great land owner having unwillingly acquired about half the Indian land on our side of the Rio Grande." Although she portrayed herself as an unwilling beneficiary, True actually served on a commission that engaged a lawyer on the side of the Mexican American defendants against the Pueblos and admitted to Samuel Brosius that she had "been in three suits brought by the U.S. to date." Furthermore, in her support of the Progressives' cause, True stood to benefit personally if more Pueblos adopted Euramerican conceptions of private property. As G. Emlen Hall pointed out, if more land became privately owned by members of the pueblo, this land could eventually be sold to non–Santa Clarans such as True.[28]

Clara True had begun her career by using women's association with moral purity to justify her work among Native Americans, but she gradually became involved in issues that were usually associated with men—politics, economics, and land. A career as an Indian reformer had enabled her to gain economic independence and a modicum of power and authority over various groups of Native Americans. Yet True was not satisfied with her influential role among Native Americans; she also sought power and influence within the BIA and white society. When she was thwarted by high officials in the BIA, who appointed men instead of her, she became deeply resentful of male power and privilege. It appears that while she was stationed at the Lower Brule Agency as principal of the boarding school in the 1890s, her superior recommended that she be made superintendent of the school. According to True, the Catholic bishop, the outgoing and incoming Indian agents, and the Indians themselves supported her promotion. However, the commissioner of Indian affairs appointed one of his friends to the job instead. True believed that the commissioner told the new appointee "that the job would be a snap as Miss True will do all the work." Embittered, she recalled, "I had my first lesson in Indian Service politics then." In 1913, she made a bid for a position as assistant commissioner of Indian affairs. Again, as in the 1890s, the BIA passed over her to hire a man for the assignment.[29]

Though True did not attain the powerful position in the BIA that she longed for, she did find other means to assert her authority. In the mid-1910s, she sought to clean up the BIA, focusing on two issues familiar to female moral reformers—stopping the liquor traffic to Indians and ending sexual immorality within the BIA. True first accused the superintendent of the Pueblo Agency, C. J. Crandall, of using his Sante Fe drugstore as a front for a "high class saloon business . . . in the same town where [the Santa Fe Indian] school holds forth."[30] In the late 1910s and 1920s, True charged the new superintendent of the Pueblo Agency, Philip T. Lonergan, with allowing officials under his supervision to keep prostitutes, drink in front of and sell liquor to Native Americans, assault an Indian woman, and rape a woman employed by the BIA.[31]

Although True held no official BIA position, her efforts paid off. In part because of her barrage of letters regarding Crandall, an investigation was conducted, and Crandall was eventually removed from his position. Due to her efforts many officials in the Indian Bureau sought to impugn True's character and implicate her in shady financial dealings. Although the record is not clear as to whether she was actually involved in any corruption, her friend and sometime attorney A. B. Renehan contended that "Miss True is being attacked not for any wrong done, but because she is a brainy, energetic, powerful personality, knowing fundamentally whereof she speaks, and not easily forced into retreat by foes from what she believes to be right and for the welfare of the Indians."[32]

True also became relatively powerful in Indian reform circles. The IRA often asked her advice about matters pertaining to Pueblo Indians, and she worked for them briefly as their only female executive employee in 1924 and 1925. Still chafing under male supervision, however, she soon became disillusioned with the IRA. The officials accused her of failing to do her assigned job—raising money and publicizing the IRA—and deemed her "disingenuous" and "unreliable." She, indeed, did shirk her assigned duties, preferring to work on her own agenda—the organization of so-called progressive Pueblo Indians. According to her New Mexico friends, she told them "she was expected to raise a lot of money to let a number of people hold easy jobs and that did not appeal to her." Wrangling with the IRA board as to whether she had resigned or been fired, True finally concluded, "It was a great mistake for me to tie up with the organization at all."[33] In part, by this time in her life, she simply could not tolerate carrying out policies designed by men—policies that she had had no voice in creating. Her experience with the IRA was not an isolated case. In the 1920s, she became alienated from many long-standing friends and associates. When a member of the IRA staff, Matthew Sniffen, traveled to New Mexico in 1925, he learned that True "had broken with nearly all her old friends." Several of her acquaintances told Sniffen that they believed True to be a "dangerous woman" and a "double-crosser." Apparently many old friends now regarded her as "brilliant, but unbalanced."[34]

True's problems with old friends in Santa Fe may have been mainly of a personal nature, but undoubtedly her steadfast commitment to assimilation set her at odds with a number of her new acquaintances, many of whom belonged to a new generation of white reformers. Influenced by novel anthropological theories of cultural relativism and the 1920s cultural movement known as primitivism, these crusaders went from defeating the Bursum bill to campaigning to discredit the BIA and its assimilation policy. Throughout the 1920s, reformers such as John Collier, Stella Atwood, Mabel Dodge Luhan, Mary Austin, Erna Fergusson, Amelia Elizabeth White, and Elizabeth DeHuff defended Pueblo dances and religion, promoted "traditional" arts and crafts, and wrote numerous articles that disparaged the BIA's assimilation policy.[35]

The issue of Indian dancing most inflamed serious conflict between these two sets of self-proclaimed "Friends of the Indian." In 1921, Commissioner of Indian Affairs Charles Burke had issued a directive to all Indian Service agents that called for the severe restriction of many types of Indian dancing. The order unleashed vituperative criticism from Collier and his colleagues. To "offset Collier's work," True and the IRA campaigned tirelessly to undermine Collier and defend the BIA. The dance issue hinged on two factors—religion and sexual morality. Champions of "traditional" Indians, such as Atwood and Collier, characterized Burke's circular as a violation of Native Americans' right to freedom of religion. True and the IRA countered with their own conception of religious freedom, arguing that "Mr. Collier [and] the pagan Pueblo caciques (or priests) [are calling for] the so-called religious 'liberty', . . . which is in reality liberty to tyrannize the Christian and progressive Pueblo Indians who refuse to participate in revolting customs and ceremonies of such a nature that they cannot be described in print." True, other reformers, and many BIA officials also charged the Pueblos with enacting obscene dances that allegedly encouraged sexual immorality.[36]

Although she vigorously defended Burke's order to restrict Indian dancing, True had grown increasingly out of step with the times. Collier and his associates' primitivist and culturally relativist visions gained favor and influence. Because of their agitation, Congress commissioned a special investigation of conditions among American Indians. The result—the Meriam Report, published in 1928—confirmed the allegations made by Collier and his associates. In the meantime, True's contempt for the new generation of Indian reformers only grew. Settling problems among the Indians "can't be done at dude ranches," she wrote, "not at teas in the art colonies [nor by] boy scoutish persons from the Atlantic seaboard who have been successful in inducing Greek bootblacks to use tooth brushes, [or] rich women who have graduated from Birth Control and the Soviet to find a thrill in Native Art."[37]

True was severely disappointed when Collier was selected as commissioner of Indian affairs in 1933. In the next year, Collier confirmed True's worst fears when he shepherded the Indian Reorganization Act through Congress. This Indian New Deal put a halt to the allotment process, closed down many boarding schools, protected Indian religious freedom, and extended a policy of limited self-determination to Native American tribes. True still believed "in civilization of Indians through education—not in the bunk of 'inner growth' and that other chestnut revived by Secretary [of Interior Harold] Ickes of 'leading their own lives' . . . I rise to ask, 'Whose lives have the Indians been leading?' It is rubbish to suppose that we can keep the Indians from developing along the same lines we have traveled, arriving at the same destination."[38] Equally disappointing was the fate of True's beloved Progressive Indians. By the late 1920s at Santa Clara, she estimated that the Progressives numbered 172, a majority of the pueblo. Yet just a few years later, in 1931, the Progressives wrote to True to express their regret that many of their members had defected to the more traditionally oriented Conservative Party.[39]

Despite signs of change among Indians themselves and the whites who advocated for them, True always retained her fervent belief that she knew what was best for the Indians and that their cultures could not survive but must inevitably assimilate to Euramerican standards. "I'll make the Indians save themselves," she declared, fully confident that she could force Native Americans to see the error of their ways and the rightness of hers. Ultimately, however, it was her ideology regarding gender and race that had become outmoded and untenable. Lacking authority in American life, she and many other white women in the late nineteenth and early twentieth centuries had attempted to claim a form of public power through their role as Indian reformers and educators. For a time, work for the assimilation and uplift of Native Americans had afforded these women a recognized position of authority and influence in society.

Ultimately, however, white women's enhanced status proved short-lived and elusive. Such power rested on the Native Americans' acquiescence to the agenda of the reformers. But many Native Americans sought to maintain and fortify their cultural identities, landholdings, and independence; they resisted True's agenda with all their might. Eventually, they found white supporters. By the late 1920s and 1930s a generation of new white reformers, led by John Collier, disdained True's beliefs that Indians needed to be changed and that white women could lead the way in accomplishing the transformation. If Collier and his followers did believe Indians needed to be saved, it was *from,* not *by,* women such as Clara True.

As her story reveals, basing white women's empowerment on the control and manipulation of other women (and men) proved to be a poor strategy for attaining an enduring voice and presence for all women in American society.

Notes

1. Clara True to Samuel Brosius, March 22, 1913, reel 27; True to Matthew Sniffen, June 16, 1919, reel 34; and True to Herbert Welsh, April 19, 1922, reel 38, Indian Rights Association Papers, Historical Society of Pennsylvania, Philadelphia (Glen Rock, NJ: Microfilming Corporation of America, 1975, microfilm) (hereafter cited as IRA Papers); *Official Register of the United States, Containing a List of the Officers and Employees in the Civil, Military, and Naval Service,* vol. 1 (Washington, DC: Government Printing Office, 1893, 1895, 1899, 1901, 1903).

2. "History of Schools in Santa Clara," reel 29, John Collier Papers (Sanford, NC: Microfilming Corporation of America, 1980, microfilm) (hereafter cited as Collier Papers); True to Superintendent Crandall, August 29, 1902, Record Group 75, Pueblo Records, Entry 38, Box 1, National Archives and Record Service, Rocky Mountain Branch, Denver, Colorado (hereafter cited as Pueblo Records, NA); True to Sniffen, January 29, 1912, reel 25, and True to Brosius, March 22, 1913, reel 27, IRA Papers.

3. For more on assimilation policy, see Frederick Hoxie, *A Final Promise: The Campaign to Assimilate the Indians, 1880–1920* (New York: Cambridge University Press, 1984); Francis Paul Prucha, *The Great Father: The United States Government and the American Indians,* vol. 2 (Lincoln: University of Nebraska Press, 1984); David Wallace Adams, *Education for Extinction: American Indians and the Boarding School Experience, 1875–1928* (Lawrence: University Press of Kansas, 1995).

4. White women's efforts to assimilate Native Americans paralleled similar endeavors by white women to Americanize Hispanic and Chinese women in the West. See Sarah Deutsch, *No Separate Refuge: Culture, Class, and Gender on an Anglo-Hispanic Frontier in the American Southwest, 1880–1940* (New York: Oxford University Press, 1987), 63–86; Vicki L. Ruiz, *From out of the Shadows: Mexican Women in Twentieth-Century America* (New York: Oxford University Press, 1998), 33–50; Peggy Pascoe, *Relations of Rescue: The Search for Female Moral Authority in the American West, 1874–1939* (New York: Oxford University Press, 1990).

5. Linda Gordon, *Pitied but Not Entitled: Single Mothers and the History of Welfare* (Cambridge, MA: Harvard University Press, 1994), 55.

6. Adams, *Education for Extinction,* 82, 90.

7. For more on the Women's National Indian Association and its concern for the "uplift" of Native American women, see Valerie Sherer Mathes, "Nineteenth-Century Women and Reform: The Women's National Indian Association," *American Indian Quarterly* 14 (Winter 1990): 1–18; idem, *Helen Hunt Jackson and Her Indian Reform Legacy* (Austin: University of Texas Press, 1990), 1–17; Helen M. Wanken, "Woman's Sphere and Indian Reform: The Women's National Indian Association, 1879–1901" (Ph.D. diss., Marquette University, 1981); Lisa Emmerich, " 'To Respect and Love and Seek the Ways of White Women': Field Matrons, the Office of Indian Affairs, and Civilization Policy, 1890–1938" (Ph.D. diss., University of Maryland, 1987).

8. For "true womanhood," see Barbara Welter, "The Cult of True Womanhood, 1820–1860," *American Quarterly* 18 (Summer 1966): 151–74.

9. Quote in True to Sniffen, January 21, 1912, reel 25; Edward S. Curtis to the IRA, September 8, 1924, reel 41, IRA Papers.

10. Carroll Smith-Rosenberg, "The Female World of Love and Ritual," in *Disorderly Conduct: Visions of Gender in Victorian America,* ed. Carroll Smith-Rosenberg (New York: Alfred A. Knopf, 1985), 53–76; Blanche Wiesen Cook, "Female Support Networks and Political Activism: Lillian Wald, Crystal Eastman, and Emma Goldman," in *A Heritage of Her Own: Towards a New Social History of American Women,* ed. Nancy Cott and Elizabeth Pleck (New York: Simon and Schuster, 1979), 412–44.

11. Amelia Stone Quinton, "Care of the Indian," in *Woman's Work in America,* ed. Annie Nathan Meyer (New York: Henry Holt, 1891), 383.

12. Clara D. True, "The Experiences of a Woman Indian Agent," *Outlook* 92 (June 5, 1909): 333; Francis E. Leupp's remarks included in *Report of the 26th Annual Meeting of the Lake Mohonk Conference of Friends of the Indian and Other Dependent Peoples* (Philadelphia: Lake Mohonk Conference, 1908), 14, 25.

13. True, "Experiences of a Woman Indian Agent," 334–35.

14. True to Brosius, March 22, 1913, reel 27, IRA Papers.

15. True, "Experiences of a Woman Indian Agent," 332.

16. True to Crandall, September 5, 6, and 10, 1902, October 9, 1902, December 20, 1902; Dr. Holterman to Superintendent of Santa Fe Indian School, February 20, 1903; and quotes in True to Francis McCormick, January 20, 21, 1903, Entry 38, Box 1, Pueblo Records, NA.

17. True to Crandall, January 28, 1903, RG 75, Entry 38, Box 1, Pueblo Records, NA; Emmerich, "'To Respect and Love,'" 200–218; Margaret D. Jacobs, *Engendered Encounters: Feminism and Pueblo Cultures, 1879–1934* (Lincoln: University of Nebraska Press, 1999), 31–32.

18. First quote in True to Sniffen, May 3, 1929, reel 45; second quote in Marah Ellis Ryan to Sniffen, September 16, 1924; and True to Welsh, December 9, 1924, reel 41, IRA Papers.

19. At least since contact with the Spanish, the Pueblo Indians deemed it men's work to engage in politics and religious ceremonies and women's work to keep up the home. See M. Jane Young, "Women, Reproduction, and Religion in Western Puebloan Society," *Journal of American Folklore* 100 (October-December 1987): 436–45; Alice Schlegel, "Male and Female in Hopi Thought and Action," in *Sexual Stratification: A Cross-Cultural View,* ed. Alice Schlegel (New York: Columbia University Press, 1977), 245–69; idem, "The Adolescent Socialization of the Hopi Girl," *Ethnology* 12 (1973): 451–53; Sue Ellen Jacobs, "Continuity and Change in Gender Roles at San Juan Pueblo," in *Women and Power in Native North America,* ed. Laura F. Klein and Lillian A. Ackerman (Norman: University of Oklahoma Press, 1995).

20. True to Brosius, May 26, 1924; True to Welsh, December 9, 1924; Superintendent C. J. Crandall to Mr. Charles Burke, December 4, 1924, with accompanying petition from Pedro Cijite et al. to Mr. C. J. Crandall, reel 40; and True to Board of Directors, IRA, February 28, 1925, reel 41, IRA Papers. The petition contains a misspelling of Pedro's last name; in other documents, it appears as Cajete.

21. True to Father Schuster, May 4, 1925, reel 42; "The State of the Progressive Pueblo Indians," n.d. [ca. 1928]; Margaret Tafoya to Filario Tafoya, September 27, 1929; Joseph

Tafoya to Samuel Brosius, November 7, 1929; and True to Brosius, November 27, 1929, reel 45, IRA Papers.

22. J. Tafoya to Brosius, fragment of letter [September 1929], reel 45, and transcription of article, "All Lies, Declare Governors of Pueblos, and Village Officials," from *Santa Fe New Mexican,* July 2, 1924, reel 41, IRA Papers.

23. True to Sniffen, May 3, 1929, and True to J. F. Tafoya, June 4, 1929, reel 45, IRA Papers.

24. True to Sniffen, June 4, 1929, reel 45, IRA Papers.

25. Quote of Nina Otero-Warren in Matthew Sniffen, report, "The Pueblo Country," September 18, 1925, reel 42, IRA Papers.

26. Ryan to Sniffen, September 16, 1924, reel 41, IRA Papers.

27. Both Mexican Americans and Anglos had squatted on Pueblo land for many decades. After living on this land for years, squatters often claimed it as their own by right of preemption. Bursum's bill would have allowed many non-Indians to claim Indian land. For more on the controversy surrounding the bill, see Kenneth Philp, *John Collier's Crusade for Indian Reform* (Tucson: University of Arizona Press, 1977), and Lawrence Kelly, *The Assault on Assimilation: John Collier and the Origins of Indian Policy Reform* (Albuquerque: University of New Mexico Press, 1983). For True's support of the bill, see True to Brosius, October 29, 1922, reel 38, IRA Papers.

28. Brosius to Sniffen, March 23, 1919, reel 34, and True to Brosius, February 15, 1921, reel 36, IRA Papers (my emphasis); G. Emlen Hall, "Land Litigation and the Idea of New Mexico Progress," *Journal of the West* 27 (July 1988): 48–58.

29. Quotes in True to Welsh, April 19, 1922, reel 38; True to Sniffen, January 21, 29, 1912, reel 25; True to Brosius, March 22, 1913, reel 27; and Mary Dissette to Brosius, April 18, 1913, reel 27, IRA Papers.

30. True to Dissette, April 27, 1919, reel 34; quote in True to Sniffen, June 2, 1919, reel 34; True to Sniffen, August 31, 1919, reel 34; and True to Brosius, October 18, 1919, reel 34, IRA Papers.

31. True to Sniffen, January 29, 1912, reel 25, and True to Welsh, April 19, 1922, reel 38, IRA Papers.

32. True to Sniffen, January 21, 1912, reel 25, August 31, 1919, reel 34; September 8, 1924, reel 41; A. B. Renehan to Matthew Sniffen, September 7, 1924, reel 41, and Ryan to Sniffen, September 16, 1924, reel 41, IRA Papers.

33. See correspondence between True and Brosius, Sniffen, and Welsh throughout 1924 and 1925; first quote in Minutes of Meeting of Board of Directors, IRA, February 20, 1925, reel 42, True to Board of Directors, IRA, February 28, 1925, reel 42, and second quote in True to Mrs. Markoe, April 22, 1925, reel 42, IRA Papers.

34. Sniffen report, "The Pueblo Country," September 18, 1925, reel 42, and Sniffen to Welsh, September 21, 1925, reel 42, IRA Papers.

35. See Jacobs, *Engendered Encounters.*

36. Brosius to Sniffen, May 29, 1924, reel 40; quote in Sniffen to Kenneth Chorley, September 4, 1924, reel 41; and Telegram from Sniffen to Mrs. Thomas G. Winter, June 2, 1924, reel 40, IRA Papers; Jacobs, *Engendered Encounters,* 106–48.

37. Quote in True to Sniffen, January 15, 1932, reel 48, November 12, 1932, reel 49, and April 23, 1933, and May 14, 1933, reel 50, IRA Papers.

38. True to "Sane Friends of the Indians," February 8, 1933, reel 49, IRA Papers. For more on the Indian New Deal, see Philp, *John Collier's Crusade,* and Kelly, *Assault on Assimilation.*

39. True to Sniffen, May 3, 1930, reel 46, and Desiderio Naranjo to True, November 11, 1931, reel 48, IRA Papers.

Suggested Readings

Bannan, Helen M. *"True Womanhood" on the Reservation: Field Matrons in the U.S. Indian Service,* Southwest Institute for Research on Women, working paper no. 118. Tucson, AZ: Women's Studies, 1984.

Hoxie, Frederick. *A Final Promise: The Campaign to Assimilate the Indians, 1880–1920.* New York: Cambridge University Press, 1984.

Jacobs, Margaret. *Engendered Encounters: Feminism and Pueblo Cultures, 1879–1934.* Lincoln: University of Nebraska Press, 1999.

Kelly, Lawrence. *The Assault on Assimilation: John Collier and the Origins of Indian Policy Reform.* Albuquerque: University of New Mexico Press, 1983.

Pascoe, Peggy. *Relations of Rescue: The Search for Female Moral Authority in the American West, 1874–1939.* New York: Oxford University Press, 1990.

8

Joseph W. Brown
Native American Politician

Paul C. Rosier*

The process of cultural exchange and mutual accommodation in the West often involved the mediation of tribal cultural brokers. The lives of such individuals, including Joseph W. Brown, support the contention that cultural mediation was an exercise in biculturalism. The son of a white rancher and a full-blooded Blackfeet Indian woman, Brown lived on or near the reservation during much of his life. He defended Indian self-determination throughout a public career that was largely a product of changing federal Indian policy during the interwar years of the twentieth century. As the theme of self-rule inherent in the Indian New Deal of the 1930s eclipsed the assimilation policy of the past, the center of power began to shift while intratribal factionalism intensified. Brown himself often provoked intratribal conflicts in the course of defending the U.S. government's paternalistic agenda, which he contended could be manipulated for the betterment of the tribal nation.

Becoming bicultural is hardly a matter of accepting all change—of becoming 100 percent American. Although Brown adapted well to the politics of Indian-white relations, he was mindful of the value of Indianness in forging the future. His life story also illustrates that mediation is akin to a juggling act: when the juggling fails dire consequences may ensue. Rosier's account, like Richmond Clow's (see Chapter 12), stresses Indian agency. Indians may be victimized, he suggests, but they are hardly simple victims. They are also actors and resisters.

Paul C. Rosier received his Ph.D. in American history from the University of Rochester in New York in May 1998. His forthcoming monograph, *Rebirth of the Blackfeet Nation, 1912–1954,* examines the impact of the 1934 Indian Reorganization Act on the social, economic, and political relations of the Blackfeet Indians. He has published in numerous journals and has taught at Princeton University, in Princeton, New Jersey, and at Rutgers University, in New Brunswick, New Jersey.

In a 1968 essay on the Blackfeet Indians of Montana, anthropologist Malcolm McFee presented the idea of "the 150% man." He was referring

*I would like to thank Lorraine Brown Owens for contributing her memories, family photos, and a box of her father's papers. Thanks also to Vicky Santana, Joe Brown's grandniece, who provided a photo and offered her insight into Blackfeet political culture.

to someone who had assimilated white mores while retaining support for or practice of Native customs and who served as a cultural "interpreter" among a "bicultural people" facing social stress created by economic, demographic, and political changes.[1] As the U.S. government's allotment policy began reordering American Indian society in the late 1800s, 150-percent Indian men and women assumed prominent roles in shaping Indian-white social relations, tribal politics, and reservation economic development in the American West.[2]

Joseph W. Brown (1874–1963) was both a 150-percent man and a representative of a new generation of community leaders. For nearly two decades, he chaired the Blackfeet Tribal Business Council (BTBC), the Blackfeet Nation's governing body; he also mediated ethnic conflict between mixed-bloods and full-bloods and championed Blackfeet employment, education, and sovereignty. Brown also worked as a stockman for the federal government, served on or chaired the county school board for three decades, and sat on the local Selective Service Board. His story illustrates the politics of Indian-white and intratribal relations and the evolving ethnic and social composition of the American West. His is also a tale of personal triumph, of overcoming physical disability and educational limitations to become a loving father to eleven children and a respected citizen in both white and Indian communities. He, more than any of his peers, strove to preserve the Blackfeet past in order to create a tribal entity capable of determining its own future.

Brown was born August 18, 1874, in Fort Benton, near present-day Great Falls, Montana. His white father, James William Brown Sr. (1841–1927), was of Pennsylvania Dutch ancestry. His mother was Sarah Bull (1854–1912), daughter of Melting Marrow and Bird Sailing This Way, both full-blooded members of the Piegan Band of Indians, one of three groups comprising the great Blackfoot Confederacy that occupied much of northern Montana until treaties greatly reduced its land base in the late nineteenth century.[3] Joe Brown was of the first generation of mixed-blooded Blackfeet Indians, born a decade before a significant demographic change occurred in Blackfeet society resulting from nineteenth-century intermarriages between white men and full-blooded women—a process set in motion by the arrival of the fur trade, gold fever, and the Great Northern Railroad. In 1885 only 18 tribal members were mixed-bloods, compared to roughly 2,000 full-bloods. In 1914, 1,189 full-bloods lived among 1,452 mixed-bloods. And by 1940, when Brown was sixty-six, mixed-bloods outnumbered full-bloods by a 5-to-1 margin.[4] This expansion of the mixed-blood population created great stress for the Blackfeet.

Yet, mixed-blood mediators, Brown in particular, became increasingly important advocates of cultural integrity and social peace.

Before settling in Choteau, Montana, and marrying into the Blackfeet Tribe in 1868, Joe's father had served in the Union army and as a guard for Abraham Lincoln. Joe, one of seven children, spent his formative years near Choteau and Fort Benton; at Fort Benton, he attended school to the eighth grade. Two boyhood accidents blinded his right eye and scarred his face. His limited education and his disability would later compel him, on his entry into Blackfeet politics, to advocate for education for his people and to improve his own communication skills.

In 1893 his father purchased a 1,000-acre cattle ranch on the Blackfeet Reservation. (The reservation is located in northwestern Montana, to the east of Glacier National Park; the park is situated on land once owned by the Blackfeet people.) Joe bought his own ranch on the Milk River seven miles to the south, where he raised cattle and horses. In 1897 he married Frances Arnoux (1877–1952), whose father was white and mother was of half Blackfeet blood. The first of the couple's eleven children—two daughters and nine sons, four of whom died young—was born the following year. Brown worked for the Bureau of Indian Affairs (BIA) in several capacities: first as the tribal butcher and then as an allotment commissioner, a range rider patrolling the 1.5-million-acre reservation, and a superintendent of livestock, a post he held for over twenty years.[5] Brown's personal experience and professional service working with livestock would inform and influence his agenda once he assumed leadership of the tribe.

Brown became active in Blackfeet politics in the second decade of the twentieth century, briefly serving on a tribal business committee and accompanying to Washington, DC, a delegation of mixed-blood ranchers advocating a controversial land sale. In the early 1920s he championed the BIA's agricultural subsistence program and the development of tribal oil resources. Though his involvement in these activities was limited, busy as he was with a growing family and his BIA employment, his influence in the tribe grew rapidly in the late 1920s. Elected to the BTBC in 1928, Brown assumed the mantle of tribal leadership when his colleagues selected him to chair the council. Throughout his BTBC career, he stressed that improved health, education, irrigation, and resource development would bring the Blackfeet Reservation into the twentieth century and expand the scope of his people's self-government. He cautioned, however, that to secure these advantages the tribe would have to overcome divisions between acculturated mixed-bloods and community-oriented full-bloods and between stock owners and non–stock owners. Brown would use his

Joseph Brown as a young lad. *Courtesy of Vicky Santana*

power to help create a unified Blackfeet voice in demanding the right of self-government, which he deemed necessary for economic progress.

Increasing dissatisfaction with the BIA's management of tribal oil and grazing resources helped unify factions on the eve of a 1929 Senate investigation of the BIA, whose incompetent and corrupt practices had engendered distrust on many Indians reservations in the American West. Brown organized several meetings on the reservation so that Blackfeet citizens could define the tribe's agenda, an open-door policy that would characterize his stewardship of the Blackfeet political process. The Senate investigation revealed that corrupt Blackfeet agency officials had neglected Indian interests in favor of white leaseholders and concluded that the Blackfeet were thus "entitled to a bigger return."[6] Mixed-bloods and full-bloods alike thus wanted expanded control of the tribe's natural resources, which had the potential to provide each tribal member with loans or per capita payments.

Brown worked closely with full-bloods to construct this common ground and to preserve the tribal entity. During the 1931 meeting of the Piegan Farming and Livestock Association (PFLA), which was dominated by full-bloods, Mountain Chief, the last "hereditary chief," told his fellow full-bloods that mixed-bloods "belong on the reservation and we should try to get along together as a tribe." Brown followed by pointing out that "when the Blackfeet work together" they can "accomplish something but where you are divided you accomplish nothing."[7] Mountain Chief later protested a plan to deny tribal membership and benefits to Blackfeet of less than one-half blood, arguing, "I have many grandchildren amongst the mixed-bloods." Brown, whose mother was full-blooded, said shortly afterward that "the mixed blood question" had been answered: "I think just as much of [full-bloods], and I will work just as hard for them as I will for my own children."[8] He used occasions such as the PFLA meeting to stress his people's shared ethnic heritage so as to secure backing for tribal self-determination that would allow them to promote a common interest in oil leasing. During the early 1930s and beyond, Brown in a sense assumed a role similar to a hereditary chief, gaining respect from Blackfeet of all degrees of blood quantum and securing loyalty to the tribal ideal.

Brown demonstrated his ability to facilitate tribal unity during the Blackfeet's 1934 debates on the Wheeler-Howard bill, which proposed granting to Indian communities expanded powers of self-government, federal credit, and BIA employment opportunities—demands that Brown had been requesting since assuming office. During a 1933 return visit by the Senate committee, he forcefully requested that the federal government hire Indian rather than white workers and allow Blackfeet to gradually assume responsibility for managing economic programs.[9] Brown's stewardship of the tribe during community meetings, negotiations with federal officials, and testimony to congressional committees represents one of his signal accomplishments as a bicultural mediator.

During the winter of 1934, Brown moderated several nonpartisan debates on the bill's merits. The principal issue was whether the Blackfeet should sanction the charter of one central government or numerous self-governing "communities," an option that the Wheeler-Howard bill made possible. During one meeting, Brown told the large crowd that "the whole bill means to gradually take over the range of government on your reservation," and he recommended that the Blackfeet "control our government right here from this office." It is not surprising that Chairman Brown and other mixed-blooded council members preferred the BTBC to control future economic development, but a consensus also emerged that centralized decision making was the only option worth considering. A few opponents simply did not trust the mixed-blood leadership, but most influential full-bloods, particularly those active in the PFLA, testified in favor of one central government, principally because the distributed decision making of the PFLA had been fractious and unproductive. The tide in favor of a central government was shown in a nonbinding vote taken during one open meeting—eighty-eight for and twenty-four against.[10] Council leaders, Brown in particular, also recognized the need to strengthen tribal sovereignty. Brown insisted that any future changes in Blackfeet affairs required "the consent of the Indian" and that the tribe retain the right to determine the "definition" of a Blackfeet individual. Neither blood quantum nor residence status should affect the "rights and privileges" of any enrolled Blackfeet, he said—a statement that symbolized his desire to preserve the "family," as full-bloods called the tribe, and his recognition that "being Blackfeet" was a quality of both the heart and the mind.[11]

Armed with the support of his people, Brown went to Washington in May 1934 to offer the tribe's support for the bill, appearing before the House and Senate Indian Affairs Committees debating the legislation. Sen. Burton Wheeler of Montana was a cosponsor of Commissioner of Indian Affairs John Collier's original bill, but by April 1934, he had lost faith in Collier's agenda and resolved to weaken it. During the Senate hearings, Wheeler told Collier that his home rule proposal would create racial conflict and "set back the Indians" in Montana.[12] Brown addressed this concern in his testimony to Wheeler's Senate committee. He first explained that tribal leaders had studied the bill and were especially excited about the proposed revolving credit fund, testifying that Blackfeet farmers and ranchers were "aching to get a chance at that $10,000,000" sum. Brown also requested that the BIA employ more Indians, to which Wheeler politely suggested, "You could take over the superintendency, more than likely?" Brown humbly offered that the job was too difficult for him.[13] Despite his vote of confidence in Brown, Wheeler attacked him for asserting that the Blackfeet needed the bill for economic and political progress, arguing that Indians such as Brown "practically run that community up there now." Brown countered that the Blackfeet wanted to determine "what laws would be [made] under the [new] government" in order to extend the tribe's sovereign control of the reservation and to reflect the needs of the Blackfeet rather than those of local whites. His statement was precisely what made Wheeler "fearful" of an indigenous form of Indian community government. If the Blackfeet Tribe passed its own laws, Wheeler assumed, the result would be "a great deal of bitterness and strife between two classes of people."[14] Several days later, Brown faced a similar contumely from proassimilation House members. He again championed the credit fund, expanded Indian educational opportunities, and Indian employment. There were Blackfeet who could "fill every position on that reservation" except for chief clerk and superintendent, Brown claimed, and if the bill passed, it would "not be long before [they] could develop men that would take those places."[15] But House leaders refused to believe that Brown understood the complex legislation, asking him if he had "given very careful study to this bill." Brown responded, "Careful in my humble way. I am not a lawyer."[16]

Brown gave reasoned and judicious testimony to the members of Congress, who were generally hostile to the idea of Indian self-determination. Despite his blindness in one eye and his lack of a formal education, he acquitted himself well in front of congressional committees, as well as at tribal meetings. According to his daughter, he overcame his disabilities by hiring a tutor to help him improve his diction, grammar, and presentation skills.[17] Smartly dressed in a business suit, soft-spoken yet confident, Brown represented an intelligent and moderate Indian voice seeking what most members of Congress wanted: an end to government supervision of Indian affairs. Brown had indeed given careful study to the bill and understood quite clearly that its merits outweighed its limitations. The pending legislation appealed to him because it gave the Blackfeet options for economic growth and the "privilege" to choose their own path, based on their own interpretations of those options. The Blackfeet may have been "dominating" public life in Glacier County, as Wheeler claimed, but they were not dominating economic life. Without credit, employment opportunities, and the political authority to negotiate with white businesses, they never would.

Signed into law on June 18, 1934, the Indian Reorganization Act (IRA) enabled tribes to develop a constitution and bylaws through which a central government could manage domestic affairs and to adopt a charter of incorporation to enhance this government's power to manage tribal resources.[18] The bill was imperfect, the result of a struggle between two competing visions of Indian America. The vision shared by Collier and Brown sought to protect Indians' right to construct their own version of the American community; Wheeler's vision, by contrast, was designed to sustain Indians' adoption of white mores and institutions.[19]

On October 27, 1934, 823 Blackfeet voted to adopt the IRA, and 171 voted against it. The Blackfeet's support for the IRA reflected the majority Indian voice on this question; in the end, 181 tribes voted for it, and 77 did not.[20] The BTBC, under Joe Brown's steady and pragmatic leadership, had created an environment for debate and discussion among the reservation's various factions. The Blackfeet's acceptance of the IRA resulted from Brown's leadership, this open debate, and the BIA's past failure to provide them with a coordinated economic policy that benefited Indians rather than whites.

Brown's judicious handling of the IRA debate and vote enhanced his status as tribal leader among both his BTBC colleagues and the Blackfeet citizenry. This leadership was quickly tested in February 1935 when the popular agency superintendent Forrest Stone was transferred to Wyoming. During the February 18 BTBC meeting, Brown spoke angrily of Collier's "betrayal," contending that Collier "has seen fit to make a change" without consulting Blackfeet leaders. The council then voted unanimously to adopt Brown's protest resolution to Collier, stating that the tribe would hold Collier responsible for any failures of the post-Stone era.[21] Stone's departure forced the council into a more prominent role of representing tribal interests, which coincided with the IRA's intent, and it thrust Brown into a highly visible role as leader of the newly empowered Blackfeet Nation. He was regarded highly by his people and by his BTBC colleagues, who repeatedly elected him chairman. He also was respected by white residents of Browning, the largest reservation town and the Blackfeet Nation's largest electoral district. Brown, who lived in the town, was a long-standing member of the local board of education and had once campaigned for a seat in the Montana state senate; being a stockman once employed by the BIA as well as former rancher, he was seen by white ranchers as a hardworking man of their ilk. The council members had such confidence in him that they asked him to succeed Stone, issuing a resolution stating that Brown "is one of the most competent and influential members of the

Joseph Brown in Washington, DC, 1913. *Courtesy of Lorraine Brown Owens*

Blackfeet Tribe; is universally honored and looked up to by all the members of the Tribe; and is known and respected throughout the State of Montana." Brown declined the nomination, feeling that he was not ready to assume that responsibility.[22]

Joe Brown was eager to prove himself worthy of leading the Blackfeet Nation. In March, he asserted his people's right to receive the same amount of state welfare aid as white Montana residents. He and BTBC secretary Leo Kennerly had discovered that Blackfeet received a monthly check of $4.27 whereas checks sent to white residents were more than twice that amount. Brown then made several trips to the state capital to demand action, which compelled Montana's governor to issue an additional $5,000 in aid.[23] Brown also led the fight to preserve the "Blackfeet Strip," a stretch of territory bordering Glacier National Park, which lay on land once owned by the Blackfeet Nation. The National Park Service (NPS) had long tried to annex the strip, but since it contained the Blackfeet's only timber reserve, the BTBC refused to sell it. Hearing reports that the government planned to try again now that Stone could no longer defend the Blackfeet, Brown stepped into the breach to do the job himself. On May 2 he responded to criticism that he was not protecting the tribe's interests, delivering an impassioned speech that left no doubt as to his leadership. He considered the annexation plan another act of betrayal, asking, "What wrongs have we committed that the [BIA] should turn around and treat us in this manner?" Brown's normally solid support of Collier and the BIA had vanished. He concluded, to great applause, "I have laid my cards on the table and I am ready to defend my position. This might cost me my job, but I would rather be a respected citizen among my people than to be a dog in the Indian Service."[24] This moment was a crucial juncture in Brown's political career. Questioned by some citizens as to where his loyalties lay—to his employer, the federal government, or to the Blackfeet people—he made it clear that he was willing to challenge anyone who threatened the Blackfeet Nation's newly made promise of independent action. The IRA required the government to secure Indian consent for any land sale, and thus the NPS backed down after Brown registered a formal protest. Yet these events—these betrayals—reinforced in Brown the need for an IRA constitution and charter to buttress the tribe's authority to prevent future attacks on its sovereignty.

In July 1935, Brown and his BTBC colleagues worked with BIA officials to produce a Blackfeet constitution. Significantly, government review committees made no substantive changes to that document, in part because Collier warned committee members against making further encroachments on the tribe's fragile emotional state.[25] On November 13 the tribe, by a vote of 884 to 157, decided overwhelmingly to adopt the constitution.[26] Before the vote the new superintendent, Warren O'Hara, had organized a series of meetings to discuss the constitution in detail. His efforts almost certainly would have failed without Brown's support. At O'Hara's urging, Collier thanked Brown for supporting the IRA program, the "foundation upon which to build a better civic and economic structure for the Blackfeet Nation."[27] Collier's letter, in using the term "Nation" rather than "Tribe," illustrated the BIA's growing recognition of the Blackfeet's sovereign rights that Brown had so forcefully defended during the NPS fight.

Brown and other tribal leaders then focused on securing an IRA charter, in part because it would enable the Blackfeet Nation to participate in the Revolving Credit Fund (RCF) program. In late March 1936 a delegation headed by Brown spent a month in Washington, DC, discussing a charter. Again, Brown was very pleased that BIA officials acceded to the delegation's requests, preserving the Blackfeet Nation's right to "terminate" by popular referendum the Interior Department's supervision of the tribe's economic affairs. After a series of debates the Blackfeet Nation adopted the charter on August 15 by a vote of 737 to 301. Despite the victory, however, the voting numbers signified a declining support of the IRA program, as many Blackfeet had become impatient for evidence of the economic progress promised by Brown and other backers of the IRA.[28]

Brown and his colleagues thus turned to rebuilding the reservation political economy and establishing the BTBC as a political body with authority equal to that of the superintendent. The council reörganized its fiscal affairs by devising a budget, established a Blackfeet Indian court and jury, wrote fish and game regulations, and funded a tribal arts and crafts program.[29] Then Brown worked with a BIA credit agent in September 1936 to complete the tribe's application for RCF moneys to fund its economic development program, which would provide low-interest loans to stock owners and farmers, help tribal members to finance business or commercial enterprises, and fund tribal enterprises. The BIA approved a loan of $100,000, and the BTBC began the distribution process in April 1937.[30]

The Blackfeet economy suffered from two distinct problems. By 1936 the tribe's oil-leasing program generated only a small percentage of the $162 average per capita income. A more substantive problem was that Blackfeet ranchers utilized merely 28 percent of the tribal rangeland, considered some of the best in the West. Furthermore, those who used this rangeland did so for below-market rates.[31] Brown believed that the Blackfeet needed to earn income through labor rather than to simply wait for the per capita distribution of oil and grazing revenues; otherwise, they would simply trade the federal government's form of relief for the BTBC's. He considered the livestock industry to be his people's best hope for long-lasting economic development. During the 1933 Senate hearing, Brown had asked, "Why can not we, the Indians who own the land . . . and do not have to pay for the grazing, make a success of the stock industry?" Stone had called Brown's goal of creating a livestock industry "the ultimate solution" to the Blackfeet's problems, and Senator Wheeler said that it was the tribe's "only salvation."[32] To this end the federal government in late 1934 sent the Blackfeet Nation 5,523 head of cattle through its Cattle Repayment Program (CRP).[33] Brown, as government stockman, helped distribute the cattle to over 500 Blackfeet.

As the livestock population expanded, Brown and other BTBC leaders became concerned that the tribe needed to use its irrigation projects to produce sufficient winter feed for the cattle. In November 1937 the BTBC debated the federal government's offer to finance the tribe's "rehabilitation program," which was designed to improve grain production by reviving the Two Medicine Irrigation Project (TMIP) while also protecting the Blackfeet Nation's water rights from its thirsty white neighbors.[34] The BTBC, needing funds for infrastructure improvements, voted unanimously to accept the offer and, as the offer stipulated, to commit tribal funds for TMIP, an action that one BIA official said would "save the tribe."[35]

This political action also precipitated a new round of tribal dissension and cost Brown his council seat. Although his agenda of modernizing tribal administration and rebuilding the livestock industry was supported by the BIA, the Interior Department, and the BTBC, it also angered a large and vocal segment of the population. Some Blackfeet, especially elderly full-bloods unwilling or physically unable to raise livestock, opposed the use of tribal oil revenues to fund "rehabilitation" and instead demanded per capita payments. In the January 1938 election, ten of the thirteen incumbents lost their seats. In his first defeat in six elections, Brown lost by nearly a three-to-one margin to Stuart Hazlett, whose vicious (and captious) attacks on the BTBC were unprecedented in Blackfeet political culture; Hazlett, of one-eighth Blackfeet blood, had returned to the reservation a year earlier to acquire political influence.[36] After campaigning to reform Blackfeet politics and provide per capita distributions, Hazlett spent his term building on Brown's agenda. He failed to keep his promises, however, and was booted from office in January 1940.

Reelected to the council in 1940, Brown helped steer the tribe through the difficult years of World War II. The Blackfeet, like most Americans, mobilized to both contribute to the U.S. cause and profit from the opportunities it presented them. The BTBC donated tribal money to the local Red Cross chapter and to the Browning War Mothers Club, which sent care packages to soldiers; it also purchased $100,000 in war bonds and allocated moneys for the planting of victory gardens. By 1943 over 250

Blackfeet men and women were serving in the military, including 6 of Brown's 7 surviving children.[37] Another 300 Blackfeet migrated to defense jobs on the West Coast.[38] The BTBC facilitated this off-reservation employment, providing grants for Blackfeet seeking defense work and allotting tribal funds to help them obtain training. Brown made a special effort to ensure that full-bloods had an opportunity to get this training. In late 1941, he traveled to Seattle to check on the living conditions of Blackfeet laborers.[39] He also served his country as a member of the Glacier County Selective Service Board, earning citations from President Roosevelt and President Truman. His wartime actions spoke to his commitment to securing practical education for his people, ensuring that all constituencies had access to it, and serving the American as well as the Blackfeet cause.

For Brown the ideological nature of the war likely reinforced his strong belief in democracy. Although a staunch supporter of the IRA, he believed the Blackfeet electorate should be allowed to make important decisions affecting the tribe as a whole. In a series of public meetings in 1944 and 1945, Brown resolutely defended the IRA and the democratic process it created, while demonstrating his solicitude for Blackfeet full-bloods who remained critical of the BTBC's distribution of tribal income. In August 1944 full-blood witnesses told a congressional special investigating committee that the IRA should be "abolished" and "erased." Brown and Senator Wheeler, who supported the full-bloods' interests, sparred over the IRA's merits just as they had ten years earlier. Brown reminded Wheeler that the tribe had adopted the IRA because "it gave us powers that we had never had before. . . . And we fear that if the act were thrown out and we had to go back to the old system that we could not get the advantages that we have now." However, Brown did offer to hold periodic referenda on abolishing the IRA. "That is democracy," he told the committee members.[40]

In this spirit, Brown helped organize a "constitutional convention" to consider amendments to the Blackfeet Nation's constitution and to prepare for changes in Indian-white relations. On April 23, 1945, he welcomed BTBC members and twenty-five delegates from the reservation's various communities to open what would become a nine-day meeting.[41] For BTBC leaders the convention represented a chance to discuss in public the IRA constitution's benefits and to defend their record of economic management. Brown used the occasion to celebrate the tribe's successes. He told the delegates that the Blackfeet had "progressed" further and were "smarter" than most Indians; tribal members, he noted, were attending college, teaching school, and working in the county government. Blackfeet politicians had secured federal funds for a reservation hospital and supported a sick fund and a funeral fund created by democratic vote. The Blackfeet Nation's leaders were always "planning ahead," Brown asserted, largely by taking responsibility for tribal affairs using the IRA constitution, which "protected" their people from "the white man's intrusions." Addressing the full-blood delegates, he affirmed that council members were "just as red-blooded and their feeling for you people is paramount, and they are doing everything that is humanly possible to help you."[42] To demonstrate this, Brown outlined his personal vision of sanitary homes, improved health, and expanded stock operations—and the BTBC's funding of the effort. The council, usually at Brown's urging, helped fund full-bloods' annual encampment, paid for special medical treatment, devised the "Special Loans to Aged Indians" fund, and included full-bloods in most council deliberations. Brown acknowledged that some Blackfeet did not wish to support stock owners and wanted per capita payments instead. He also warned that the tribe had to diversify its economy in case oil revenues declined; at that time, Blackfeet were dependent on oil revenues of roughly $350,000 per annum to fund the social welfare, investment, and administrative programs that he outlined.[43] Testimony of full-bloods and a nonbinding vote supportive of the IRA indicated that his efforts had educated delegates about the IRA's value.

In a subsequent four-day meeting with full-bloods, Brown and others again defended the BTBC against dissidents' attacks on its fiscal policies.[44] The constant criticism angered Brown. "You [full-bloods] do not give us credit for any help whatever," he said. Once again, he passionately defended the BTBC's health, education, and economic programs. D'Arcy McNickle, a mixed-blooded BIA official, later thanked Brown directly for doing "everything humanly possible" to facilitate a productive discussion of tribal affairs, noting the "time, effort and money you have already expended in behalf of achieving harmony in the Tribe."[45] Brown got little back in return for this effort. For a man who had devoted much of his adult life to economic development and the health, education, and welfare of all tribal members, the criticism was particularly painful.[46]

Now in his seventies, Joe Brown devoted the rest of his political life to helping the Blackfeet Nation protect and expand its governmental powers, traveling to Washington on several occasions to champion its right to define itself and to determine its own public policy. In 1947 he testified before a House subcommittee on Indian affairs debating various "emancipation bills," part of Congress's postwar efforts to "terminate" unilaterally the government's trust responsibilities to American Indians. Brown articulated his moderate philosophy of allowing Indians to gradually take responsibility for reservation management, arguing that the IRA had provided tribal members with the tools to achieve independence from BIA supervision. The Blackfeet, he contended, could do this in part because education, one of his priorities, had produced capable high school and college graduates who were now filling positions in the tribal and county governments. He told House members that "we feel that if you will just let us take care of ourselves and not put too many stumbling blocks in our road, then we are going to come out all right."[47] For Brown the matter of "emancipation" was best left to Indians themselves. During his final appearance before Congress in 1951, at age seventy-six, he proposed deep cutbacks in BIA personnel and an attendant increase in Indian personnel. He argued that Blackfeet citizens could fill twenty-four of the twenty-six federal positions, leaving a stenographer and a superintendent who would assume the role of an ambassador.[48] This last point reflected both his confidence in his people and his sharpened sense of Blackfeet sovereignty. A year later, in one of his final appearances as a BTBC member, these two issues came together when he blasted the agency superintendent for subverting tribal politics and for trying to "perpetuate the power that the Indian Bureau has on the Indian."[49] Like many community leaders in the American West, Brown resented the presence of large numbers of federal workers. For nearly twenty-five years, he had worked against an entrenched bureaucracy while dealing with the paternalism that it engendered on Indian reservations. Brown's long-term employment with the government had, for those twenty-five years, demonstrated that the Blackfeet could, if given the opportunity, take responsibility for their affairs.

In the summer of 1952, Brown lost both his eyesight and his wife of fifty-five years, Frankie. He retired from the BTBC and, on November 17, 1963, died from cancer. He had spent his final years grieving his wife's absence but comforted by the presence of his extended family. Called "the Governor" by his older sons, Brown was a loving father who made many sacrifices to ensure that his children were educated. Lorraine Brown Owens, his youngest daughter, recalled that "he never grumbled about it because he truly believed in education." Asked about her father's service to the Blackfeet Nation, Owens said simply, "He did a lot to try to help the people."[50]

Brown lived during three dynamic eras of Indian-white relations: the allotment, New Deal, and termination eras. He had seen the worst of these relations and the promise of better. He had survived political infighting, criticism of the IRA that he championed, and charges of

BTBC corruption, which forced several members to resign. His own integrity was challenged on only one count, that of inflating the assessed value of land sold to the tribe, but this charge was neither pursued nor proven. Half-Indian and half-white, Brown also spent his career defending his Indianness and the right of Indians to define their future. In the process, he was the most forceful advocate of maintaining the tribal entity, consistently extolling the value of blood unity and respect for elders. He had, using the IRA as a "guide," helped to modernize the Blackfeet economy and administration, supervised a democratic process that benefited all citizens, and encouraged Blackfeet to assume more control of their affairs.[51] Brown was both a statesman who represented the Blackfeet Nation on the reservation and in Washington, DC, and a respected citizen who served the multiple interests on the reservation. His obituary in *The Glacier Reporter* stated that no Blackfeet "has in larger degree retained the confidence and respect of his people." He "undeniably deserves the title Elder Statesman," the article noted, and would be "remembered as an honest, upstanding man and a credit to his community."[52] That community was large and diverse, and Brown walked between two worlds, believing in the value of both. His eyesight may have faded, but his vision of making that community a productive and peaceful bicultural entity did not.

Notes

1. Malcolm McFee, "The 150% Man, a Product of Blackfeet Acculturation," *American Anthropologist* 70 (December 1968): 1096–107.

2. The General Allotment Act of 1887 forced many Indians to adopt farming programs that were chronically underfunded and, in many cases, implemented on land that was not suitable for agriculture. The result was, to use a common phrase, the "dispossession of the American Indian": Indian peoples lost nearly ninety million acres between 1887 and 1934, when allotment was halted.

3. For a summary of Blackfeet treaties, see Charles J. Kappler, comp., *Indian Affairs: Laws and Treaties,* 5 vols. (Washington, DC: Government Printing Office [hereafter cited as GPO], 1904–1941).

4. See Freal McBride, "Ten-Year Program for the Blackfeet Reservation, Montana: Population and Trend," 3, Central Classified Files (hereafter cited as CCF)-2 [1940–1956] File 7056-1944-Blackfeet (hereafter cited as BF)-071, Record Group 75, Bureau of Indian Affairs, National Archives and Record Service (hereafter cited as NA); E. B. Linnen and F. S. Cook, "Report of Investigation of Affairs on the Blackfeet Indian Reservation, Montana," CCF-1 [1907–1939] File 30650-1915-BF-150, NA.

5. "Resume, Training and Experience of the Tribal Officers," in "Loan Application of the Blackfeet Tribe of the Blackfeet Indian Reservation for a Loan from the Revolving Fund for Loans to Indian Corporations," September 3, 1936, CCF-1 File 19522-1936-BF-259, Part IA, NA.

6. For examples of Brown's handling of tribal meetings, see "Minutes of the Blackfeet Tribal Business Council," July 16, 1929, and "Speeches of a General Tribal Council Held July 20, 1929," CCF-1 File 40274-1929-BF-054, NA. For details of the Senate investigation, see "Report of Walter W. Liggett on Blackfeet Indian Reservation," in U.S. Congress, Senate, *Survey of Conditions of Indians of the United States,* Hearings before a Subcommittee of the Committee on Indian Affairs, 72d Cong., 1st sess., pt. 23 (Washington, DC: GPO, 1930).

7. "Minutes of the Meeting Held at Heart Butte," May 7 and 8, 1931, CCF-1 File 30804-1931-BF-057, NA.

8. "Minutes of the Blackfeet Tribal Business Council," January 4, 1934, CCF-1 File 3599-1934-BF-054, NA; for Brown's comments, see "Minutes of the Meeting of the Blackfeet Tribal Business Council," March 14, 1934, CCF-1 File 27648-1934-BF-054, NA.

9. U.S. Congress, Senate, *Survey of Conditions of Indians of the United States,* Hearings before a Subcommittee of the Committee on Indian Affairs, 73d Cong., 1st sess., pt. 31 (Washington, DC: GPO, 1933), 16716.

10. "Minutes of the Meeting of the Blackfeet Tribal Business Council," March 31, 1934, Records Concerning Wheeler-Howard Act (hereafter cited as RCWHA), CCF-1 File 4894-1934-BF-066, Part 2A, NA.

11. Ibid.

12. U.S. Congress, Senate, *Hearings on S. 2755, to Grant to Indians Living under Federal Tutelage the Freedom to Organize for Purposes of Local Self-Government and Economic Enterprise,* 73d Cong., 2d sess., pt. 2 (Washington, DC: GPO, 1934), 68.

13. Ibid., 167. For a complete review of the Blackfeet's IRA debates and congressional testimony, see Paul C. Rosier, *Rebirth of the Blackfeet Nation, 1912–1954* (Lincoln: University of Nebraska Press, 2001), and idem, " 'The Old System Is No Success': The Blackfeet Nation's Decision to Adopt the Indian Reorganization Act of 1934," *American Indian Culture and Research Journal* 23, no. 1 (1999): 1–37.

14. U.S. Congress, Senate, *Hearings on S. 2755,* 170–71.

15. U.S. Congress, House, *Readjustment of Indian Affairs,* Hearings before the Committee on Indian Affairs, 73d Cong., 2d sess., pt. 5 (Washington, DC: GPO, 1934), 244.

16. Ibid., 60.

17. Lorraine Brown Owens, interview with author, August 28, 1996. In author's files.

18. *U.S. Statutes at Large of the United States,* 48 Stat. 984 (1934).

19. Brown's assertion of his tribe's right to pass laws had alarmed Wheeler, who wielded his power to weaken Collier's vision of Indian self-government. Wheeler viewed the Blackfeet in many ways as a model for assimilation and acculturation.

20. Stone to Indian Office, telegram, October 28, 1934, General Records Concerning Indian Organization (hereafter cited as GRCIO), Box 2, File 9522-1936-BF-066, NA.

21. "Minutes of the Meeting of the Blackfeet Tribal Business Council, February 18, 1935," CCF-1 File 25146-1935-BF-054, NA.

22. "Minutes of the Blackfeet Tribal Business Council Meeting, April 4, 1935," CCF-1 File 20858-1935-BF-054, NA. Oscar Boy petitioned the council to nominate Brown, arguing that Brown was qualified to fill that position because he "understands the conditions of our people and is one of our own kind."

23. Ibid.

24. "Minutes of the Blackfeet Tribal Business Council Meeting Held at the Community Hall, May 2, 1935," CCF-1 File 29288-1935-BF-054, NA. See "Memorandum to the Director of National Park Service and Commissioner of Indian Affairs" (Exhibit C), and Brott to CIA, April 25, 1935 (Exhibit D), CCF-1 File 29288-1935-BF-054, NA.

25. "Memorandum for the Acting Secretary," Nathan Margold to Acting Secretary of the Interior Charles West, October 14, 1935, Felix Cohen Papers, Box 8, Folder 106, Yale Collection of Western Americana, Beinecke Rare Book and Manuscript Library, Yale University, New Haven, Connecticut.

26. O'Hara to CIA, November 14, 1935, GRCIO File 9522-A-1936-BF-068, NA.

27. Ibid.; Collier to Brown, December 23, 1935, GRCIO file 9522-A-1936-BF-068, NA.

28. "Results of Charter Election August 15, 1936," GRCIO File 9522B-1936-BF-061, NA. See also the *Browning (MT) Glacier County Chief,* August 21, 1936. The charter allowed the Blackfeet Nation to terminate federal supervision of resource development, contracts, loans, fund deposits, and per capita distribution.

29. *Constitution and By-Laws for the Blackfeet Tribe,* see Article VI (Powers of the Council), Section 1: Enumerated Powers, k, m, and p, and "Tribal Budget, March 1 to June 30, 1937," CCF-1 File 15708-1937-BF-050, NA.

30. "Loan Application of the Blackfeet Tribe of the Blackfeet Indian Reservation for a Loan from the Revolving Fund for Loans to Indian Corporations," September 3, 1936, CCF-1 File 19522-1936-BF-259, Part IA, NA.

31. This statistic was compiled from the tables of the "Annual Report of Extension Workers," 1936, CCF-1 File 4634-1937-BF-031, NA.

32. U.S. Congress, Senate, *Survey of Conditions of the Indians in the United States,* pt. 31, see pp. 16716–43.

33. The terms of the CRP gave the Indian allottee, provided he or she met certain requirements, title to the cows after three years. See A. C. Cooley, "Indian Cattle Purchase Program," *Indians At Work* 2, no. 4 (October 1, 1934).

34. See "Minutes of the Blackfeet Tribal Business Council, November 5, 1937," GRCIO File 9522-E-1936-BF-O54, NA.

35. Ibid.

36. For Hazlett's clever but divisive campaign, see the following issues of the *Browning (MT) Glacier County Chief:* September 3, 1937; October 8, 1937; October 15, 1937; October 29, 1937; December 3, 1937; and January 7, 1938.

37. "Project—Assisting in the Nation's War Effort," in "Annual Report of Extension Work, 1942," 11, CCF-2 File 1332-1943-BF-031, NA; Owens, interview.

38. "Ten-Year Program for the Blackfeet Indian Agency," March 1944, 27, CCF-2 File 7056-1944-BF-071, NA. For a good history of Indian America during World War II, see Alison R. Bernstein, *American Indians and World War II: Toward a New Era in Indian Affairs* (Norman: University of Oklahoma Press, 1991).

39. "Minutes of Meeting Held by the Blackfeet Tribal Business Council in Special Session," December 20, 1941, and February 1, 1941, GRCIO File 9522-E-1936-BF-054, NA.

40. U.S. Congress, House, *Investigate Indian Affairs,* Hearings before a Subcommittee of the Committee on Indian Affairs, pt. 3: Hearings in the Field, 78th Cong., 2d sess. (Washington, DC: GPO, 1944), 400.

41. "Minutes of the Blackfeet Tribal Constitutional Convention under Sponsorship of the Blackfeet Tribal Business Council," April 23, 1945, CCF-2 File 36128-1945-BF-054, NA.

42. Ibid., April 24, 1945.

43. Ibid., April 26, 1945.

44. "Meeting of Blackfeet Tribal Business Council and D'Arcy McNickle on the Wheeler-Howard Act," November 3, 1945, and November 6, 1945, CCF-2 File 36128-1945-BF-054, NA. Brown's speech runs from p. 13 to p. 22.

45. McNickle to Assistant Commissioner of Indian Affairs William Zimmerman, November 13, 1945, CCF-2 File 174-1943-BF-056, NA; McNickle to Brown, November 20, 1945, GRCIO File 9522-1936-BF-066, NA.

46. After the war a new generation of younger Blackfeet politicians would adopt a "corporatist" approach to tribal economics and attempt to dismantle the social programs set up under Brown's tenure; these politicians considered each tribal member a shareholder rather than a citizen deserving assistance.

47. U.S. Congress, House, *Emancipation of Indians,* Hearings before the Subcommittee on Indian Affairs of the Committee on Public Lands, 80th Cong., 1st sess., H.R. 2958, H.R. 2165, and H.R. 1113. (Washington, DC: GPO, 1947), 132.

48. See "Economies in Indian Bureau Program," in U.S. Congress, House, *Interior Department Appropriations for 1952,* Hearings before the Subcommittee of the Committee on Appropriations, 82d Cong., 1st sess. (Washington, DC: GPO, 1951), 1127–43.

49. "Public Hearing," February 27, 1952, CCF-2 File 1141-1946-BF-068, Part 2, NA.

50. Owens, interview.

51. For economic data and political analysis, see Rosier, *Reconstructing the Blackfeet Nation.*

52. *Browning (MT) Glacier Reporter,* November 22, 1963.

Suggested Readings

Ewers, John C. *The Blackfeet: Raiders on the Northwestern Plains.* Norman: University of Oklahoma Press, 1958.

Farr, William E. *The Reservation Blackfeet, 1882–1945: A Photographic History of Cultural Survival.* Seattle: University of Washington Press, 1984.

McFee, Malcolm. "The 150% Man, a Product of Blackfeet Acculturation." *American Anthropologist* 7 (December 1968): 1096–103.

Rosier, Paul C. *Rebirth of the Blackfeet Nation, 1912–1954.* Lincoln: University of Nebraska Press, 2001.

Taylor, Graham D. *The New Deal and American Indian Tribalism: The Administration of the Indian Reorganization Act, 1934–45.* Lincoln: University of Nebraska Press, 1980.

Washburn, Wilcomb E. "A Fifty-Year Perspective on the Indian Reorganization Act." *American Anthropologist* 86 (1984): 279–89.

9

Eugene Pulliam
Municipal Booster

Lara Bickell*

Eugene C. Pulliam (1889–1975) exemplifies the business and civic leaders who have traditionally served as one-person public relations machines in the West. Called "boosters," they have promoted the West in an effort to settle an area they have grown to love and hope to develop. Pulliam, a midwesterner, was a highly successful newspaperman who frequently wintered in Phoenix, Arizona. After purchasing two Arizona newspapers in the 1940s, he and his wife moved to Phoenix in 1954, and he spent the next twenty years promoting the city he had adopted as his own. Throughout his career, Pulliam encouraged tourism and civic and business development, and he sang the praises of Phoenix and the Valley of the Sun.

His endeavors reflected the growth of the Sun Belt region in the post–World War II years, an outcome of heavy federal investment in military bases and factories during the war years. This subregion soon became the pacesetter for the West and the rest of the United States. Developments in high-tech and defense industries, a thriving tourism, and government investment in public works in this area continue in the twentieth-first century and remind us that the "frontier" has yet to close. This situation is supported by ongoing labor migration and the flow of capital from within and without the United States, particularly from the Pacific Rim. Indirectly the efforts of boosters such as Pulliam, along with those of the central government and urban entrepreneurs, have connected the West to regional, national, and global markets.

Lara Bickell is currently working on her doctorate in history at Claremont Graduate University, Claremont, California. Currently she is curator at the Civil Engineer Corps/Seabee Museum in Port Hueneme, California. This essay is drawn from her master's thesis, completed at Pepperdine University, Malibu, California.

Since World War II the American West has experienced astronomic urban growth because of the millions of Americans who relocated there during and after the war. The population of Phoenix, Arizona, for example, grew almost eightfold between 1940 and 1980.[1] At first the growth

*I would like to thank Bruce Dinges, Amy Essington, Mike Logan, Linda Mollno, and William Schoeffler for suggesting changes and expansions. I am also indebted to the encouragement and criticism of my family and my mentor, W. David Baird.

appeared to be sporadic and random, with new industrial parks, cultural conveniences, and groves of suburban tracts popping up overnight. But behind the seemingly out-of-control urbanization, there was a method to the madness. In the case of numerous western cities, prominent residents in the community who were referred to as "boosters" took the lead in shaping the identity of the postwar West. These boosters had definitive visions of what the new West should look like, and they used their wealth and power to attract the elements necessary to make their visions a reality.

The purpose of this essay is to examine post–World War II boosterism and how it shaped the West. Boosters were active in many western cities after World War II, including Denver, Oklahoma City, and Salt Lake City. Although the specific situation in each city differed, the career of newspaper publisher Eugene C. Pulliam and his role as a booster in Phoenix, Arizona, illustrates the phenomenon of boosterism. This essay looks at three aspects of local culture that Pulliam directly affected: the expansion of tourism, the construction of new cultural amenities, and the reform of municipal government.

"Boosterism" is not an easy term to define because it encompasses many aspects of the cycle of urban growth and because it has both positive and negative effects.[2] At its core, it is the promotion of a region by either individuals or groups to encourage growth. In its ideal cycle, boosterism attracts people to an area for either relocation or tourism purposes, which increases the economy and draws in more money for reinvestment in the community. The reinvestment creates newer and better amenities, thus attracting more people and perpetuating the cycle. A contemporary example of boosterism is the "Texas: It's Like a Whole Other Country" campaign sponsored by the Texas Department of Economic Development. This program provides information about a wide variety of tourist attractions and facts for new residents.

Although boosterism often increases the economy of targeted cities, it also has negative side effects. Historian Hal Rothman argues that regions suffer from such effects when boosters make the "devil's bargain." Communities embrace a new economy without considering the cost of the irrevocable changes that the arrival of new money will cause.[3] In post–World War II Phoenix, for example, boosterism engendered overpopulation, increased environmental strain, and altered the sense of local identity.

Boosters have existed on the American frontier as long as there has been a profit to be made. Their primary goal is to promote their cities for the purpose of increasing their personal wealth. Boosters are always highly invested in their towns, and they profit in tandem with urban growth. Land speculators exemplified the boosters of the 1800s. In the late nineteenth and early twentieth centuries, many boosters purchased arid and seemingly worthless tracts of desert land at low prices, such as those in the Imperial Valley in California. After establishing fundamental infrastructures—canals, banks, general stores, homes, and saloons, for example—the boosters sold the converted desert Eden for exorbitant prices. They took tremendous personal financial risks to create communities where none existed previously. Yet because they owned both land and the infrastructures, they also made a profit off every person who relocated into the area.

Although they had similar intentions, post–World War II boosters differed from their predecessors because they had to maneuver within the established political and economic infrastructure of existing cities and towns. These boosters might have owned the local department store or the local newspaper, but the population of the West had grown large enough that only rarely would one person control an entire town. After World War II, boosters served as growth networks or alliances of the elite echelon of businesspeople—real estate agents, bankers, lawyers, publishers, and corporate executives—and held a single vision of prosperity.[4] Like the nineteenth-century land speculators who convinced homesteaders of the desert's Edenic virtues, post–World War II boosters had to convince people to move to their towns. They achieved this by promoting tourism and urban renewal, with an emphasis on cultural resources such as parks, museums, and theaters. In addition, they attracted new businesses by offering tax reform and political favors.

Post–World War II boosters extensively employed local media to advance their agendas. Newspaper publishers were integral members of the business elite because urban growth translated into more people, increased newspaper circulation, and greater profit. Many of these individuals used their newspapers as a mouthpiece for the progrowth booster agenda. Often the local newspaper served as the primary source of news for a town, as there were few, if any, other sources to dispute the information they disseminated. Newspapers, therefore, helped to gain popular support for the boosters.

One man who used his medium to advocate a booster agenda was Eugene C. Pulliam, publisher of the *Arizona Republic* and the *Phoenix Gazette.* Pulliam was born in a frontier sod house in Ulysses, Kansas, in 1889, the son of a traveling Methodist preacher who moved his family across the Midwest as he ministered to as many as seven churches simultaneously. Though not a churchgoer as an adult, Pulliam supported Christian values, and his beliefs were reflected in the topics of his editorials and in the masthead of one of his papers: "Where the spirit of the Lord is, there is Liberty" (2 Cor. 3:17).

As a boy, Pulliam attended Methodist schools. Among these was Baker Academy, a small Methodist preparatory school in Baldwin, Kansas. After finishing high school, he attended Depauw University in Greencastle, Indiana. There, he became acquainted with journalism when he and a group of friends launched a daily campus newspaper, of which Pulliam was the vice president and lead correspondent. In 1909, as a means of making journalism a more respectable profession, Pulliam founded the oldest journalism fraternity in the United States, Sigma Delta Chi. Although he never completed his degree, his accomplishments and his financial contributions to Depauw earned him a monument on the university campus, erected in his honor.

Pulliam made his fortune and reputation by buying small-town midwestern newspapers cheaply, reviving them, and selling them for a good profit. During his career, he owned a total of fifty-one papers in thirteen states, including Kansas, Oklahoma, Texas, Indiana, and Arizona. Along with many other wealthy midwesterners, Pulliam frequently wintered in Phoenix, Arizona, and in October 1946, he spread his sphere of influence to the Southwest by purchasing the *Arizona Republic* and the *Phoenix Gazette.* These two newspapers were major purchases in terms of influence: the *Arizona Republic* was the only newspaper distributed across the entire state of Arizona, and though the *Phoenix Gazette* had a smaller area of circulation, it was the favored evening paper in Phoenix, the population and political center of the state.[5] Pulliam had recently liquidated all but one of his other newspapers (the *Indianapolis Star*), but he purchased the Arizona papers because he believed that Phoenix had the potential to be one of America's most beautiful and lucrative cities.

He explained his vision for Phoenix to a reporter from the *Arizona Republic* the winter before he bought the paper: "I am very bullish on Arizona. You know, next to water, air, food and sex, Americans want sunshine most. They love to live outdoors and they can do it here to their hearts content. You need to awaken more to your opportunities and possibilities of the Salt River valley as a mecca for sun-hungry Americans. So I say, 'Sell it to the American people.' That's your God-given asset, and you should tell the whole nation about it."[6] "Sell it to the American people" operated as the unofficial motto of the Pulliam press as the publisher used his newspaper to tell his readers of all the attributes Phoenix had to offer.

Pulliam believed the residents and businesses of Phoenix were not sufficiently utilizing their natural assets to promote tourism. As early as 1946 he suggested that the city invest more money in traditional tourist accom-

From the *Arizona Republic,* March 1965. *Courtesy of Phoenix Neswpapers, Inc. (permission does not imply endorsement)*

modations, such as outdoor, shaded, pedestrian shopping areas, better horse-racing tracks, new park facilities, and more golf courses.[7] However, during his early years as a publisher in Phoenix, he used his newspapers to support less-traditional tourist campaigns.

Pulliam wanted Phoenix to glorify its western heritage, but he failed to understand that the area had emerged as a predominantly Anglo city and rarely highlighted aspects of its Hispanic and Native American history. Despite the local aversion, during his first few years as a publisher in Phoenix, Pulliam suggested several ways to incorporate the state's multi-ethnic heritage and attract more tourists. For example, in a 1951 editorial titled "More Injuns and Cowboys," the publisher encouraged the Phoenix Chamber of Commerce to provide people dressed up as cowboys to greet incoming tourists at the airport. He also suggested that Phoenix create an ethnic area celebrating the influence of Hispanic culture, similar to Olvera Street in Los Angeles.[8] Because Pulliam did not understand the image that local Phoenicians wanted to portray, such suggestions fell on deaf ears and were never implemented.

Pulliam's tourist campaigns also emphasized local industry. Within a few months of purchasing the newspaper, the publisher decided that Phoenicians were not taking full advantage of the local grapefruit harvest: he argued, for instance, that resorts ought to serve fresh-squeezed Arizona grapefruit juice rather than reconstituted juice from Florida. Pulliam believed that ignoring the importance of grapefruit was a disservice not only to the tourist and the Arizona grapefruit growers but also to the fruit itself, "for nowhere have the desert grapefruit . . . been less honored than in this, their own homeland."[9]

To rectify this situation, Pulliam began a full-scale campaign, called the "Squeezin' Season," to promote grapefruit in Phoenix. Using editorials and cartoons, he criticized Phoenicians for their ignorance regarding the grapefruit industry and explained the importance of the fruit. Six weeks of editorials culminated during the week of May 7, 1947, with the "Season for Squeezin' " celebration. Luncheons, parades, contests for the biggest grapefruit and sweetest juice, and even the designation of six girls as the "Grapefruit Squeezettes" marked the event.

Pulliam argued that the almost humorous fervor with which he supported the "Squeezin' Season" was justifiable. A new era in Phoenix community spirit had begun. He claimed that there was increasing support for the Arizona grapefruit industry, which illustrated a resurgence in community awareness. Moreover, he hoped that Phoenix could provide this same degree of support to other community projects, such as the assembling of a symphony orchestra, the building of a civic auditorium, and the expansion of city limits.[10]

The success of the "Squeezin' Season" remains dubious, although Pulliam stated that it had elicited a widespread positive response and garnered support from resorts, schools, merchants, the chamber of commerce, and housewives. However, little or no evidence of this influence survives, and it is questionable whether the campaign actually brought the community together in a united front.[11] In addition, despite the supposed popularity of the grapefruit festival among locals and tourists alike, as extolled in the pages of the *Arizona Republic,* an annual citrus festival was never established in Phoenix.

Local Phoenicians did not lend their full support to Pulliam's early tourist campaigns. Because the campaigns emphasized groups and matters deemed extraneous to Phoenix's urban identity—such as Native Americans, Hispanics, and agriculture—Phoenicians considered them promotional rather than seriously business-minded. However, Pulliam's focus changed in March 1954 when he and his wife, Nina, purchased a house and made Phoenix their permanent home. Perhaps because he was now a local himself, the publisher came to understand how Phoenix wanted to be seen by the rest of the nation. Whatever his motivation, Pulliam clearly changed his approach toward the question of tourism.

The publisher continued to promote the tourist industry in Phoenix but without the unconventional focus of his earlier days. Editorials discussing tourism decreased in frequency, and those that he wrote had a much more conservative tone, usually only reminding Phoenicians of the vital economic importance of the tourist sector. His enthusiasm resurfaced briefly in 1964 when he published a series of six front-page articles highlighting the positive and negative features of Phoenix as a tourist attraction.[12]

Pulliam's greatest contribution to tourism was putting Phoenix in the national spotlight. Over the course of his career, he befriended a plethora of political dignitaries. When he invited these people to his new hometown, they brought the national press with them. For example, Pulliam invited President Dwight D. Eisenhower to visit Phoenix in 1958. When *Air Force One* landed at Sky Harbor Airport, Pulliam, acting as primary host, welcomed the president and his wife to their first visit to Arizona. The presidential event received national news coverage, displaying the advantages of Phoenix as a tourist destination for the entire country. Eisenhower's visit also increased local support for Pulliam and his papers in Phoenix. The photograph of the president arriving at the Phoenix airport on the front-page of the *Arizona Republic* made the publisher look like the official ambassador for the city.[13]

Pulliam believed the weather and the natural beauty of Phoenix could attract visitors initially, but he worried that without cultural amenities, it would be impossible to convince them to return—and boosters of course needed people to return, as either tourists or transplants, to sustain the economic cycle. To publicize his concern the *Arizona Republic* examined Phoenix's cultural status in a front-page article in 1950. After a scathing assessment, it recommended immediate cultural enrichment for the city.[14]

In addition to donating headlines to the effort, Pulliam, under the auspices of his Phoenix Newspaper Corporation, funded many cultural enrichment projects in the Valley of the Sun. The Phoenix Zoo stands as a shining example of the degree of support cultural enrichment projects received from the publisher and his newspapers. Constructing a zoo in Phoenix first became an issue in 1954. The severe summers of the Sonoran Desert had previously precluded a zoo, but the introduction of new technology, such as affordable air-conditioning, now made it possible. The dilemma of cost effectiveness became paramount: would the type of animals that would thrive in a temperature-controlled desert attract enough visitors to pay the bills? Eugene Pulliam believed in the cause and argued that people enjoyed going to a zoo and would be impressed by the variety of animals that the desert could sustain.[15] Others agreed, and plans for the Phoenix Zoo moved forward.

Financial difficulties threatened the scheduled opening of the zoo in November 1962. Robert and Nancy Maytag, the founders and primary financiers of the Phoenix Zoo, attributed the problem to lack of financial support from the community. "Phoenicians have every reason to believe my financial support will continue," said Mrs. Maytag, "but, such support will not meet the needs of the zoo now nor in the next five years."[16] She pleaded publicly for Arizona families and businesses to donate money to the cause.

Pulliam printed two articles on the front page of the *Arizona Republic* to explain the plight of the zoo and emphasize its cultural potential. The articles brought both public attention and funds to the project. The Phoenix Newspaper Corporation donated $130,000 to the zoo, the largest single contribution besides the Maytag investment. Pulliam made the following comment about the zoo on the day the contribution was announced: "I know of no institution which will contribute more to the education and pleasure of Arizona people, both the young and the old. The zoo deserves the enthusiastic support of all the people of the state, because it will be in reality an Arizona Zoo."[17] The funding he himself provided was used to construct and maintain an exhibit of native Arizona flora and fauna, though no public recognition of the donation acknowledged his contribution.[18]

Although boosters such as Pulliam placed much emphasis on promoting tourism and improving cultural amenities, they also needed more residents to secure their visions of the new West. An increased population delivered a steady supply of new income and justified major changes in the local infrastructure. For example, additional schools were needed to accommodate the influx of baby boom children, and increased tax revenues supplied by the new residents funded the school construction. To attract new residents to their area, boosters needed to guarantee a quality of life characterized by virtues such as stability and economic prosperity, and prosperity was a product of a stable municipal government.

In the 1940s the municipal government in Phoenix was in a state of disarray. Many of the problems stemmed from the relationship between the city and the burgeoning military presence immediately outside the city limits. Beginning in June 1941, with U.S. involvement in World War II seemingly unavoidable, Phoenix and the surrounding areas had become a hub of military growth. Several air force bases and pilot-training facilities were rapidly established. Many troops traveled to these training camps and passed through Phoenix. In 1943 alone, Camp Hyder housed over 30,000 troops at one time. To accommodate personnel there and at the other bases, as many as fifteen military trains shuttled troops through Phoenix on a daily basis. On one occasion, volunteers tallied a minimum of 6,900 troops passing through Union Station in downtown Phoenix.[19]

The military presence proved economically beneficial for Phoenix businesses. The military permitted off-duty troops to visit the city to spend their money and time, providing Phoenix with tens of thousands of regular visitors. Hotels were always full, and restaurants and bars had a constant flow of customers. In fact, there were so many people in Phoenix that at times there were even food shortages. Stores ordered extra supplies and would still sell out. Realizing the possibility of profit, owners of retail establishments such as Goldwater's Department Store ordered a much larger and more varied inventory than they would have carried for civilian Phoenix. For many retailers, accommodation of the troops quickly translated to economic dependence on the military personnel.

The relationship between Phoenix and the military turned sour on November 30, 1942, when Col. Ross G. Hoyt, commander of Luke Field, declared Phoenix off-limits for his troops because sexually transmitted diseases were infecting so many of the soldiers. Earlier in the year the military authorities had asked the Phoenix city council to clean up their "red-light district," but months later, prostitutes still walked the streets and advertised their services with neon signs. The military felt that Phoenix officials lacked the ability and integrity to enforce their own laws and that the city had not made a sincere effort to curtail prostitution. The city council took a renewed stance against prostitution, but four months later the cases of venereal disease had tripled at Luke Field. Colonel Hoyt barred troops from Phoenix until further notice.

The military ban hurt businesses badly. Phoenicians could not buy all of the excess merchandise that retailers had acquired to sell to military personnel. Merchants realized they needed to restore their relationship with the military to perpetuate Phoenix's booming wartime economy. In reaction to the economic crisis, the Phoenix Chamber of Commerce and a group of concerned citizens demanded that new members replace the sitting council. Confronted with the tense situation, the old council members stepped down, allowing more-progressive leaders to take charge. The new city council succeeded in reinstating off-duty military visits.

Despite the immediate success of the new council, certain aspects of the city charter stymied long-term reform. The root of the problem was that the city manager position was an elected post, open only to residents of Phoenix. As a result, candidates were often underqualified, and unscrupulous relationships developed among political bedfellows. In November 1948, Phoenicians voted on a charter that made the Phoenix municipal government a council-manager system, with the city manager hired on the basis of professional qualifications.[20] The amendment passed with a popular vote of 6,595 to 2,949.[21] A provision of the charter amendment demanded the immediate removal of the present city council manager, marking the beginning of a new era in Phoenix municipal government.

In July 1949 a group of concerned citizens who supported the charter amendment established the Charter Government Committee (CGC). Most members of the CGC were white, upper-middle-class males, and all were involved in some type of public-dependent business, such as retail or publishing. Religion played no obvious role, as Protestants, Catholics, and Jews promoted the CGC with equal zeal. Only a small percentage of the membership of the CGC were women, though, and most of these were wives of prominent men who were too busy to serve themselves. Racial ethnic minorities had little or no input in CGC. The committee's purpose was to choose candidates for the city council who not only supported the charter amendment but also embraced a vision of growth for Phoenix. In other words the CGC was a political booster club, choosing members and representatives based on their ability to promote the city. In the November 1949 election, all of the candidates slated on the CGC ticket won, just as their successors would over the next twenty-five years.

One of the masterminds behind the CGC and the charter reform was Eugene Pulliam. The publisher shied away from the limelight, never holding a public office or government position, and since much of his business was conducted on the telephone, he left little written evidence of his interaction with other movers and shakers. Therefore, his role as a political booster must be assessed on the basis of his influence rather than any direct role. In this instance, Pulliam influenced the success of the CGC by choosing the candidates, swaying the elections, and supporting the CGC agenda.

Some historians claimed that Pulliam picked or at least approved all of the candidates on the CGC ticket. He supposedly began this practice during the first election in 1949, when he handpicked Barry Goldwater for the city council race. Running for a council seat seemed out of character for Goldwater, a department store owner who said that "[Pulliam] talked [him] into it."[22] The image of Pulliam as the ultimate decision maker in the CGC was suggested by other comments, as well. James E. Cook, a longtime Phoenician and writer for the *Arizona Republic,* argued that Pulliam was one of three men who comprised the top tier of leadership in Phoenix. Apparently, Pulliam, banker Walter Bimson, and lawyer Frank Snell ultimately decided the public policy of the city. According to Cook, "Consensus needed only the opinion of these three men."[23]

Although Pulliam's behind-the-scenes role remained somewhat obscure, there was no question that he used his newspapers to sway city elections in favor of the CGC: "The *Arizona Republic* and *Phoenix Gazette* actively supported Committee candidates in [the election in 1949] and subsequent city elections and unquestionably have been an important factor in Charter Government victories."[24] Since his newspapers were the largest in the city, the majority of Phoenix residents read Pulliam's opinions. Thus, he used both direct and indirect methods to advocate the CGC nominees.

In fact, no other newspaper advocated specific candidates quite as ardently as Pulliam's. In them, he published the names of the candidates to whom he threw his support. Indeed, just before every city election, the *Arizona Republic* printed its list of recommended candidates—sometimes in the form of a listing of favored candidates and their party affiliation and at other times in a narrative giving the candidates names' and reasons why they deserved to win. Regardless of the style the message remained the same: an explanation that the individual belonged to the CGC and had done much to further its agenda. Often the lists would be printed in such a way that they could be easily clipped out of the newspaper and carried to the polling place.[25]

The Arizona Supreme Court case *Phoenix Newspaper, Inc. v. Choisser* (1957) further illustrated Pulliam's influence on the success of the CGC. On November 4, 1953, the Phoenix Chamber of Commerce sponsored a forum and debate for the city council candidates. Candidates from the CGC and from an opposing organization known as the Economy Ticket were both present. All of them had the opportunity to explain their platforms to the press before entering a series of discussions about the future of the city council.

The next morning the *Arizona Republic* reported the events of the previous evening: "Opposing candidates in the forth-coming city election collided head-on last night over the issue of prostitution and gambling."[26] Jack Choisser, the mayoral candidate, and others running with him on the Economy Ticket were highly offended by the article, which they believed depicted them as promoters of prostitution and gambling. They argued that Pulliam favored the CGC ticket and purposefully discredited the Economy Ticket in an attempt to secure victory for his candidates. In response to the article, Choisser and the others filed a libel suit against the Phoenix Newspaper Corporation.

After the state superior court found in favor of the plaintiff, awarding Choisser $154,000 in damages, Pulliam appealed the case to the state supreme court. In a written decision by Justice Porter Murry, the high court reversed the original finding. However, though Pulliam prevailed, the decision illustrated that his peers acknowledged that his newspapers were used to support the CGC. As Judge Murry wrote, "There is no question that the articles and editorials here involved showed a desire on the part of the defendant to defeat the plaintiffs for elections."[27]

Providing a stable municipal government was key in attracting new businesses to the Valley of Sun, but the triumphant CGC members did not want to attract just any industry. They understood that tourism was the most lucrative industry in Phoenix and that they could not permit industrial growth that would encroach on the natural beauty of the desert. What Phoenix needed was low-polluting, "clean-air" industries, such as electronic and computer plants that produced little smoke and would not lower the air quality. They also wanted industries that enticed well-educated, middle-class residents to move to Phoenix.

Pulliam strongly supported the relocation of clean-air industries to Phoenix. For instance, when Goodyear Aircraft first moved there in 1947, he paid tribute to Paul Litchfield, the company's chairman of the board, for choosing the city as the site of the new plant. Pulliam realized that industry was the future of Arizona, and he argued that "that the postwar future of Arizona will be what we who live in the state make it. The opportunity for growth and progress and prosperity is present."[28]

Although Phoenix had already welcomed large companies such as Motorola, Goodyear Aircraft, and AiResearch, the CGC had its sights set on Sperry Rand, a large electronics company that had relocation offers from many cities in the West. Company officials had reservations about moving to Phoenix because of the previous instability of the municipal government and their employees' fears of relocating to an isolated desert city.

In 1955 the Municipal Industrial Development Corporation, a private special interest group consisting of members from both the chamber of commerce and the CGC, met Sperry Rand's terms. The company had given the organization a list of demands, which, if met, would convince them to move to Phoenix. Within seventy-two hours after receiving these terms, the group raised $650,000. With this money the organization bought Sperry Rand a tract of land for a factory and paid for improvements to a nearby airport through which the company would conduct the majority of its business. The remainder of the money paid for other, unnamed inducements. How the group collected such a large amount of money in such a short amount of time was unknown, though it has been assumed that community business leaders used private resources to fund the transaction.

A change in the Arizona state tax code also enticed Sperry Rand and others to move to Phoenix. Influential Phoenicians wanted Arizona to eliminate state sales taxes on goods manufactured for sale to the federal government. Such a repeal would make items such as automotive and airplane parts sold to the government tax-free. In Phoenix the CGC supported similar tax breaks for businesses on a local level.

Pulliam championed corporate tax-incentive initiatives long before they became a public issue. As early as 1950, he wrote editorials promoting Arizona's adoption of tax repeal. Arguing that industries would see repeal as an open and warm invitation, he asked both the chamber of commerce and the state legislature to consider its value.[29] Prior to the legislature's vote on tax repeal in 1955, Pulliam made his opinion known, loud and clear. On the front page of the *Arizona Republic,* he said outright that the new tax laws should be passed in order to ensure the expansion of Sperry Rand.[30] Three days later the repeal was passed. Sperry Rand officials immediately announced that they were planning to build a second plant in Phoenix.

Ironically Pulliam's political influence can be seen most clearly in the demise of the CGC. When he died in 1975, the CGC was left without his support in the elections held later that year, and for the first time in twenty-five years, it lost control of the city council, never to regain it. Some argue that the CGC lost because its members were getting too old to govern and because the younger, more ethnically diverse residents of Phoenix wanted more appropriate representation. Yet criticisms had been hurled at the CGC for almost a decade and had not caused it to lose elections. Perhaps the reproach had weakened the infrastructure of the CGC, but the loss of the group's most powerful supporter was its deathblow.[31]

Months before his death, Pulliam invited thirty-seven people to join a civic organization known as the Phoenix 40. In effect, he was attempting to preserve the power structure of the city's politics as established since 1949. Despite the dedication of the Phoenix 40 to the Pulliam style of politics, this group never achieved the same degree of success because their predecessors had created an environment that made their ideology obsolete.

Eugene Pulliam and other boosters across the West envisioned urban growth and worked hard to make their visions a reality, and through their dedicated efforts western cities boomed. However, growth also diversified the character of the cities, attracting a more ethnically mixed population to the region. By the 1970s many western cities sustained a large, diverse citizenry—people who vocalized their dissatisfaction with the boosters—and national cultural shifts caused by the Vietnam War and the civil rights movement gave a political voice to groups who had been muted in the past. The opinions of women, blacks, Hispanics, and members of other ethnic groups affected mainstream politics, and the youth of America took the future of the nation into their own hands. These vocal groups elected representatives of various races, genders, and ages who advocated more liberal agendas, in effect ousting the very people who had created the attributes that drew them to the West in the first place.

Both contemporary critics and historians have criticized Eugene Pulliam for using his newspapers to promote public agendas that achieved primarily personal benefits.[32] The accusation of greed has been the albatross around the necks of all post–World War II boosters. As is the case with many of his cohorts, no documentary evidence of Pulliam's motivation remains. Therefore, despite his critics' insistent condemnation, some questions about him remain unanswered. Did he fully understand the long-term ramifications of his devil's bargain? Did he really believe that Phoenix could be the most sophisticated city in the West? Or was he only trying to make the city profitable to serve his own purposes and line his own pockets? Similar questions linger regarding the intentions of most post–World War II boosters.

For all their faults, boosters played a major role in shaping the identity of western cities. Assuming the urbanization of the West was inevitable given the injection of funds and people into the region after the United States became involved in World War II, boosters were simply the people with a vision. They had grandiose plans for their cities—plans that, if accomplished, would make their hometowns the most beautiful and lucrative urban centers in America. When looking at photographs of some of these cities in the 1940s, one wonders if the divine or the deranged inspired their visions. Nonetheless, it is clear that, despite its inherent flaws, boosterism was a successful movement that created an outline for future growth in the West. The framework created by the boosters—for the infrastructure of the economy, for municipal government, and for the supply of natural resources—continues to support many western cities today.

Notes

1. The following numbers from the U.S. Census Bureau refer to the population within the city during the corresponding years: 65,414 (1940); 106,818 (1950); 439,170 (1960); 654,153 (1970); 789,704 (1980).

2. For more detailed information about urban growth in the West, see Carl Abbott, *The Metropolitan Frontier: Cities in the Modern American West* (Tucson: University of Arizona Press, 1993); Richard M. Bernard and Bradley R. Rice, eds., *Sunbelt Cities: Politics and Growth since World War II* (Austin: University of Texas Press, 1983); Robert B. Fairbanks and Kathleen Underwood, eds., *Essays on Sunbelt Cities and Recent Urban America* (College Station: Texas A&M Press, 1990); Raymond A. Mohl, ed., *Searching for the Sunbelt: Historical Perspectives on a Region* (Knoxville: University of Tennessee Press, 1990); Gerald D. Nash, *The American West Transformed: The Impact of the Second World War* (Bloomington: Indiana University Press, 1985); David C. Perry and Alfred J. Watkins, eds., *The Rise of Sunbelt Cities* (Beverly Hills, CA: Sage Publications, 1977); Peter Wiley and Robert Gottlieb, *Empires in the Sun: The Rise of the New American West* (New York: G. P. Putnam's Sons, 1982).

3. Hal K. Rothman, *Devil's Bargain: Tourism in the Twentieth-Century American West* (Lawrence: University Press of Kansas, 1998), 10–28.

4. Richard White, *"It's Your Misfortune and None of My Own": A New History of the American West* (Norman: University of Oklahoma Press, 1992), 541–46.

5. Throughout the rest of this essay, I refer only to the *Arizona Republic.* It was and is the morning paper, whereas the *Phoenix Gazette* was the afternoon paper (it ceased publication in early 1997). In most cases the editorials in the two newspapers were identical.

6. *Arizona Republic,* February 10, 1946, 1.

7. Ibid.

8. Ibid., September 21, 1951, 6.

9. Ibid., April 16, 1947, 6.

10. Ibid., May 12, 1947, 6.

11. During the late 1940s and early 1950s the Phoenix Chamber of Commerce printed a monthly magazine entitled *Phoenix Action,* which prided itself on making Phoenix the most publicized city in the country. Neither the "Squeezin' Season" nor anything about the Arizona grapefruit industry was mentioned in that publication.

12. *Arizona Republic,* November 22–27, 1964, 1.

13. Ibid., February 24, 1958, 1.

14. Ibid., January 1, 1950, 1, 5.

15. Ibid., July 24, 1954, 6.

16. Ibid., May 31, 1962, 1, 4.

17. J. Morris Richards Collection, Box 5, Folder 6, Arizona Historical Foundation, Tempe, Arizona.

18. *Arizona Republic,* November 20, 1962, 1.

19. Bradford Luckingham, *Phoenix* (Tucson: University of Arizona Press, 1989), 139. Luckingham's monograph is the most complete and most concise history written on Phoenix.

20. *Arizona Republic,* August 15, 1948, 6.

21. Michael F. Konig, "Election of 1949: Transformation of Municipal Government in Phoenix," in *Phoenix in the 20th Century,* ed. G. Wesley Jr. (Norman: University of Oklahoma Press, 1993), 171.

22. Russell Pulliam, *Publisher* (Ottawa, IL: Jameson Books, 1984), 135.

23. James E. Cook, "1966–1996: Coming of Age," *Phoenix Magazine* 31 (August 1996): 30–31.

24. Paul Kelso, "A Decade of Council-Manager Government in Phoenix, Arizona" (Tempe, AZ: n.p., 1960), 10.

25. *Arizona Republic,* November 7, 1950, 1.

26. Ibid., November 5, 1953, 1.

27. *Phoenix Newspapers, Inc. v. Choisser,* 82 Ariz. 271 (1957). Other court cases against the Pulliam press expressed similar concerns regarding favoritism.

28. *Arizona Republic,* January 16, 1947, 6.

29. Ibid., March 21, 1950, 1; March 23, 1950, 1; March 24, 1950, 6.

30. Ibid., December 18, 1955, 1.

31. A 1981 quantitative study by Graham Robertson analyzed the relationship between editorial endorsements by the *Arizona Republic* and the election results during the time Pulliam owned the newspaper. Robertson found that the *Arizona Republic* made 508 positive endorsements and 150 negative endorsements of candidates running in Arizona State, Maricopa County, and Phoenix elections between 1947 and 1974. There was a high correlation between the newspaper's endorsements and the election results. According to Robertson, "Only once during the period Pulliam was publisher did a candidate for city council or mayor who was endorsed by the newspaper lose." See Graham J. Robertson, "Editorial Endorsements by the *Arizona Republic* from 1947 to 1974, and Arizona Election Results" (Master's thesis, Arizona State University, 1981).

32. One example of contemporary criticism of Pulliam was a pamphlet entitled "Arizona Crisis: The People of Arizona v. Eugene C. Pulliam—The Man Who Likes to Play God." The author and publication date of the eight-page pamphlet are unknown, but the piece has been attributed to the Arizona Democratic Party. Published in either 1956 or 1962, it responded to Pulliam's conservative political views and the unfair use of his newspapers to expound his agenda.

Suggested Readings

Luckingham, Bradford. *Minorities in Phoenix: A Profile History of Mexican American, Chinese American, and African American Communities, 1860–1992.* Tucson: University of Arizona Press, 1994.

Pomeroy, Earl. *In Search of the Golden West.* New York: Alfred A. Knopf, 1957.

Rothman, Hal K. *Devil's Bargain: Tourism in the Twentieth-Century American West.* Lawrence: University Press of Kansas, 1998.

Sheridan, Thomas E. *Arizona.* Tucson: University of Arizona Press, 1995.

Zarbin, Earl. *All the Time a Newspaper.* Phoenix: Arizona Republic, 1990.

10

William O. Douglas
The Environmental Justice

Adam M. Sowards

William O. Douglas (1899–1980) is best known for his tenure as a justice of the U.S. Supreme Court. Appointed by President Franklin Delano Roosevelt in 1939, the forty-year-old Douglas became the Court's second-youngest appointee ever. Less well known, however, are Douglas's contributions to the environment. Though born outside the West, he grew up near the Cascade Mountains, and personal tribulations shaped his lifelong ties to the physical landscape. His career later took him to the East, but outdoor leisure activities repeatedly pulled him back to the Pacific Northwest. Like the preservationist John Muir, Douglas was reverent toward nature, and like the conservationist thinker Aldo Leopold, he embraced an ethical response to the land. His understanding that the wilderness frontier made men and women strong and Americans great—which reminds one of the ideas of Frederick Jackson Turner and Theodore Roosevelt—also shaped his commitment to the environment.

This love of wilderness was articulated in several decisions the Court handed down during his tenure, as well as in his books on nature. Douglas's public life reflected the emergence of an early environmentalism in the West, one that stressed the health of ecosystems and the biological well-being of the planet. Certain changes after World War II gave this movement its momentum. The prosperity experienced in U.S. cities in the postwar years made Americans less concerned with scarcity and more concerned with the quality of life. Yet that same prosperity also fueled more investments, which engendered continual opposition from wilderness preservation advocates.

Adam M. Sowards earned his doctorate at Arizona State University in Tempe. Currently, he is completing an environmental history of the Pacific Northwest's Cascade Range that analyzes the dynamic interaction between nature and culture since human occupation. He has published essays and articles on John Muir and the American Southwest.

In early 1939, U.S. Supreme Court Associate Justice Louis Brandeis announced his plans to retire. President Franklin D. Roosevelt made no secret that he wished to appoint a westerner to the nation's highest tribunal to balance regional representation on the Court. A front-runner for the position seemed to be a senator from Washington State named Lewis Schwellenbach, a loyal New Dealer who even faithfully supported

Roosevelt's ill-advised Court-packing plan.[1] William O. Douglas, chair of the Securities and Exchange Commission (SEC), was also a possibility, but Roosevelt initially dismissed him as an easterner. To borrow Schwellenbach's characterization, Douglas, though he had grown up in Washington state, "was anything but a 'technical' Westerner." In fact, he had been a member of the eastern intelligentsia since the 1920s—as a Wall Street attorney, a law professor at Columbia and Yale University Law Schools, and a commissioner and eventually the chair of the SEC. An individual who had spent his entire professional life on the East Coast clearly would not fit Roosevelt's bill.[2]

Despite those nonwestern qualifications, Douglas and his allies maneuvered to emphasize his western experience and sensibilities, as well as demonstrate regional support. The pro-Douglas campaign worked, especially after the well-known William Borah, a Republican senator from Idaho, announced that Douglas would make a fine representative of the West on the Court. In March, Roosevelt sent his name to the Senate for confirmation, and in short order, William O. Douglas became a U.S. Supreme Court justice.[3]

That Roosevelt could have considered Douglas too "eastern" in 1939 comes as a surprise today, for no member of the Court or perhaps all of Washington, DC, during his tenure could match his image as a westerner—rugged individualist, expert outdoorsmen, famous for his marked informality. He cultivated this image deliberately and linked it inextricably to the West's reputation of individualism and its celebrated landscapes. Douglas may have spent his professional life largely in Washington, DC, but his heart remained in his native Pacific Northwest. His favorite cause, conservation, confirmed that western identity, for environmental debates and activism were always a central feature of western politics and culture. As the Supreme Court's environmental justice, he drew deeply from his western roots and experiences.

In the foreword to his 1950 autobiography, *Of Men and Mountains,* Douglas remarked, "The boy makes a deep imprint on the man." That truism seems especially apt in the case of William O. Douglas. Orville, as he was known as a child and youth, was born in Maine, Minnesota, in 1898 to Julia Fisk Bickford Douglas and William Douglas, a Presbyterian minister. Later in life, he recalled little about Minnesota, since soon after his birth his father transferred to a new pastorate in Estrella, California, and soon thereafter the family made another move to Cleveland, Washington. From Cleveland, Douglas first glimpsed the two principal natural features of the Pacific Northwest that would ultimately prove so important in his upbring-

Courtesy of the Yakima Valley Museum

ing and later career—the Cascade Mountains forty miles to the west and the Columbia River thirty miles to the south. For Douglas the river and the range formed an emotional, almost spiritual, bond to this land.[4]

Now settled in the Northwest, which he would call home in one way or another for the rest of his life, Douglas's attachment to the dry, sagebrush-covered hills of central Washington developed intensely. That affection only deepened during the funeral for his father, who had died in August 1904 of complications following surgery for stomach ulcers. Now fatherless and understandably afraid, the five-year–old boy wanted to escape the church service, but at the cemetery, he "became afraid—afraid of being left alone, afraid because the grave held my defender and protector." As young Orville started to cry the minister told him, "You must be a man, sonny." Douglas's gaze gradually lifted to Mount Adams in the distance: "As I looked, I stopped sobbing. My eyes dried. Adams stood cool and calm, unperturbed by the event that had stirred us so deeply that Mother was crushed for years. Adams suddenly seemed to be a friend. Adams subtly became a force for me to tie to, a symbol of stability and strength." As Douglas remembered the episode, no doubt embellishing it over the years, the Cascades became an anchor for him and remained so from that day forward.[5]

If being fatherless at age five was not difficult enough, Douglas contended with extreme poverty and his own severe illness. Julia Douglas moved her family—three children under the age of seven—to Yakima, Washington. There, she built a house at 111 North Fifth Avenue with part of the life insurance money her husband left behind, and she invested the remainder in a highly speculative irrigation project that soon failed. Housed but penniless the Douglas family struggled financially. Orville washed store windows, swept out businesses, picked fruit in the productive Yakima Valley, and worked at other odd jobs. The money that he, his older sister, Martha, and his younger brother, Arthur, earned "often meant the difference between dinner and no dinner." At Christmas time the Douglases received a box from the Presbyterian Home Mission. This and other charity made Christmas a "grubby occasion" for Douglas, who felt such welfare mostly assuaged the psyche of the rich who donated the cast-off clothing, with only slight benefit to the poor recipients. These childhood holiday episodes helped form his substantial distrust toward what he routinely referred to throughout his career as "the Establishment" and created an indelible class consciousness. Even in Yakima, a small but growing center for agricultural production, the Establishment affected Douglas, as it contrasted sharply with his family's poverty. "Because of our poverty," he wrote in *Go East, Young Man* (1974), the first volume of his autobiography, "we did occasionally feel that we were born 'on the wrong side of the railroad tracks.' " That feeling of being outcast and the resentment it engendered remained strong within Douglas and later permeated his jurisprudence and extrajudicial writings, speeches, and other activities.[6]

Although poverty made a deep impact on Douglas's worldview, another factor more profoundly shaped the course of his life. While still in Minnesota, he contracted a minor case of polio. Despite his mother's near constant attention, including massaging Douglas's limbs every two hours and praying constantly for weeks, the young boy's legs remained weak. However, contrary to doctors' prognostications and in contrast to the experiences of many other polio victims, Douglas eventually regained the use of his legs, though his mother still made excuses for his understandable weakness. "He's not as strong as other boys," he remembered her telling others, "he has to be careful what he does—you know, his legs were almost paralyzed." Predictably, he was afraid of "being publicly recognized as a puny person—a weakling." On the way to school, classmates teased, "Look at that kid's skinny legs. . . . Did you ever see anything as funny?" At a loss, Douglas cried, confirming, at least in his own mind, his weakling status. He resolved to rise above his peers in academics, which he did. Yet a boy's world, especially in the American West just past the turn of the century, required strength. Men were expected to exemplify the strenuous life that Theodore Roosevelt celebrated in his early-twentieth-century salute to the masculine accomplishments of the American westering spirit. Drawing a parallel with the natural world and heavily incorporating Darwinian language, Douglas later explained his fears: "The physical world loomed large in my mind. I read what happened to cripples in the wilds. They were the weak strain that nature did not protect. They were cast aside, discarded for hardier types. . . . Man was the same, I thought. Only men can do the work of the world—operating trains, felling trees, digging ditches, managing farms. Only robust men can be heroes of a war." The western world in which he wished to live and which was enshrined in popular culture had no room for a "cripple" or a weakling.[7]

So in a fashion to be repeated time and again, Douglas set out to meet a challenge and conquer his fear, for he knew that "man is not ready for adventure unless he is rid of fear." He longed for adventure, and the foothills north of Yakima provided an ideal testing ground. After meeting a Sunday school classmate who had been climbing those hills under a doctor's orders, Douglas knew instinctively that he would strengthen his legs similarly. "First I tried to go up the hills without stopping," the justice explained. "When I conquered that, I tried to go up without change of pace. When that was achieved, I practiced going up not only without a change of pace but whistling as I went." After several seasons of regular hiking, Douglas's legs grew strong. He defeated his weakness, learned to appreciate nature in the mountains, and developed a passion for hiking in magnificent western landscapes. In the process, his childhood disease, the method he used to overcome it, and the place of his recovery made lasting imprints on a young man destined for a life that led him away from his beloved hills near the Cascade Mountains.[8]

Douglas's uncommon determination and his imposing intellect led to his graduating as valedictorian of his high school class and earning a scholarship to Whitman College in Walla Walla, Washington. He worked his way through college at a Norwegian immigrant's jewelry store, as a janitor, and as an agricultural worker in summertime, where he worked and conversed with Wobblies—members of the radical Industrial Workers of the World union. At Whitman, Douglas met influential science and literature professors, rebelled against religious dogma, and nursed his suspicion of the Establishment. His successful college career led first to a stint teaching high school back in Yakima and then on to Columbia Law School in 1922, after shepherding a flock of sheep on the railroad from eastern Washington to Chicago to pay for his transportation. The departure from his beloved West was not without misgivings: "All the roots I had in life were in the Yakima Valley." Whenever he thought of the Cascades while in the urban corridors of New England, New York, and Washington, DC, Douglas "felt an almost irresistible urge to go West. It was the call of the Cascade Mountains." For him, then, the West was home in spirit, if not always in fact.[9]

As Douglas made his meteoric rise from professor of law to SEC commissioner to SEC chair to Supreme Court justice in just a few years, he garnered national press attention as a leading New Deal liberal. Notably this attention fixed partly on his previous western life. Richard L. Neuberger, Oregon journalist and eventual U.S. senator, wrote a feature entitled "Mr. Justice Douglas" in the August 1942 edition of *Harper's*. The complimentary article depicted the young justice dressed in "the five-gallon Western hat he invariably wears." Neuberger maintained that everyone called Douglas "Bill," emphasizing an informality cultivated from his western background. Finally, the journalist explained Douglas's political appeal, drawn unmistakably from his humble Yakima beginning: "He has a grassroots personality, a homespun Lincolnesque appearance, and the nearest thing to a log-cabin background there is in American politics today." Neuberger's portrait was an accurate homage from a friend. He made clear to readers of *Harper's* that William O. Douglas personified the West. As was revealed in a 1946 letter to the editor of *American Mercury*, the public accepted such an image and early on identified the justice with the outdoors: "Douglas suggests the strength and ruggedness of the giant oaks of his own Wallowa Mountains of Oregon." Surely this characterization would have pleased Douglas, even if his botanical knowledge and outdoor experience told him oaks were relatively rare in the pine-dominated Wallowas. Throughout American political history a western identity held appeal, conveying as it did the image of a rugged individual from the frontier past.[10]

At the time Neuberger's article appeared in *Harper's*, rumors that President Roosevelt might reshuffle his cabinet for the wartime emergency led to conjectures that Douglas might receive a cabinet appointment.

Neuberger speculated and actively promoted Douglas for such positions as director of the War Production Board or secretary of war. Douglas's leading qualifications were, first, his proven administrative acumen and, second, his ability to represent the needs and desires of the Far West. For their part western liberals and progressives readily praised his qualities and urged his reassignment. "The west has an especial regard for Justice Douglas," stated an editorial in southern Oregon's *Coos Bay Times.* The editorialist went on to claim that the "west" knew Douglas from his time as a student, lawyer, and perennial visitor. "The northwest has found Justice Douglas, as has the east, a man of intellectual vigor, of impeccable honesty, with a *restless physical verve* so necessary for high offices in conduct of war. Douglas gets things done. . . . This area knows he would make a valuable addition to any reconstituted cabinet the president may select." In a similar endorsement the *Oregon Labor Press* offered even higher praise. After complaining that there were "too few Westerners" in the war program, an editorialist announced "the common people of the country—and especially the common people of the West—know that Mr. Douglas understands their problems." These northwestern newspapers sanctioned Douglas's westernness and accepted him as an able regional representative. If these editorials at all reflected their readers' opinions, western communities, especially the liberal constituencies, happily claimed him as one of their own.[11]

The national and regional press clearly offered praise and prominence for this symbol of American liberalism. Although Douglas would always wear with pride the liberal badge he earned in the 1930s and 1940s, he increasingly donned other political apparel. Beginning in 1949 he became a world traveler extraordinaire, visiting Asia, the Middle East, and the Soviet Union and writing books filled with observations and policy recommendations not always popular with conservative politicians during the Cold War. With his considerable stature as a public figure and his self-conscious image as an outdoorsman, Douglas brought to conservation a ready influence. By the mid-1950s he regularly took a visible public role in conservation matters. A hiker and fisherman nearly all his life, he found it necessary to lead environmental causes into the public fray. In that role, he may have achieved his greatest lasting significance.

Occasionally, Douglas wrote letters in the 1940s to friends and acquaintances about fishing resources or trail conditions in the Pacific Northwest. Not until the 1950s, however, did he bring his penchant for outdoor activities and his weighty influence to bear on conservation causes. His first publicized fight involved the Chesapeake & Ohio Canal near Washington, DC, adjacent to which some hoped to build a scenic highway.

Douglas frequently hiked along the historical canal and enjoyed the birds and other wildlife and especially the solitude. In 1954, long before most Americans were aware of or interested in environmental matters, he challenged the editors of the *Washington Post,* who had publicly approved the idea of a parkway, to a hike along the 189-mile canal from Cumberland, Maryland, to Washington, DC. Soon the Wilderness Society, private citizens, and government officials clamored for a voice and a place among the hikers. For a week the hike held the national news media's attention. The *Washington Post* editors changed their minds, and in 1961, after a long battle and annual reunion hikes to maintain the issue's prominence in the public's eye, President Dwight D. Eisenhower declared the canal a national monument. In 1971, it was designated a national historic park, and by 1977, it was dedicated to Douglas. Assuredly, the controversy surrounding the Chesapeake & Ohio Canal was an Eastern environmental battle, and that was fitting for a justice who lived three out of four seasons in the beltway. Nevertheless Douglas's early foray into public conservation activism served as a significant precedent and established patterns for his later environmental contests in the West.[12]

Not long after beginning his activism on behalf of the canal, Douglas took up a cause closer to his favored home in the Pacific Northwest. On Washington's Olympic Peninsula, where he owned a summer cabin, local business interests wanted to build a new road that would wind along an ocean beach contained within the Olympic National Park. Although such a roadway would make automobile travel for commercial and tourist purposes easier within the relatively remote peninsula, Douglas wrote Conrad L. Wirth, director of the National Park Service, in 1957 to express his concern. "I have hiked this primitive beach," he explained, "[and] as a result of that hike I fell in love with that primitive beach and its great charm and beauty, and its abundant wildlife." He continued, citing his worry that if the road was allowed close to the beach, the traffic would "drive out the game and we'd end up with just another *ordinary* beach." The justice wanted anything but an *ordinary* beach. Taking a page from his C & O Canal book, he led a three-day, twenty-two-mile hike to protest the road, with sponsorship and organization provided by the Wilderness Society and the Federation of Western Outdoor Clubs. Despite evidence to the contrary, he maintained the group was "not fighting a road." Clearly, of course, they were fighting a road, but Douglas meant more was at stake than merely this strip of macadam.[13]

In his first book of nature writing, *My Wilderness: The Pacific West,* published in 1960, Douglas devoted a chapter to this Pacific beach and explained the deeper issues involved in the 1958 fight. He described the flora and fauna of the region and wove human and natural history together by commenting on the native history of the coast and even describing how the ocean connected, rather than divided, North American and Asian populations. Besides offering these portraits, Douglas embedded his prose with ecological lessons. He carefully explained how downed timber littered the forest floor, making traveling with a horse quite treacherous; however, he noted that the timber was "being reclaimed and turned to humus," returning basic nutrients to the soil. He extended his ecological discussion to the marine life as well, offering a series of miniature biology lessons for readers who were likely ignorant on the subjects he addressed.[14]

Moreover the beach proved inspiring at a spiritual level. Like many before him, Douglas felt an almost obligatory humility before the force of the oceans: "I realize how small and minute man is in the cosmic scheme." Furthermore, he coupled that humility with fear of humans' growing technological prowess and ability to despoil natural areas. Humans had become "bold and aggressive and dangerous," Douglas warned, adding that "now [humanity] has unlocked the secrets and can destroy and sterilize for eons the good earth from which we all came." He emphasized how threatened the beach had become in the technological world of post–World War II America.[15]

With his reasons for protecting the Pacific beach outlined, Douglas's protest hike in the late 1950s seemed justified. By the time the hike began the group had grown to seventy individuals—"safari proportions," according to a Seattle newspaper. Among the safari members were the central leaders in American conservation circles, including Harvey Broome, president and cofounder of the Wilderness Society; Olaus J. Murie, famed wildlife biologist and director of the Wilderness Society; Howard Zahniser, secretary of the Wilderness Society; and Conrad Wirth, director of the National Park Service. The group represented some of the most important founders of the postwar environmental movement, suggesting the significance of the event and the esteem in which the participants held Justice Douglas. Such a notable roster inevitably led to media exposure.[16]

The ocean strip of the Olympic National Park should be off-limits to road building, the protest group maintained, primarily because it was wilderness protected in a national park. Through Douglas, their spokesperson, group members suggested alternatives to a road in the park. "We can have both the road and a stretch of wilderness sea shore," Douglas explained. "Let's not put roads everywhere. Let's leave some of the state, some of the country, free from roads and from the effects of civilization that roads always bring." Confronting a protester who met the hiking group at the trail's end, he elaborated, "We'll settle for a road east of Lake Ozette. We'll give you 99 per cent of the U.S. but save us the other 1 per cent, please." Proponents of the highway hailed those very "effects of civilization"—tourist dollars for fuel, food, and lodging—that Douglas and the others hoped to avoid.[17]

It is important to note that, given the weak economy of the region based on forest exploitation, the peninsula economy needed to turn to tourism. The conflict involved a cast of characters that presaged countless environmental battles in the American West. Areas with economies that were dependent on natural resources increasingly looked to tourist development to cure their economic ills and frequently encountered opposition from environmentalists. Moreover, opponents of preservation often equated wilderness protection with locking up resources and the eventual and certain onset of poverty. This episode on the Pacific beach portended the western environmental future. In this instance, Douglas and the road's opponents emerged triumphant. No road has yet been built.[18]

This Olympic Peninsula protest was not the only instance when Douglas faced environmental issues before most others recognized them, and *My Wilderness: The Pacific West* was not the only forum he used to popularize his ideas. A companion volume—*My Wilderness: East to Katahdin*—was published the following year, in 1961. Both books consisted of chapters devoted to different places and landscapes, such as the Brooks Range in Alaska, the Middle Fork of Idaho's Salmon River, Baboquivari in southern Arizona, and the Florida Everglades. Douglas described the natural features of each place and typically educated the reader on a specific issue of ecology or conservation politics. Thus, readers were treated to portraits of some of America's fabulous landscapes while simultaneously being imbued with an environmentalist ethic. Perceiving an especially dire environmental situation in Texas, Douglas devoted an entire book to the state, titled *Farewell to Texas: A Vanishing Wilderness* (1967). Although he employed many of the same rhetorical devices as in his earlier works, his stance was decidedly more strident and his message more pessimistic because he grew increasingly exasperated that progress in raising environmental consciousness proved so slow. In each of these books of nature writing, Douglas allowed the western landscape to fill the pages, as he hoped readers would share his profound awe of the places and his fervent hope to prevent industrial and agricultural economies from wreaking ecological havoc. His books seldom addressed the people who made their livelihood from working the land, thus revealing a weakness shared by many others in the wilderness movement—the inability to reconcile the conflicting needs of humans and nature.[19]

In addition to leading protest hikes and writing books, Justice Douglas used his position on the Supreme Court to argue on nature's behalf. After people began farming and ranching more extensively and intensively in the arid American West in the nineteenth century, obtaining sufficient water became a ubiquitous concern. In the twentieth century new and expanding western manufacturing and population centers also needed cheap power. For both reasons, dams blocked portions of all the major western rivers, generating hydroelectricity and storing water for irrigation and against drought. By the middle of the twentieth century dam proponents became a favored target of environmentalists. Douglas, an avid fisherman and frequent rafter, joined the antidam sentiment.

Delivering the opinion of the Court in *Udall v. Federal Power Commission* (1967), Douglas questioned the wisdom of building another dam on the Columbia-Snake river system, this time at High Mountain Sheep on the Snake River. Douglas quickly turned to "the question whether any dam should be constructed." He looked to three existing laws to argue against the Federal Power Commission (FPC) granting a private power company a permit to build the proposed dam. Using a phrase in the 1920 Federal Power Act that named "recreational purposes" as a public use in river development, the justice claimed the dam would likely destroy or significantly diminish the salmon population and thus ruin recreational possibilities. In addition, the Fish and Wildlife Coordination Act of 1958 forced agencies to address wildlife conservation in water development projects with "equal consideration" given to other development factors. Finally, the recently passed Anadromous Fish Act (1965) discouraged river development that would harm salmon runs. Douglas had all the law he needed to determine that no dam should be built. According to western legal expert Charles F. Wilkinson, his opinion in the case was "trailblazing." The justice located relatively minor parts of relevant statutes and forced the FPC to reexamine the potential dam site further before issuing a permit, effectively quashing the power project by emphasizing recreational and conservation values for free-flowing rivers. Wilkinson claimed that the opinion "has stood as a bright model of vigilant judicial review in complex natural resources litigation." It would be difficult to find a better Supreme Court case that encompassed so many aspects of western history.[20]

For most of Douglas's tenure, though, comparatively few cases with environmental components came to the tribunal. When they did, Douglas as often as not dissented from the majority opinion. Thus, he made little actual impact on existing law, which is how constitutional scholars tend to evaluate a justice's importance. However, in Douglas's estimation, a dissent was "an appeal to the brooding spirit of the law, *to the intelligence of a future day,* when a later decision may possibly correct the error into which the dissenting judge believes the court to have been betrayed." So it was from his position as a dissenting justice that Douglas most commonly expressed his environmentalist values. Although his arguments rarely won over legal scholars or his brethren on the Court, hopeful environmentalists await "the intelligence of a future day."[21]

His most important dissent came in the early 1970s when he argued his most radical philosophy in *Sierra Club v. Morton* (1972). In the 1960s, Walt Disney Enterprises, the company who brought the West the idealized Frontierland and unrealistic depictions of wildlife, wanted to transform the Sierra Nevada's Mineral King Valley into a ski resort, carving it out of a portion of the Sequoia National Forest. In protest the Sierra Club touched off a long legal debate focusing on the issue of legal standing. Traditionally, litigants must prove they suffered some injury themselves to be able to sue. The Sierra Club hoped to establish a new precedent by arguing that Mineral King Valley itself had legal standing to sue. Such a ruling would have expanded greatly the notion of natural rights. The majority of the Court held that the Sierra Club had suffered insufficient harm and thus lacked standing. The Court would not grant inanimate natural objects rights.[22]

In his dissent, Douglas embraced an expansive reading of the law on legal standing and pushed the envelope of environmental ethics, law, and philosophy, reaching the zenith of his environmental thinking. He began simply arguing that a federal rule was needed to allow "environmental issues to be litigated before federal agencies or federal courts in the name of the inanimate object about to be despoiled, defaced, or invaded by roads and bulldozers and where injury is the subject of public outrage." The case, he explained, would then properly be named *Mineral King v. Morton,* reflecting the valley's legal interest that superseded any human representation. Giving inanimate objects rights was surely not revolutionary: as Douglas pointed out, ships had legal personalities, and corporations acted as "people" in the law. These legal fictions were unproblematic, "so it should be as respects valleys, alpine meadows, rivers, lakes, estuaries, beaches, ridges, groves of trees, swampland, or even air that feels the destructive pressures of modern technology and modern life," he maintained. To solve the logistical question, he suggested that people who know and have "a meaningful relation" to the inanimate natural system are "its legitimate spokesmen." With such advocates, "the voice of the inanimate object . . .

should not be stilled." Douglas's reasoning failed to move a majority of his colleagues, although two other justices dissented from the Court's ruling.[23]

Judging Douglas as an environmental advocate on the bench becomes a complicated task. Compared to the opportunities presented to the Supreme Court after his retirement in 1975, few cases of lasting environmental significance were presented in his record thirty-six-year career. In those that did, Douglas could be counted on to vote for what he believed was nature's best interest. In the two examples offered here, one can see how he at times worked within the law, finding obscure passages to support his viewpoint, as in *Udall v. FPC.* At other times, he pioneered new legal terrain—something critics fault him for doing—as he did in *Sierra Club v. Morton.* Environmental law specialist Christopher D. Stone argued that with his dissent in *Sierra Club v. Morton,* Douglas "instated himself as the leading judicial champion of the environment." Wilkinson concurred, explaining that the opinion was "daring," but adding that, nonetheless, "its influence is intangible and lies in the scholarship and the public mind rather than in Supreme Court's opinions." Such ambiguity establishes the complexity of evaluating Douglas's role as a justice.[24]

Judged by any standard, Douglas's life story is remarkable. Whether he could have lived in the same way had he been born and raised in the East is unlikely. The ready access to public lands in which to hike and explore, so common in the West, influenced him to take an interest in conservation. It is telling that the entirety of his first *My Wilderness* book and nearly half of the second concerned western places. In addition, he devoted an entire book to Pacific Northwest mountains and another to Texas. Douglas traveled widely through America and the world, and the places he came to know, love, and revere were, by and large, located within the American West. Consequently, many of the causes he hiked for, wrote about, or passed judgment on involved western landscapes and ways in which to prevent them from what he perceived as further despoliation or exploitation.

In a memorial written the year after his death in 1980, Cathy H. Douglas, the justice's widow, reflected on how he led his life. She acknowledged that Douglas drew from his own life experience: "He may . . . be best remembered for the way in which he incorporated the experiences of his own life into the fabric of the law and his work on the Court." Of the many experiences that shaped his life, Cathy wrote at length about his time in Goose Prairie, Washington, his summer retreat in the Cascade Mountains. On one occasion there, Douglas led a hesitant deer to safety, away from a pack of wild dogs. That rescue, Cathy was certain, played in his mind during the following term, when the justice wrote his dissent in

Sierra Club v. Morton. In her memorial, Cathy only discussed two cases with any depth, and the inclusion of the Mineral King case resonates with the argument that Douglas was, at heart, a western environmentalist. He built that identity self-consciously and deliberately but also from lived experience. It is a legacy for which he shall always be remembered.[25]

Notes

1. During the New Deal, the Supreme Court declared several of Roosevelt's reforms unconstitutional. To counter the seeming obstinacy of the Court, the president proposed granting his office the power to add federal judges once sitting judges turned seventy. The proposition was a thinly veiled power play designed to force conservative judges off the bench, and it would be Roosevelt's most serious political blunder of his presidency.

2. "Douglas, Jurist: Appointment to Supreme Court Puts Hard Hitter on the Bench," *Newsweek,* March 27, 1939, 13.

3. James F. Simon, *Independent Journey: The Life of William O. Douglas* (New York: Harper and Row, 1980), 191–94; William O. Douglas, *Go East, Young Man: The Early Years—The Autobiography of William O. Douglas* (New York: Random House, 1974), 456–63.

4. William O. Douglas, *Of Men and Mountains* (1950; reprint, San Francisco: Chronicle Books, 1990), XI.

5. Douglas, *Go East, Young Man,* 11, 12; idem, *Men and Mountains,* 29.

6. Douglas, *Go East, Young Man,* 15, 19.

7. Douglas, *Men and Mountains,* 32, 33–34; for Roosevelt and the "strenuous life," see Roderick Nash, *Wilderness and the American Mind,* 3d ed. (New Haven: Yale University Press, 1982), 149–50.

8. Douglas, *Men and Mountains,* X, 35.

9. Douglas, *Go East, Young Man,* 94–113; quotes in Douglas, *Men and Mountains,* 15, 5.

10. Richard Neuberger, *They Never Go Back to Pocatello: The Selected Essays of Richard Neuberger,* ed. Steve Neal (Portland: Oregon Historical Society Press, 1988), 108–25, quotes on 112, 116, 125; Hugh Russell Fraser, letter to "The Open Forum," *American Mercury* 62 (February 1946): 251; Michael P. Malone and F. Ross Peterson, "Politics and Protests," in *The Oxford History of the American West,* ed. Clyde A. Milner II, Carol A. O'Connor, and Martha A. Sandweiss (New York: Oxford University Press, 1994), 501–33.

11. Neuberger, *They Never Go Back,* 109; "Douglas for the Cabinet," *Coos Bay (Oregon) Times,* May 9, 1942, 2 (emphasis added); "When Will Douglas Enter War Effort," *(Portland) Oregon Labor Press,* n.d., 2.

12. See letters concerning the C & O Canal in William O. Douglas, *The Douglas Letters: Selections from the Private Papers of Justice William O. Douglas,* ed. Melvin I. Urofsky and Philip E. Urofsky (Bethesda, MD: Adler and Adler, 1987), 236–41; "The C and O Walkathon," *American Forests* 60 (May 1954): 18–19, 54; William O. Douglas, *My Wilderness: East to Katahdin* (Garden City, NY: Doubleday, 1961), 181–211; Stephen Fox,

The American Conservation Movement: John Muir and His Legacy (Madison: University of Wisconsin Press, 1981), 241–43.

13. Douglas, *Douglas Letters,* 241–42 (emphasis added); "Justice Douglas, 70 Hikers to Begin Wilderness Trip," *Seattle Times,* August 18, 1958, 10.

14. William O. Douglas, *My Wilderness: The Pacific West* (Garden City, NY: Doubleday, 1960), 32–49 passim, quote on 34.

15. Ibid., 40.

16. Byron Fish, "Olympic Wilderness Hikers Hope to Chill Coast-Road Plan," *Seattle Times,* August 19, 1958, 30; "Highway Boosters, Primitive Lovers Will Take Hike along Coastline," *Seattle Times,* August 10, 1958, 22; "Justice Douglas and Hiking Party Complete Trip," *Seattle Times,* August 21, 1958.

17. "Justice Douglas"; "68 Footsore Hikers Wind Up Beach Trek near LaPush," *Port Angeles (WA) Olympic Tribune,* August 22, 1958.

18. For tourism and resource economies, see Hal K. Rothman, *Devil's Bargain: Tourism in the Twentieth-Century American West* (Lawrence: University Press of Kansas, 1998); Thomas Michael Power, *Lost Landscapes and Failed Economies: The Search for a Value of Place* (Washington, DC: Island Press, 1996).

19. Douglas, *My Wilderness: The Pacific West;* idem, *My Wilderness: East to Katahdin;* idem, *Farewell to Texas: A Vanishing Wilderness* (New York: McGraw-Hill, 1967). Douglas's *A Wilderness Bill of Rights* (Boston: Little, Brown, 1965) and *The Three Hundred Year War: A Chronicle of Ecological Disaster* (New York: Random House, 1972) were concerned with environmental issues from more political and philosophical perspectives and did not focus specifically on the American West. Richard White most eloquently discussed the seemingly irreconcilable problem of humans and nature in a brilliant essay, " 'Are You an Environmentalist or Do You Work for a Living?': Work and Nature," in *Uncommon Ground: Toward Reinventing Nature,* ed. William Cronon (New York: W. W. Norton, 1995), 171–85.

20. *Udall v. FPC,* 387 U.S. 428, 436 (1967); Charles F. Wilkinson, "Justice Douglas and the Public Lands," in *"He Shall Not Pass This Way Again": The Legacy of Justice William O. Douglas,* ed. Stephen L. Wasby (Pittsburgh: University of Pittsburgh Press, for the William O. Douglas Institute, 1990), 239.

21. Quoted in James C. Duram, *Justice William O. Douglas* (Boston: Twayne Publishers, 1981), 102–3 (emphasis added).

22. *Sierra Club v. Morton,* 405 U.S. 727 (1972); Wilkinson, "Douglas and Public Lands," 242–44; Roderick Frazier Nash, *The Rights of Nature: A History of Environmental Ethics* (Madison: University of Wisconsin Press, 1989), 130–31; John Warfield Simpson, *Visions of Paradise: Glimpses of Our Landscape's Legacy* (Berkeley: University of California Press, 1999), 220–35 passim.

23. *Sierra Club v. Morton,* 741, 743, 745, 749; Wilkinson, "Douglas and Public Lands," 242–44; Nash, *Rights of Nature,* 130–31; Simpson, *Visions of Paradise,* 220–35.

24. Christopher D. Stone, "Commentary: William O. Douglas and the Environment," in *"He Shall Not Pass This Way Again": The Legacy of Justice William O. Douglas,* ed. Stephen L. Wasby (Pittsburgh: University of Pittsburgh Press, for the William O. Douglas Institute, 1990), 231; Wilkinson, "Douglas and Public Lands," 244.

25. Cathleen H. Stone, "William O. Douglas: The Man," in Supreme Court Historical Society, *Yearbook* (1981): 6–9.

Suggested Readings

Nash, Roderick. *Wilderness and the American Mind.* 3d ed. New Haven: Yale University Press, 1982.

Rothman, Hal K. *The Greening of a Nation? Environmentalism in the United States since 1945.* Fort Worth, TX: Harcourt Brace, 1998.

Simon, James F. *Independent Journey: The Life of William O. Douglas.* New York: Harper and Row, 1980.

Wasby, Stephen L., ed. *"He Shall Not Pass This Way Again": The Legacy of Justice William O. Douglas.* Pittsburgh: University of Pittsburgh Press, for the William O. Douglas Institute, 1990.

11

Margaret Chung and the Dilemma of Bicultural Identity

Benson Tong

Margaret Chung (1889–1959) was the first American-born Chinese female physician, the daughter of parents who, though natives of China, were both products of Protestant missionary backgrounds. Hence, despite her Chinese ethnicity, Chung was shaped by American culture and education. Her life reflected the turbulent changes of a period that encompassed the reform spirit of the Progressive Era, the swinging twenties of early popular icons, and the nationalism of the interwar years and 1940s. These changes gave her the freedom to carve out a niche for herself as a humanitarian, patriot, model citizen, and friend of the famous.

However, she was also a woman caught in complex circumstances that involved the intertwined strands of gender and racial oppression. As a bicultural American, Chung struggled to reconcile her Chinese ethnicity and heritage with the American lifeway and its ideals while at the same time contending with ambivalent feelings toward her own sexual identity. Like that of the other persons of color explored in this volume, her ethnic identity was never static but constantly responded to changing conditions, and like other racial ethnic minorities in the West, her agency in the dominant society was limited by anti-immigrant sentiments that reflected a circumscribed definition of what it meant to be an American.

Benson Tong, assistant professor of history at Wichita State University, in Wichita, Kansas, specializes in U.S. immigration and ethnicity. He has published *Unsubmissive Women: Chinese Prostitutes in Nineteenth-Century San Francisco* (1994), *Susan La Flesche Picotte, M.D.: Omaha Reformer and Tribal Leader* (1999), *The Chinese Americans* (2000), and several journal articles on Native American history.

"I am particularly grateful to be a citizen of the United States with all of its privileges because my parents and my forefathers were Chinese," wrote Margaret Chung in her unpublished autobiography. If she had been born in China, she noted, she "probably would have been thrown down the Yangtze River for [she] was the oldest of eleven children and most of [them] were girls."[1] Her parents' Protestant missionary background, her own western education, her knowledge of American culture, and her contributions to the war effort in the 1930s and 1940s, she hinted, shaped and secured her birthright and American identity. Yet later in this assimilationist narrative, Chung expressed regrets about her lack of ties to the Chinese American community in San Francisco, a situation she labored to rectify during the Sino-Japanese War (1937–1945) through her involvement in the *jiuguo,* or "Save China," movement in the United States. Her reflections capture the gender- and race-based tensions in her life, as she struggled to move between two seemingly disparate worlds and cope with an ambivalent sexual identity as well. As an educated, American-born Chinese, she used her familiarity with the Euramerican world to gain status and recognition in the Chinese American community, but at the same time, she also selectively used her Chinese roots to win acceptance from Euramericans.

Like many other second-generation, educated Chinese American women of the interwar years, Chung experienced an ongoing and multifaceted process of identity transformation in the context of racial prejudice, sexism, and the dichotomous pressures of Americanization and China-centered nationalism.[2] Arriving at a Chinese American identity involved negotiating multiple and often conflicting loyalties as well as navigating the shifting boundaries of race, gender, class, sex, and politics through an entire lifetime. For most Chinese Americans in the American West, ethnic identity was not fixed and bounded, but, in an era when cultural pluralism had yet to make its mark on American consciousness, moving at will between different "subject positions" (or practicing a bicultural identity) was further impeded by the hegemony of Euramerican values and popular culture.[3] Some Chinese Americans formed a syncretic identity, but others were more drawn to the dominant culture. Chung's active involvement in the Euramerican society—her links to the U.S. armed services, to white celebrities, and to politicians—reflected a desire for assimilation. However, she never entirely attenuated her relationship to the Chinese American community, as evidenced by her participation in the anti-Japanese aggression movement (although that relationship was a somewhat distant one).

The psychological and social estrangement between Margaret Chung and the Chinese American community began during her childhood years. In Santa Barbara, the site of her birth, only some 700 of the 6,000 residents were Chinese. Ten years later the Chung family moved to Ventura County, which had a similarly small Chinese population. After the turn of the century the family moved to Los Angeles. Though the number of Chinese in

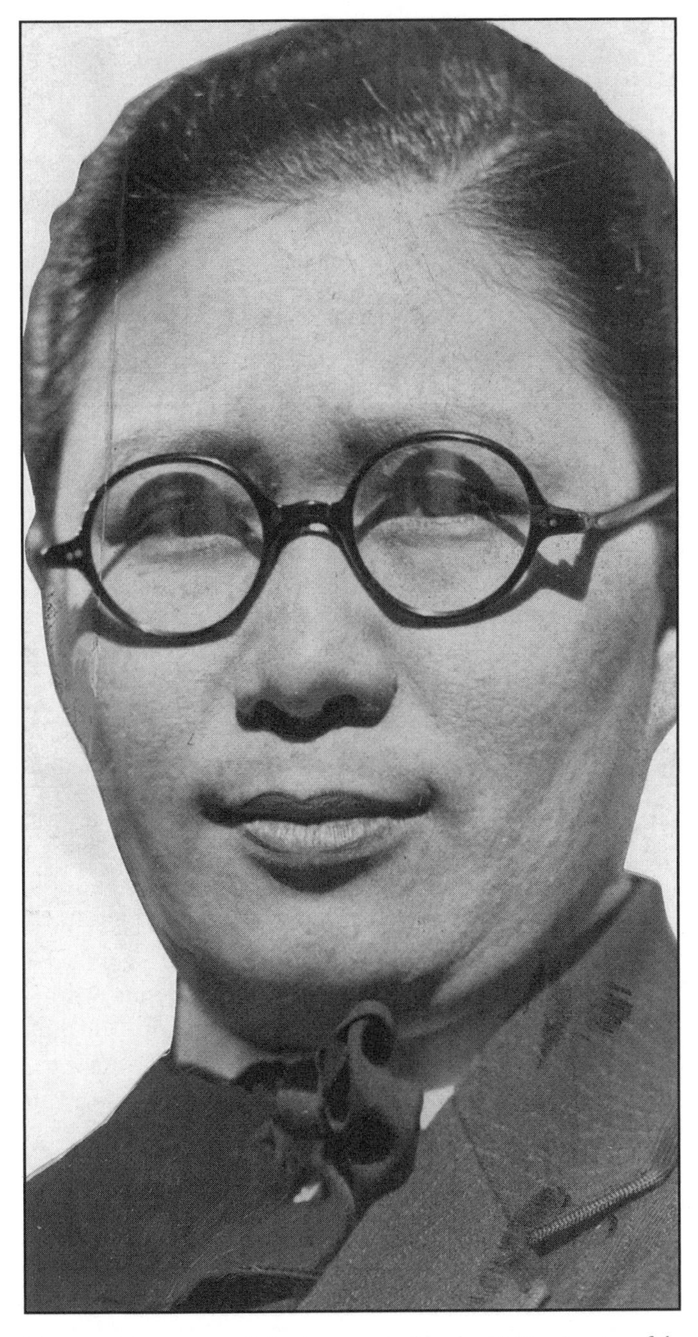

Margaret Chung, most likely photographed in the 1920s. *Courtesy of the San Francisco History Center, San Francisco Public Library*

that city was around 2,000 between 1900 and 1920, non-Chinese outnumbered Chinese 50 to 1 in 1900, and by 1920, the ratio stood at 300 to 1. Given the size of these Chinese communities the Chungs, like most southern California Chinese Americans, had to develop business and social ties with the dominant society. In Santa Barbara Margaret's father, Chung Wong, initially an unsuccessful small-time merchant of ethnic goods, eventually turned to vegetable peddling, an enterprise that depended on white patronage.[4] The family's transience probably also did little to promote Chung Wong's involvement in the ethnic economy.

Both Margaret's father and her mother, Ah Yane, were tied to Protestant America socially. Chung Wong came under the tutelage of Presbyterian missionaries soon after his immigration to the United States at the age of fifteen in 1875. He was baptized in 1886 and attended the local Presbyterian church in Santa Barbara. So did Ah Yane, who also relied on missionary support to help her adapt to American society. On arrival in the United States, she most likely served as a *mui tsai,* or servant girl, and at age six, in 1880, she was arrested in a brothel and then placed in the Presbyterian Mission Home in San Francisco.[5] Considered victims of male abuse, she and other *mui tsai* came under the maternal "rehabilitation" of women missionaries. These female Protestants sought to imbue the girls with Victorian values of "true womanhood," such as moral influence and domesticity, which the girls could parlay into social authority later in life. Ah Yane seemingly did not disappoint her maternal guardians. She served as an interpreter for the home mission women and eventually married a fellow Chinese Christian.[6]

As practiced by the family, Protestantism infused young Margaret Chung with the missionary zeal to become an educated, professional woman who would serve society. In later years, she recalled the role Christianity played in her family: "Each night before our bedtime father would gather us in front of the fireplace and sing hymns which he dearly loved." She remembered, too, that her mother encouraged her to become a medical missionary. While living in the mission home as a young girl, Ah Yane had joined other inmates in raising funds to support the work of female medical missionaries in China. Chung recalled the following: "When I announced at the age of 10 that I was going to be a medical missionary, my mother answered, 'I hope you can, Daughter.' " From her family, Chung learned that Presbyterian reformers were interested in securing women medical missionaries who could use their supposed innate nurturing quality to help convert "heathen" women even as they were ministering to their bodies.[7]

Family privation and illness, along with racial prejudices, also probably shaped Margaret's desire to earn a medical degree. As medical historian Regina Morantz-Sanchez has observed, "A childhood or adolescent encounter with illness—either their own or that of a close friend or relative"—often is a motivation to pursue medicine as a profession.[8] As a young girl, Chung witnessed the declining health of her mother. "For twenty-six long years," she dramatically recalled, "each month there would be several nights that I would stand, agonized with terror, watching her die a little at a time." Suffering from tuberculosis, Ah Yane was also burdened by the domestic role of raising seven children in the midst of poverty. She and her children augmented Chung Wong's limited income by planting potatoes, yams, and other vegetables and working as farmhands. Margaret did her part by holding odd jobs, ranging from pitting prunes to waiting tables at a chop suey restaurant.[9]

Limited evidence also suggests that young Margaret suffered derision and ridicule both in school and on the streets. Though they were U.S. citizens, Chung and other second-generation Chinese Americans were still considered, to quote scholar Sucheng Chan, "inassimilable aliens and perpetual foreigners." The evidence sheds little light on Chung's immediate response to such racism, but her resistance, like that of so many second-generation Asian Americans, involved a strategy of avoidance and a resolute commitment to self-fulfillment.[10] Given the economic insecurity of her family, she probably eventually understood that education and the attainment of professional skills would enable her to leave poverty and the endless racial struggle behind.

On graduating from high school, Chung entered the University of Southern California (USC) Preparatory School in 1907. The school, part of an institution founded by the Methodist Episcopal Church in 1881, provided the college training necessary for study at USC's College of Medicine. But gaining admittance was one thing; completing the program was another. Chung's class background meant that she had little, if any, financial support from her family. Apparently, however, she paid for part of her education with the prize she received for winning the *Los Angeles Times* scholarship contest, a competition selling newspaper subscriptions. Subsequent participation in several oratorical contests provided additional funding. Margaret also held service and clerical jobs to help pay for her higher education; one acquaintance recalled seeing her "reading a medical book propped on a shelf while doing dishes in a restaurant."[11]

Unlike the preparatory school, where the ratio of males to females in the student body was nearly equal, the medical college enrolled only a few women in its classes. Both institutions also showed a marked absence of students of color; in her medical school classes, Chung was the only non-white student.[12] In this context her racial marker as well as her gender identity became problematic. As was the case during her precollege days, racism dogged her at USC; one journalist who interviewed her years later reported that "she knew the bitterness of racial prejudice during the years when she was working her way through medical school."[13]

Chung could do little about that situation, except to assimilate into the dominant American culture. She showed only slight interest in Chinese herbal medicine and presumably believed that western medicine could save lives and improve society. She avoided Chinese clothes and wore only western garb. A professional friend noted that "she never wore Chinese clothes, but on all occasions appeared in a thin black tailored suit." Her clothing was also masculine. In adopting this style, Chung, like so many other professional women of the early twentieth century, was trying to assimilate into a masculine arena, in her case medicine. Though the institutional barrier for aspiring female physicians and other professionals had been lowered somewhat by that time, social acceptance from male colleagues was still elusive. For Chung, clothing became a symbolic expression of both the attainment of "civilization" (western) and privileged gender identity.[14]

Partially to compensate for gender exclusion, Chung joined women's organizations, which offered not only companionship and support but also the opportunity to participate in oratorical contests. She eventually drew on that experience to lecture "on China at churches and clubs."[15] In exploiting her ethnic roots, which rationalized such an interest in China, she promoted her image as a politicized, cosmopolitan American citizen. Some of Chung's speaking engagements seemed to have focused on the issue of China's role in shaping worldwide politics; others presumably, given USC's religious mission, addressed the question of international exchange and cooperation. The scholars who wrote the history of USC noted that Chung was a "leader in her class in the College of Medicine," hinting that she was a popular and well-known figure on campus.[16]

In 1916, after completing her medical studies, Chung applied to serve as a Presbyterian medical missionary in China. Her family's association with missionaries, USC's interest in the poor and the "heathens" in Asia, and her own growing interest in China's politics fueled this ambition. But her application was rejected, not once but twice. In the late 1930s a journalist who interviewed Chung reported that the young doctor was turned down because "there was no provision in the rules and regulations governing funds to send American missionaries to China that covered a case of an

American of Chinese descent." Most likely racial prejudice played a role here; of the forty-one names of American missionaries of the Occidental Board (Presbyterian Church) laboring in China from 1875 to 1920, none seemed to be of Asian ancestry.[17]

Following these rejections, Chung became disenchanted with Christianity and, according to one of her sisters, Dorothy Siu, she "was never known to have gone to church after she graduated from medical school." Her sense of having arrived at a crossroads in life is also hinted at in the lines of poetry she chose as her parting thought for the school annual—the opening stanza of H. W. Longfellow's poem "Maidenhood," which read: "Maiden! with meek, brown eyes, / In whose orbs a shadow lies / Like the dusk in evening skies." Leaving behind the innocence of childhood, the rest of the poem suggests, one encounters the vicissitudes of adulthood. Anxieties ebb and flow, but idealism sustains one through such challenges. In choosing this poem, Margaret was probably expressing her faith in the occupational choice she had made: to be a physician, the healer of others.[18]

Chung needed self-assurance, since she had run into a roadblock—she initially failed to secure an internship within southern California. Even in the early twentieth century and in spite of the gradual diminution of a biologically determined understanding of gender in favor of the idea of equality, women medical graduates still encountered sex-based discrimination in trying to gain access to such professional opportunities. The internship that Chung finally secured took her to Chicago. Interviewed in 1939 by a *Los Angeles Times* reporter, she remarked that a female doctor "bucks heavy odds of lay prejudice and professional resentment at usurpation of what many consider to be a man's undisputed field and when that woman is an American of Chinese descent she is granted even fewer mistakes and less leisure."[19] The memory of those early challenging years and the racial and gender exclusion they entailed apparently haunted her even in middle age.

The exclusion of women from male-dominated medical institutions was the rationale that led to the establishment of hospitals for women and children, among them the Mary Thompson Hospital for Women and Children in Chicago. In joining this institution, Chung entered a world of maternalism, a legacy of the nineteenth-century sphere of female power that stemmed from women's supposedly innate qualities of domesticity and purity. In the program that Chung went through, the interns were expected to help improve women's role and status as mothers and wives, which in turn would allow them to contribute to the progress of society.[20] Working in the Progressive Era of science and bureaucratization, Chung and her colleagues were also enmeshed in promoting modern female health reforms, ranging from sex education to birth control.

The melding of old and new ideas shaped Chung's training at the next institution she served in, as well—the Kankakee State Hospital for the Insane. Her paid residency at this hospital in late 1917 led quickly to another residency with the Illinois Juvenile Psychopathic Institute (JPI), housed in the Cook County Psychopathic Hospital. These appointments probably reminded her both of the advances made in gender equality and of the distance yet to be covered. Women psychiatrists could join their male compatriots in applying scientific expertise to help rehabilitate criminals, delinquents, and the mentally ill so that they could rejoin society as useful citizens. At the JPI, however, Chung witnessed the institutionalization of maternalist politics, as female staff members focused on the welfare and reform of delinquent children. In addition, there was a disproportionate number of women physicians in psychopathic institutions precisely because these were stigmatized positions ignored by male doctors in favor of private practice.[21]

Chung's training in Chicago would serve her professional career well enough, although emotionally and socially these years seemed to last forever. Her observations on her first day in that city perhaps foreshadowed her lasting impression of those years: "The trees were leafless, the wind was cold, and the welcome in the hospital was hardly warmer." Moreover the training in psychiatry would prove emotionally draining and "too depressing" for Chung. Though she was exploited as cheap labor in these institutions, she maintained her steady course of work and more work only because she needed to support the education of four of her siblings.[22]

In late 1919 family obligations, along with a general dissatisfaction with her life in Chicago, led Chung back to southern California, returning her to the familiar landscape of the West. She set roots in Pasadena and became a staff physician with the Santa Fe Railroad Hospital. There, Margaret thrived as staff and patient curiosity about the "exoticness" of this Chinese American doctor quickly turned into respect and admiration when she demonstrated her medical acumen. But imagined gender difference never dissipated; in the eyes of male employees, she was still a woman first and a physician second. In a 1939 interview, Chung recalled that her advice for preventive medicine was considered motherly, and her surgical skills were seen as the natural outcome of the nurturing quality possessed by all women.[23]

While working at the Santa Fe Railroad Hospital, she also maintained a private practice, which gradually relied more on non-Chinese than Chinese patients: the minuscule number of Chinese in Pasadena, along with Chung's unmarried status and poor command of Chinese (which marked her as "different" in the eyes of southern Californian Chinese), translated into just a few coethnic patients.[24] However, her friendship with coethnic outcast and B-movie "temptress" Anna May Wong—the first well-known Chinese American actress—led to ties to the Euramerican-dominated artistic community comprising musicians, actors, and other entertainers. A friend remembered that soon after Chung began practicing, "she had removed Mary Pickford's tonsils."[25] Her growing list of celebrity patients suggests that Chung, finding it difficult to fit into the Chinese American community, was more comfortable moving in the circles of the unconventional—those whose lives society idolized.

In the early 1920s, Chung relocated to San Francisco. It is unclear how and why she arrived at the decision to move. Perhaps self-interest propelled her northward; in her autobiography, she wrote that "there were no Chinese Doctors practicing American medicine and surgery in Chinatown, and I thought I saw a great future [in San Francisco]."[26] The city's Chinatown population could expand her practice, although she did not suffer from want of clientele in Pasadena. The desire to fulfill the dream of being a medical missionary may also have played a role in the relocation. San Francisco's Chinatown was the largest Chinese community in the United States. An ethnic enclave economy flourished there, but so did poverty. Poor living conditions and an ambivalent attitude toward western medicine could provide the appropriate setting for medical missionary work. Finally, in moving to San Francisco's Chinatown, Chung may have been trying to find that elusive connection to her ethnic roots—a not uncommon reaction among Asian Americans facing exclusion in the interwar years.

Establishing herself in her new community proved to be a challenge. "For a solid month I sat in my offices without a single patient," she bemoaned in her autobiography. Her potential patients had a residual suspicion of western medicine and a Chinese bias against western-trained Chinese doctors in favor of Caucasian physicians (a by-product of internalized mainstream racial attitudes). Furthermore, Chung had to contend with her own emotional and social distances.[27] When she later told stories of how her first visit to Chinatown involved traveling in Hollywood style, being driven around by a chauffeur and accompanied by movie executives, she also recalled being "shocked to see the conditions under which many of the Chinese people lived."[28] She expressed sympathy for their plight, but showing empathy seemed beyond her ability.

Eventually, Chung established a clientele in the Chinese American community. Dorothy Siu, her sister, noted that Chinese women came under her care because they were "too shy to let a man examine them."[29] At the Chinese Hospital, established in 1925 to serve the local community, Chung was listed under the department of gynecology, obstetrics, and pediatrics. A history of the Chinese Hospital duly stated that she "had a huge non-Chinese following."[30]

Chung's inability to find full acceptance in the Chinese American community also partly stemmed from the ambivalent nature of her sexuality. Resisting marriage and a heterosexual family life—a unique stance given the lopsided sex ratio in her ethnic community—Chung, unlike most Chinese American women, adopted a masculine or androgynous persona. Photographs of her from the 1910s through the 1930s showed a woman with slicked-back hair, dark-rimmed glasses, and dark suits that one reporter characterized as "professionally mannish." In addition, "Mike," as she sometimes identified herself to friends, took easily to masculine-defined activities such as gambling, drinking, and swearing.[31] This behavior and the preference for "mannish" clothing fit into the early-twentieth-century medical definition of sexual degeneracy or the "mannish lesbian"—that is, a woman who desired male privileges and adopted male dress. This scientific understanding of gender inversion and its misleading connection to homosexuality, according to one scholar, stemmed from preexisting prejudices and categorizations; what doctors now label "inverts," society had called "fairies" and "queers."[32]

Perhaps such an awareness accounts for the ambivalent nature of Chung's homoerotic relationships with the poet Elsa Gidlow and the singer Sophie Tucker. The first relationship, pursued in the late 1920s, embraced expressions of erotic feelings. The second, encompassing the 1940s, submerged such feelings in the appearance of a romantic friendship. Both, however, bore testimony to Chung's continual preference for the Euramerican world; both also attest to the role race played in shaping the definition of beauty and sexual desire. Of course, having grown up in racially mixed communities rather than in large and segregated Chinatowns and being handicapped by the absence of ethnic markers (such as speaking Chinese and accepting the subordinate status of women), Chung probably felt more at ease forging intimate relationships with whites rather than Chinese.[33]

Chung's relationship with Gidlow was marked by hesitancy and personal doubts. Though meals, gifts, and kisses were involved in this relationship, she never acted on homoerotic desires.[34] The next relationship, with Tucker, also involved homoeroticism, but Chung, by then in her early fifties, cast her romantic desires for Tucker in maternal language. A

Victorian form of romantic friendship characterized this relationship, with "Mom" (as Chung called herself in her letters to Tucker) professing her maternal love for "Boss" (the nickname for Tucker) and her appreciation of Tucker's "companionship, . . . priceless humor [and] loyalty." Yet this relationship at times appeared to cross the line between romantic friendship and homoerotic longings, as indicated by the tender endearments that appeared on good-night notes Margaret wrote to Sophie: "Goodnight Sweet Heart," "Love and Kisses Nightie Night," and "You are the most wonderful Pal in the whole world—I adore you." One scholar interprets this tension between maternal love and homoerotic passion as the outcome of trying to reconcile homoerotic desires with the rejection of a lesbian identity.[35]

Chung's attempt to suppress her sexuality stemmed from the public persona she cultivated during the World War II years, when she was involved in the U.S. war effort and the movement opposing Japanese aggression. Such involvement, which placed her in a motherly and nurturing role, probably explains why her attire became more feminine during those years; she was dressed either in the American Red Cross uniform or in evening gowns, with her hair coiffed and glamorous makeup applied.[36]

Margaret Chung's participation in the war effort included the creation of a surrogate family life that promoted American patriotism and good citizenship. In turn, she solidified her claim on the birthright that had been questioned by the discrimination she suffered in the early years. Her isolation from the Chinese American community served to encourage this search for self-definition within the dominant society. The maternal persona also allowed Chung to maintain the illusion of heterosexuality while still enjoying her independence.

When Japan attacked Manchuria in 1931, Steven G. Bancroft, an ensign in the U.S. Navy reserves and a former football player, contacted Chung, hoping that she could help him secure a commission in the Chinese military. (This contact suggests that in the eyes of some Euramericans, she was more Chinese than American.[37]) The encounter led to something of a mother-son relationship between Chung and Bancroft—a relationship that expanded to include his six housemates and before long encompassed over a thousand white male military personnel, entertainers, and politicians. The large surrogate family was divided into three branches: "fair-haired bastards" were male pilots, "Golden Dolphins" were male submariners, and "kiwis" were simply "sons" and "daughters" who did not fit into either group. This latter category included such luminous figures as Amelia Earhart and Alice Roosevelt Longworth.

As the "mother" of this family, Chung provided emotional support for the military men who were separated from their loved ones. She cooked for and even nursed them during their stopovers in San Francisco. One "son," H. Joseph Chase, suffering from malaria and blackwater fever, actually flew out to that city just so that he could be nursed back to health by Margaret. But it was her Sunday buffet dinners, attended by sons, spouses, friends, and family, that marked her as a successful matronly hostess. On these occasions, she prepared barbecued spareribs, roast turkeys, trimmings, and frosted chocolate cakes while "robed in a gingham apron." Chung also wrote an endless number of letters and sent countless packages to her sons serving in various theaters of war. Even the spouses of these men received advice and gifts and were entertained when they visited her. In the process the sons and wives had their wartime morale bolstered, and Chung had more opportunities to knit this far-flung family together.[38]

Margaret admired the masculinity and "Americanness" of her sons, calling them the "most glorious specimens of real American manhood." She also recalled that they "opened up a brand new world" for her.[39] Through her cooking, nursing, and platonic companionship, she took on the role of the American mother who supported the war cause, and in so doing, she proved her patriotism. By telling her military sons repeatedly to "bring back [to her] seven Jap scalps," she identified with the racialized patriotic rhetoric of the war years, and in sending them Christmas cards embossed with prayers and Christ's image, she presented herself as the nurturing Protestant American woman.[40] Several contemporaries recognized how important all this was to Chung. Author Gertrude Atherton described her in a way that the physician probably approved of: "The fluid in her body may be Chinese but her brain cells are American."[41] "No one refers to Dr. Chung as Chinese," wrote one newspaper reporter, "although that is her ancestry. She was born in San Francisco and got perfectly furious once because she was called 'a great Chinese American.' "[42] Yet Chung's attempt to present herself as simply American was not always successful; newspaper coverage of her exploits as late as the early 1950s still tended to highlight her "exoticness" and her Chinese heritage.[43]

Dedicated to the war effort, Chung demanded that each potential fair-haired bastard be courageous and willing to make the world "a better place because he lives."[44] Hailed as a "one-woman flyers' recruiting force," she received a steady stream of hopeful young men seeking her connections; one newspaper article reported that her typical response was: "Take this to General so-and-so. Tell him Mom sent you. Tell him you're under age but that Mom says it won't matter." It is obvious that Chung lived vicariously through the exploits of her sons. At home, she filled a room with war-related souvenirs—flags, insignia, photographs, pennants, testimonial scrolls, and other artifacts—that these men had sent to her.[45] In memorializing their exploits, she highlighted her own commitment to American values, and in celebrating their contributions, she reminded everyone of her own.

Certainly, one of her contributions has yet to receive due recognition. What began with her attempt to join the U.S. Navy turned into a crusade to help create the Women Appointed for Volunteer Emergency Service (WAVES). Barred from the navy by the absence of a precedent, Chung set in motion the legislative process to create a naval reserve for women. She mobilized her sons—naval officers, congressmen, and senators—to get bills passed in Congress. Influential women friends such as Alice Roosevelt Longworth, the daughter of President Theodore Roosevelt, and Mary Alice Holmes, the sister of Steve Early (Franklin Roosevelt's executive secretary), also helped her lobby for support within the Roosevelt administration and in Congress.[46]

Later, Chung cited her agency and the supposedly rapid passage of the bills as proof that America was indeed the land of opportunity. "What a glorious country this is!" she proclaimed. "A humble obscure woman of Chinese parentage had an idea for a woman's auxiliary, and five months later it becomes a reality."[47] Her working-class and ethnic background, she implied, did not hinder the realization of personal aspirations.

This effort to create the WAVES, however, bore fruit only because the seeds were already sown some time before. Some 10,000 women had served in the U.S. Navy reserves during World War I, an opportunity reversed by subsequent legislation. Against the backdrop of a labor shortage in noncombat positions during World War II, the establishment of the Women's Auxiliary Army Corps (WAAC), which preceded the WAVES, raised the interest in reviving women's participation in the navy.[48]

But interest did not necessarily mean unequivocal support. There were gender- and race-based objections from the navy, the White House, members of Congress, and senators. Women, especially women of color, some argued, simply did not belong in the military. Chung's response to the race issue is telling: "Well, the people from the South are going to have to make up their minds very soon as to whether they prefer to have colored people fighting for them or have the Japs and Germans in our hair." Casting aside the idealism of equality, she relied on the pragmatism of waging a war—a strategy that was in step with her fervent desire to prove her own patriotism. Much to Chung's disappointment, her application to be part of the WAVES was turned down thrice. The last time she applied, her age—she was over the maximum age of fifty allowed for WAVES officers—was cited as the reason for rejecting her.[49]

Chung's interest in the war effort was expressed in other equally attention-grabbing ways. In 1939, she and the American Red Cross set up a disaster relief station in San Francisco, which apparently played a critical role in rapidly mobilizing relief for victims of the Pearl Harbor attack in 1941. As the war years plodded on, she went on lecture tours—one reportedly lasted as long as four months—across the country. Extolling traditional American values such as responsibility, virtue, and honor, Chung dramatically urged her fellow citizens to recognize that the "virtues of human brotherhood . . . can save mankind from the dictatorship of evil ambitions."[50]

During the war years, Chung also took part in the *jiuguo* movement—the national salvation movement afoot in Chinese American communities across the United States. Here, too, she faced both personal triumphs and disappointments. Like any cultural broker, she mediated between Chinese Americans and non-Chinese. She used her connections in the larger society to lobby U.S. support for China, but she also used the fund-raising opportunities rooted in the anti-Japanese movement to promote in the larger society the image of Chinese Americans as loyal allies of the United States. Along the way, she improved her own image within the San Francisco Chinese community, even as she was increasingly celebrated in American popular culture as the voice of the oppressed Chinese and China. But for Chung true intraethnic acceptance still seemed elusive.

When war broke out in China in the 1930s, she offered her medical skills to her parents' homeland. What Chung did was not unusual; following the Mukden Incident of 1931, which initiated the Sino-Japanese conflict in Asia, Chinese in America started a boycott of Japanese products, a propaganda campaign to rally moral support among Chinese and non-Chinese, and a fund-raising drive to back anti-Japanese forces in China. Furthermore, an estimated 20 percent of American-born Chinese in the 1930s returned to China to help rebuild the war-torn country. Chung offered her medical service to the Chinese authorities twice, but they turned her down on both occasions. The negative response for her first application centered on the absence of urgency for such involvement. The second application was rejected because her American citizenship could apparently complicate her service in China.[51] Since other Chinese Americans, both men and women, had worked for Chinese authorities, this rejection, in the absence of more evidence, is difficult to fathom; perhaps a language barrier, coupled with Chung's cocksure attitude that sometimes bordered on arrogance, did little to encourage the authorities to accept her into civil service.

This rejection may have forced Chung to rely on involvement in the national salvation movement to fulfill the "purely humanitarian motives" that she claimed had driven her to apply to work in China. As she capitalized on her connections to the Euramerican world to further the cause of China-centered nationalism, she nurtured her own selfless image in the dominant society. Just two months after the Marco Polo Bridge Incident of 1937, which launched renewed Japanese aggression on China, Chung organized a benefit show to raise money for medical supplies for the ancestral land. Show participants included both American artists and Chinese celebrities, whom presumably Chung had personally enlisted for the occasion.[52]

Chung also promoted the "Rice Bowl parties"—communitywide extravaganzas in the late 1930s and 1940s that featured cultural shows, parades, and carnival concessions. Designed to help raise funds for the anti–Japanese aggression movement, the festivities in San Francisco, raising a total of $235,000 and eventually involving other Chinese communities across the country, were the brainchild of B. S. Fong, a Chinese community leader, Paul C. Smith, the editor of the *San Francisco Chronicle,* and Margaret Chung. Within California, Chung attended various Rice Bowl parties, where she hosted fund-raising auctions. In San Francisco, she most likely played a role in shaping the nature of these parties. The festivals celebrated the cuisine, decorations, architecture, dress, and cultural activities of the Chinese even as they mourned the human losses in Asia through live performances.[53] Emphasizing both the exotic quality of Chinatown (and its residents) and the desperate plight of bombed-out China, the festivals manipulated "Oriental" tourism to serve politics. The overall nature of the festivals seemed to coincide with Chung's larger-than-life character and her interest in celebrities; it also hints of her conscious assertion of certain "positive" aspects of Chinese life so as to win acceptance from American society.

As a spokesperson for the Chinese war effort, Chung was able to capture the limelight and attain minor celebrity status as well as craft a pro-China image of herself that was acceptable to Chinese America. Using her well-honed oratorical skills, she lectured all over the country on behalf of the Chinese war cause. In one radio interview, published in a mainstream newspaper, she dramatically declared, "Today women and children are suffering in China—dying without even a chance to be saved." That sentence echoed her early public justification for her involvement in this human conflict: simply to save the lives of the innocent and defenseless. Chinese American newspapers, however, tended to portray her as a Chinese patriot who contributed to the war against Japan, though not a community leader. Chung's understanding of her political identity seemed ambivalent and was further complicated by a milieu that involved heightened wartime patriotism, Chinese Americans' belief that China's eventual victory over Japan would improve their image in the United States, and her own fragile relationship to the Chinese American community. Perhaps her claim of having recruited some two hundred white male American pilots for China—who became known as the Flying Tigers—during the war years symbolically served as the personal reconciliation of her conflicting ties.[54]

In June 1945, Chung received the People's Award from the Republic of China. The first American woman to earn this recognition, she also received an American Red Cross citation signed by President Harry Truman for "meritorious personal service performed in behalf of the nation, her Armed Services, and suffering humanity in the Second World War."[55] Her sons also remembered her deeds. When her generosity during the war years had led her into financial straits and she was in danger of losing her own home, her sons, with the encouragement of Sophie Tucker, rallied around and paid the balance of the house mortgage in late 1945 as a Christmas gift. Interviewed at her home three years later, Chung offered this poignant reflection: "If you keep too busy doing for others to seek your own personal happiness, its apt to come to you, unsought."[56] When Chung died on January 5, 1959, the victim of ovarian cancer, one friend commented that at the funeral, "all creeds, all colors, all types of people, rich and poor came to pay homage."[57]

Chung's life story demonstrated some of the challenges American-born women of color encountered in twentieth-century U.S. society. Her story is also a reminder of the power of human creativity in the face of boundaries of race and ethnicity that served to shape the perceptions and representations of self and community in the West. Becoming American was, and perhaps is, never easy.

Notes

1. Margaret Chung, "Autobiography," typescript, Box 1, Folder 1, Margaret Chung Collection, Asian American Studies Library, University of California, Berkeley.

2. See Judy Yung, *Unbound Feet: A Social History of Chinese Women in San Francisco* (Berkeley: University of California Press, 1995); Huping Ling, *Surviving on the Gold Mountain: A History of Chinese American Women and Their Lives* (Albany: State University of New York, 1998); Sucheng Chan, "Race, Ethnic Culture, and Gender in the Construction of Identities among Second-Generation Chinese Americans, 1880s to 1920s," in *Claiming*

America: Constructing Chinese American Identities during the Exclusion Era, ed. K. Scott Wong and Sucheng Chan (Philadelphia: Temple University Press, 1998), 127–64.

3. For an explanation of "subject positions," see Lisa Lowe, "Heterogeneity, Hybridity, Multiplicity: Marking Asian American Differences," *Diaspora* 1, no. 1 (1991): 24–44.

4. Maryann Hellrigel, "A Social History of Presidio Area Occupants, 1900 to the Present," and Richard Piedmonte, "The Chinese Presidio Community," both in *Santa Barbara Presidio Area, 1840 to the Present,* ed. Carl V. Harris, Jarrell C. Jackman, and Catherine Rudolph (Santa Barbara, CA: Presidio Research Center, 1993), 28 and 119–20; Roberta S. Greenwood, *Cultural Resources Impact Migration Program, Los Angeles Metro Rail Red Line Segment 1* (Los Angeles: Los Angeles County Metropolitan Transportation Authority, 1993), 33; Kim Fong Tom, "The Participation of the Chinese in the Community Life of Los Angeles" (Master's thesis, University of Southern California, 1944; reprint, San Francisco: R & E Research Associates, 1974), 12; *New Directory of the City of Santa Barbara, Cal.* (Santa Barbara, CA: Independent Publishing, 1888), 144; "Chinese Women of Santa Barbara in Fight for Country," newspaper clipping, Margaret Chung File, Santa Barbara Historical Society, Santa Barbara, California.

5. Dorothy Siu, interview conducted for the Southern California Chinese American Oral History Project, Department of Special Collections, University Research Library, University of California, Los Angeles; "Report of the Mission Home," *Ninth Annual Occidental Board Report* (San Francisco: n.p., 1882), 14; "Mission Home," *Eleventh Annual Occidental Board Report* (San Francisco: n.p., 1884), 24.

6. In China the *mui tsai* system was a form of indentured servitude for girls who hailed from poverty-stricken families. See Benson Tong, *Unsubmissive Women: Chinese Prostitutes in Nineteenth-Century San Francisco* (Norman: University of Oklahoma Press, 1994), 40, 43. Margaret Culbertson, "Report of Mission Home," *Thirteenth Occidental Board Report* (San Francisco: n.p., 1886), 47–49; idem, "Report of Mission Home," *Fifteenth Occidental Board Report* (San Francisco: n.p., 1888), 54–56; idem, "Report of Chinese Mission Home," *Sixteenth Occidental Board Report* (San Francisco: n.p., 1889), 48–49.

7. Quotes in Chung, "Autobiography"; Margaret Culbertson, "Annual Report for 1890," *Eighteenth Annual Occidental Board Report* (San Francisco: n.p., 1891), 48–49; Mrs. J. B. Stewart, "Medical Missions," *Occidental Leaves* (1893): 38. For Protestant women missionaries and their work, see Peggy Pascoe, *Relations of Rescue: The Search for Female Moral Authority in the American West, 1874–1939* (New York: Oxford University Press, 1990).

8. Regina M. Morantz-Sanchez, *Sympathy and Science: Women Physicians in American Medicine* (New York: Oxford University Press, 1985), 107.

9. Quotes in Chung, "Autobiography."

10. Judy Tzu-Chun Wu, "Mom Chung of the Fair-Haired Bastards: A Thematic Biography of Doctor Margaret Chung (1889–1959)" (Ph.D. diss., Stanford University, 1998), 24–25. For identity formation of second-generation Chinese Americans during the adolescent years, see Chan, "Race, Ethnic Culture, and Gender," 127–64, quote on 145. For the strategies of empowering the "weak," see James C. Scott, *Weapons of the Weak: Everyday Forms of Peasant Resistance* (New Haven: Yale University Press, 1985).

11. Chung, "Autobiography"; anonymous quoted in Wu, "Mom Chung of the Fair-Haired Bastards," 33.

12. Wu, "Mom Chung of the Fair-Haired Bastards," 33.

13. George F. West quoted in ibid., 36.

14. Bertha Van Hoosen, *Petticoat Surgeon* (Chicago: Pellegrini and Cudahy, 1947), 219; Lillian Faderman, *Odd Girls and Twilight Lovers: A History of Lesbian Life in Twentieth-Century America* (New York: Penguin, 1992), 21; the classic work on the significance of cross-dressing is Vern L. Bullough and Bonnie Bullough, *Cross Dressing, Sex, and Gender* (Philadelphia: University of Pennsylvania Press, 1993).

15. "Friendship Theme of Y. W. Address," *Los Angeles Daily Southern Californian,* October 30, 1913, 3–4; Gerald J. O'Gara, "The Ministering Angel of Chinatown," *Sunset Magazine* 53 (December 1924): 28.

16. Wu, "Mom Chung of the Fair-Haired Bastards," 37; quote in Manuel P. Servin and Iris Wilson Engstrom, *Southern California and Its University: A History of USC, 1880–1964* (Los Angeles: Ward Ritchie Press, 1969), 60.

17. Helen Satterlee, "Two Remarkable Women: The Story of a Persevering Chinese Girl Who Reached the Heights of a Surgical Fame," *Los Angeles Times Sunday Magazine,* June 25, 1939, 20; *Forty-Seventh Annual Report of Woman's Occidental Board of Foreign Missions* (San Francisco: n.p., 1920), 48–54.

18. *El Rodeo* (University of Southern California class annual), 1917, 432; Dorothy Siu quoted in Wu, "Mom Chung of the Fair-Haired Bastards," 42.

19. Mary Roth Walsh, *"Doctors Wanted: No Women Need Apply": Sexual Barriers in the Medical Profession, 1835–1975* (New Haven: Yale University Press), 219–21; Van Hoosen, *Petticoat Surgeon,* 218; quote in Satterlee, "Two Remarkable Women," 20.

20. Morantz-Sanchez, *Sympathy and Science,* 73; Mary Harris Thompson, "The Chicago Hospital for Women and Children," in *In Memoriam, Mary Harris Thompson,* ed. Mary S. Iberne (Chicago: Board of Managers, 1896), 59; Rose V. Mendian, "Bertha Van Hoosen: A Surgical Daughter's Impression," *Journal of American Medical Women's Association,* April 1965, 349.

21. Wu, "Mom Chung of the Fair-Haired Bastards," 52; for reform in mental health care, see David J. Rothman, *Conscience and Convenience: The Asylum and Its Alternatives in Progressive America* (Boston: Little, Brown, 1980); Robert M. Mennel, *Thorns and Thistles: Juvenile Delinquents in the United States, 1825–1940* (Hanover, NH: University Press of New England, 1973); Anthony M. Platt, *The Child Savers: The Invention of Delinquency,* rev. ed. (Chicago: University of Chicago Press, 1977); Morantz-Sanchez, *Sympathy and Science,* 153.

22. Chung, "Autobiography."

23. Ibid.; Satterlee, "Two Remarkable Women," 5.

24. Chung's unmarried status and how it might have undermined her efforts to connect with the larger Los Angeles Chinese population are hinted at in "Born in Los Angeles—Reared in Oriental Fashion," in *Orientals and Their Cultural Adjustment: Interviews, Life Histories, and Social Adjustment Experiences of Chinese and Japanese* (Nashville, TN: Social Science Institute, Fisk University, 1946), 25.

25. For an overview of Wong's life and career, see Neil Okrent, "Right Place, Wong Time: Why Hollywood's First Asian Star, Anna May Wong, Died a Thousand Movie Deaths," *Los Angeles Magazine,* May 1990, 84–96; quote in Van Hoosen, *Petticoat Surgeon,* 219.

26. Chung, "Autobiography."

27. O'Gara, "Ministering Angel of Chinatown," 28.

28. Pearl S. Puckett, "She's Mom to Two Thousand Flyers," *Independent Woman,* January 1946, 32.

29. Siu, interview.

30. "The Opening of the Chinese Hospital," Box 3, Folder 11, Chinese Historical

Society, San Francisco Collection, Asian American Studies Library, University of California, Berkeley; *The Dawning* (San Francisco: Chinese Hospital Medical Staff Archives, 1978), 7.

31. Quote in O'Gara, "Ministering Angel of Chinatown," 28; Chung, "Autobiography."

32. See Carroll Smith-Rosenberg, "Discourses of Sexuality and Subjectivity: The New Woman, 1870–1936," in *Hidden from History: Reclaiming the Gay and Lesbian Past,* ed. Martin Duberman, Martha Vicinus, and George Chauncey Jr. (New York: Penguin, 1989), 264–80; George Chauncey Jr., "From Sexual Inversion to Homosexuality: The Changing Medical Conceptualization of Female 'Deviance,' " in *Passion and Power: Sexuality in History,* ed. Kathy Peiss and Christina Simmons, with Robert A. Padgug (Philadelphia: Temple University Press, 1989), 87–117.

33. For interracial unions, see Collen Fong and Judy Yung, "In Search of the Right Spouse: Interracial Marriage among Chinese and Japanese Americans," *Amerasia Journal* 21 (Winter 1995–1996): 77–97.

34. Elsa Gidlow, *Elsa: I Come with My Songs* (San Francisco: Booklegger Press, 1986), 207; see also Wu, "Mom Chung of the Fair-Haired Bastards," 96–101.

35. Chung quoted in Wu, "Mom Chung of the Fair-Haired Bastards," 103–105; there is only a hint of the nature of this relationship in Michael Freedland, *Sophie: The Sophie Tucker Story* (London: Woburn Press, 1978), 211; see also Wu, "Mom Chung of the Fair-Haired Bastards," 107.

36. Dr. Bessie Jeong, interview conducted for the Southern California Chinese American Oral History Project, Department of Special Collections, University Research Library, University of California, Los Angeles.

37. Chung, "Autobiography."

38. Margaret Chung, "Biography of Sons," Box 1, Folder 2, Chung Collection; quote in Ted and Dorothy Friend, "This Is the Life: Dr. Chung Cooks in Large Quantities," Chung Scrapbook, Box 10, Chung Collection; Harry Byrone, "Press Release," July 8, 1944, Box 6, Folder 4, Chung Collection.

39. Chung, "Autobiography."

40. Quote in Sigrid Arne, " 'Mom' Chung a One-Woman Flyers' Recruiting Force," *Boston Daily Globe,* February 3, 1942, Chung Scrapbook, Chung Collection; Christmas cards, Box 8, Folder 5, Chung Collection.

41. Gertrude Atherton, *My San Francisco: A Wayward Biography* (Indianapolis: Bobbs-Merrill, 1946), 272.

42. Rhea Talley, "One Beautifies Millions, One Mothers Thousands," *The Louisville Courier-Journal,* n.d., Chung Scrapbook, Chung Collection.

43. For examples, see Barbara Bancroft, "Dr. Chung's Decorative Furnishings Express Her," *San Francisco Call-Bulletin,* November 8, 1948; Jack Rosenbaum, "Our City: Check Yore Shootin' Irons," *San Francisco News,* February 6, 1950.

44. U.S. Navy, "Mom Chung Here for Air Show," press release, Box 6, Folder 1, Chung Collection.

45. Quoted in Arne, " 'Mom' Chung a One-Woman Flyers' Recruiting Force"; La Verne Bradley, "San Francisco: Gibraltar of the West Coast," *National Geographic Magazine* 83, no. 3 (March 1943): 246.

46. Chung, "Autobiography"; Mel Mass to Chung, April 16, 1942, Box 6, Folder 5, Chung Collection; Albert B. Chandler to Chung, March 18, 1942, Box 3, Folder 2, Chung Collection.

47. Chung quoted in Wu, "Mom Chung of the Fair-Haired Bastards," 181.

48. Joy Bright Hancock, *Lady in the Navy: A Personal Reminiscence* (Annapolis, MD: Naval Institute Press, 1972), 48.

49. U.S. Senate, Committee on Naval Affairs, *Women's Auxiliary Naval Reserve: Hearings on S. 2527,* 77th Cong., 2d sess., 1942; quote in Chung, "Autobiography"; Tova Petersen Wiley, "Oral History," in *The Waves in World War II,* 2 vols. (Annapolis, MD: U.S. Naval Institute, 1979), 2:28.

50. Shirley Radke, "We Must Be Active Americans," *Christian Science Monitor,* October 3, 1942.

51. Yung, *Unbound Feet,* 225; Gloria H. Chun, " 'Go West . . . to China': Chinese American Identity in the 1930s," in *Claiming America: Constructing Chinese American Identities during the Exclusion Era,* ed. K. Scott Wong and Sucheng Chan (Philadelphia: Temple University Press, 1998), 165; Andrew Lee to Chen Chung Loh, May 4, 1933, Box 2, Folder 2, Chung Collection; "Noted Chinese Woman Doctor Offers Her Aid," *San Francisco Chronicle,* August 17, 1937.

52. "Help for Stricken China: Supper Club Stars to Aid Benefit—War Victims Will Be Helped by S. F. Show," *San Francisco Chronicle,* September 15, 1957; "To Aid War Benefit: Opera Singer Featured—Plans Go Ahead for Tuesday Night Chinese Refugee Show," *San Francisco Chronicle,* September 18, 1937.

53. Yung, *Unbound Feet,* 239–40; Franc Shor, "Stanton Delaplane, Chronicle Reporter, Wins Pulitzer Prize: Journalism's Highest Honor," *San Francisco Chronicle* (1942), Chung Scrapbook, Chung Collection; "Chinatown Holds Open House Tonight," *San Francisco Chronicle,* June 17, 1938; Abe Mellinkoff, "The Parade: Thousands Marched Last Night So Millions Might Live," *San Francisco Chronicle,* February 10, 1940; Robert O'Brien, "S. F. Goes to a Party," *San Francisco Chronicle,* May 3, 1941.

54. *San Francisco Chronicle,* September 18, 1937; "Chinese in U.S. Continue Fund-Raising for China Refugee Relief," *Chinese Digest,* October 1937, 16; "Chinese Physician Sends Medical Supplies to Refugees," *Chinese Digest,* November 1937, 13; Chung, "Autobiography."

55. "Dr. Chung Decorated by Chinese," *San Francisco Chronicle,* June 5, 1945; Chung, "Autobiography."

56. Bancroft, "Dr. Chung's Decorative Furnishings."

57. Mrs. Chester William Nimitz quoted in Wu, "Mom Chung of the Fair-Haired Bastards," 207.

Suggested Readings

Chun, Gloria Heyung. *Of Orphans and Warriors: Inventing Chinese American Culture and Identity.* New Brunswick, NJ: Rutgers University, 2000.

Ling, Huping. *Surviving on the Gold Mountain: A History of Chinese American Women and Their Lives.* Albany: State University of New York Press, 1998.

Takaki, Ronald. *Strangers from a Different Shore: A History of Asian Americans.* Boston: Little, Brown, 1989.

Tong, Benson. *Unsubmissive Women: Chinese Prostitutes in Nineteenth-Century San Francisco.* Norman: University of Oklahoma Press, 1994.

Wong, K. Scott, and Sucheng Chan, eds. *Claiming America: Constructing Chinese American Identities during the Exclusion Era.* Philadelphia: Temple University Press, 1998.

Yung, Judy. *Unbound Feet: A Social History of Chinese Women in San Francisco.* Berkeley: University of California Press, 1995.

12

Robert Burnette
A Postwar Lakota Activist

Richmond L. Clow

Rising "Red Power" militancy, which peaked in the early 1970s, along with the strident African American civil rights movement and the sociopolitical turmoil of the 1960s, shaped the broad contours of Robert Burnette's life (1926–1984). But his activism on behalf of the Sioux Nation, as explained by Native American studies scholar Richmond L. Clow, was also molded by a family heritage that advocated ethnic pride and community service. This convergence of influences resulted in a unique politics of confrontation, promoting both tribal sovereignty and personal ambitions. Though intratribal politics consumed much of his public life, Burnette's attention was captured by nationally related issues such as civil rights, electoral politics, and Pan-Indianism, all of which eventually affected his ties to tribal America. An outsider for much of his life, he spoke the common language of racial conciliation even as he fostered divisions on and off the reservation.

Cultural mediation often produced conflict as well as understanding. As suggested by Burnette's story, any study of Native American lives in the West—an old theme in western historiography—is incomplete without a probing of the intratribal conflicts that the American nation engendered. Both Burnette's and Joseph Brown's stories (see Chapter 8) also clearly illustrate that tribal revitalization continued throughout the twentieth century.

Richmond L. Clow earned his Ph.D. in history from the University of New Mexico in Albuquerque in 1977. After teaching in several departments, he joined the Native American Studies Department of the University of Montana in Missoula in 1984, where he is a professor. He is the coauthor of *Tribal Government Today: Politics on Montana Indian Reservations,* (rev. ed., 1998).

Robert Philip Burnette was a post–World War II Lakota activist and crusader who opposed discrimination and tribal corruption throughout his life. His battle against these ills drove him to campaign for tribal and state offices and to serve as director of the National Congress of American Indians (NCAI). At the end of his career Burnette's idealism often clashed with his political ambition, creating gaps between his rhetoric and his actions. His was the dilemma of the radical as tribal leader.

Burnette's father, Grover Burnette Sr., was of mixed Lakota and white ancestry and was born on John Burnette's ranch south of White River, South Dakota. Grover was a cowboy early in his life and participated in the last great Rosebud cattle roundups at the turn of the century.[1] In 1921, he married Winnie Rogers, who was also a tribal member. They joined the local Episcopal church and over the next decade had ten children. To support their family, Grover and Winnie found employment on the Rosebud Reservation. In the early 1930s the family moved to Rapid City, South Dakota, and settled there for a short time when Grover found employment in a sawmill. They soon returned to Rosebud, where he worked as a tribal policeman and a heavy-equipment operator for the Indian Service road department. The family eventually moved to the Two Kettle Rehabilitation Project, a New Deal experiment in community building on the Rosebud Reservation.[2]

Robert Burnette was born in 1926 on the reservation. His education as an activist began at home, where the Burnette family standards and principles partially shaped his character. During the Great Depression his parents participated in various activities in their Swift Bear community, north of Rosebud Agency. Grover served several terms as a councilman from Swift Bear and later became chief tribal judge. At the same time, Winnie raised funds for the Episcopal church.

Despite hard times both parents stressed the importance of their Lakota heritage and emphasized the significance of maintaining tribal and self-autonomy.[3] In 1943, Winnie Burnette asked South Dakota representative Karl Mundt to introduce legislation that would free Indians from government supervision. She argued that Indians were citizens in name only. To correct that inequity, she said, the United States should treat Indians as equals, not second-class citizens, and permit them to live their lives free of government paternalism. Winnie declared, "Even if some of us do not get an education we still know some things an [*sic*] I think we can get along without a bunch of nit wits to tell us what to do."[4] Robert Burnette's autobiographical sketches also reveal that his parents taught him the importance of community service, equality, and self-respect.

Reservation schools and the U.S. Marine Corps also influenced him. In school, Burnette learned to fear and despise authority and, as he said, "the realities of power," for he quickly discovered that any political leader could be either corrupt or benevolent. Burnette served in the marines from 1943 to 1946. His stint with the corps tempered his hatred toward those in power with tolerance because he learned that "there were good men of every race who could be rallied to correct a wrong."[5] For him, as for many minority veterans, military service was as much a lesson in equality and hope as an experience with discrimination and bitterness.

After the war, Burnette returned to Rosebud, married Beatrice Briggs, had nine children, and began his public career.[6] Like his mother, he strongly stated his convictions, and, like his father, he entered tribal politics. Political office provided the young crusader a forum to deliver his equality message beyond the Swift Bear district, the political base he inherited from his father. Swift Bear, however, remained the political foundation for his public career. In 1952, Burnette was elected to the Rosebud Sioux Tribal Council from Swift Bear by four votes.[7] Eventually the northwest section of the Rosebud Reservation that includes most of Mellette County became "Burnette country" because a majority of voters from that district supported him.[8] Voters returned Burnette to the tribal council in 1956, and the council members elected him chairman.[9] Four years later Swift Bear voters once again elected him to the tribal council, and the council members selected him chairman.[10] During this last term, Burnette also served as director of the Midwestern Inter-Tribal Council.[11]

With his first election the Swift Bear councilman entered the troubled realm of tribal politics. The low standard of living on the reservation coupled with a high unemployment rate encouraged some tribal leaders to fleece their own people, and when Burnette questioned these unethical practices, his detractors branded him "a potential troublemaker."[12] Exposing government graft became a lifelong calling for him after he discovered that officials running the Tribal Land Enterprise (TLE), a tribal land-management subsidiary, had profited by approving the exchange of land for certificates that represented the land's value. Burnette's response was quick: he wanted to close the TLE forever. That was next to impossible because the secretary of the interior (acting as the trustee for the American Indian) had approved these land-for-certificates trades between TLE, representing the tribe, and individuals. Another tribal emergency arose when attorney Ralph Case lost the Lakota lawsuit against the United States for the taking of this region in the 1870s. Burnette intervened on behalf of the tribe, asking the U.S. Court of Claims to reconsider the matter because the tribe's legal counsel was inadequate, and the court agreed. Through Burnette's efforts the council selected Marvin Sonosky to revive the Black Hills claim.[13]

Despite Burnette's dedication to his tribe, his crusading ethic and his political ambition extended beyond Rosebud. George McGovern's 1956 election to the state's eastern congressional seat gave South Dakota Democrats a reason to hope for future triumphs. In 1958, Burnette

Robert Burnette as a young activist. *Courtesy of the Buechel Memorial Lakota Museum/ Rosebud Educational Society, Saint Francis, South Dakota*

entered the Democratic primary for South Dakota's western congressional seat but finished third in a six-man race.[14] Two years later, he ran as a Democrat for South Dakota's state senate from his south-central district, which had a high Indian population. Despite a substantial tribal voting block, Burnette lost because South Dakota voters generally supported Richard Nixon, and local Republicans gained control of the state legislature.[15] These state campaigns reminded Burnette of the reality of the politics of exclusion, based partially on ethnicity, that influenced South Dakota elections.

Burnette's forays into state politics, however, prepared him for his first assault against racial prejudice. He hated the cruel things that people did to each other, particularly the discrimination against Indians that dominated South Dakota's post–World War II decades. Many storeowners in areas bordering the reservation placed "No Indians Allowed" signs in their windows, revealing deep racial prejudices.[16] The 1953 passage of Public Law 280 escalated Indian civil rights concerns because the act gave select states the option to assume control of law and order on reservations, negating a tribe's right of self-rule. When South Dakota lawmakers began discussing the takeover of reservation law enforcement, supporters claimed they wanted to make law and order equal for all, but tribal opponents charged that tribal and individual rights would be violated. Tribal leaders mounted an opposition, claiming that Indians would be treated unfairly in state courts, given the racism of the time, and that Indians should have a voice in making this jurisdiction decision.[17] Like many tribal leaders, Burnette opposed the state's assumption of reservation law enforcement because the notion violated his sense of fairness. In 1957 he testified before a South Dakota legislative committee, arguing that Indians had to be included on juries and that a popular referendum was needed to decide this issue before Indians would accept state authority on their reservations.[18]

Burnette carried his discrimination charges to Congress, claiming in a House hearing that "Indians are getting an awful shoving-around." In February 1959, before the House Interior and Insular Affairs Subcommittee on Indian Affairs, he spoke against a proposed administration amendment to the Johnson-O'Malley Act (1934) providing funds to assist states in usurping reservation law enforcement. Burnette declared that "Indians are already victimized by prejudice and they fear the bill might lead to taking of their lands and destruction of tribal governments."[19] In his view the proposed legislation violated the Indians' freedom from state encroachment on tribal sovereignty. Burnette "decided to make [his] testimony a report of the injustices that had occurred since Public

Law 280 had been enacted." He claimed that he "had evidence to support [his] charges," which included a declaration that only one Indian ever served on a state jury.[20]

Because of the gravity of Burnette's allegations, the committee requested that he submit a detailed written statement. In writing, he opposed giving money to states to assume reservation jurisdiction "without the Indians' consent." Burnette added that there was "systematic exclusion" of Indians from serving in state court juries. He alleged that prejudiced judges imposed "heavier sentences" on Indians than on whites who committed equivalent crimes.[21]

At the hearings and in his written statement, Burnette encountered the dilemma of a crusader: the need to provide specific details. His opponents now had an opportunity to discredit him by finding exceptions to his assertions. South Dakota newspaper editors and politicians denounced Burnette's charges. A *Sioux Falls (SD) Argus-Leader* editorial headline proclaimed "Indian Report Absurdly in Error." His charge that Indians "are sent to the South Dakota Penitentiary like 'herds of cattle' " was not true, the editorial asserted, as was his claim that Indians did not serve on juries. In fact, the Indians received fair treatment in courts because "almost all judges . . . will explain that Indians have every advantage accorded whites in the courts."[22] Some tribal leaders also took exception to Burnette's accusations, favoring a less confrontational approach to racial issues and preferring to work quietly with the state's civil rights advisory group. For example, Benjamin Reifel, the director of the Aberdeen Area Office and a Lakota from Rosebud, admitted that discrimination existed but doubted "that prejudice is as aggravated as Burnette pictured."[23]

South Dakota Republican representative E. Y. Berry responded that "Burnette's testimony was one of the most devastating things that has happened." He stated that the most serious repercussion from Burnette's charges was "the impress [sic] that goes out over the nation." Berry blamed outsiders for influencing Burnette because he "spends his time with these integration outfits such as the leaders of the NAACP and NCAI, etc. He listens to their propaganda and is carried away with it." Unlike Burnette, Berry narrowly defined discrimination, concluding that because Indians voted and attended white schools, no racial exclusion existed.[24]

Local Rosebud whites, who had a special interest in tribal affairs, also described Burnette's charges as false. A group of non-Indian ranchers who leased Indian land but refused to pay a recent tribal leasing tax organized the Todd County Taxpayers League to protest the tax. The group's leaders responded to Burnette's charges by claiming no discrimination existed.

They contradicted his sweeping statements made before the House committee and added that he was "not well informed."[25]

Charges and counterclaims are not necessarily truth, and Burnette's claims required further investigation. Even Burnette encouraged an independent study.[26] The task was given to the U.S. Civil Rights Commission, which in turn requested "its South Dakota Advisory Committee to 'evaluate' broad allegations of discrimination against Indians," among them Indian exclusion from state juries, judicial prejudice against Indian defendants, and school discrimination.[27]

The state's advisory committee held hearings at Rosebud in May 1959. Bennett County state's attorney Frederic Cozad chaired the meeting and sent the state committee findings to the Civil Rights Commission. Over one hundred men and women entered the Rosebud American Legion building and listened to eighteen witnesses. This one-day hearing, according to an Associated Press story, "produced several charges of anti-Indian discrimination, some rebuttal, a lot of bi-racial humor and a general clearing of the air." The Indian testimony went both ways. Some witnesses claimed that local judges violated their civil rights; as one unidentified Indian alleged, "Court sentencing of Indians is harsher than that of non-Indians except in crimes among Indians." By contrast, a few Indians declared that "voting rights are seldom abridged."[28]

The Civil Rights Commission analyzed the Rosebud evidence, and in 1960, the committee reported that no housing, voting, or education discrimination existed in South Dakota. The study's conclusions noted that, although reservation Indians had a low housing standard due to the poor economy, there was neither racial nor cultural discrimination: Indians willing to pay the rent could live wherever they wanted. This study defined discrimination very narrowly. As a result, if Indians voted, attended integrated schools, and white neighbors said that Indians could live in an all-white community provided they could pay the rent, no racial exclusion existed.[29] Yet these pronouncements were seriously tainted because the committee apparently did not investigate Burnette's charges involving jury and court sentencing after the Rosebud hearings.

Burnette understood that racial prejudice extended far beyond the committee's simple criteria. As a result, these findings challenged his credibility and affronted his sense of justice. He described the conclusions as "an outrageous lie," demonstrating his willingness to force contentious encounters with those who disagreed with him. Burnette was an imposing man, both intellectually and physically, standing over six feet and weighing nearly two hundred pounds. In all his fury, he went to the state capitol to seek out Democratic governor Ralph Herseth. The man from Rosebud entered the building and dropped "a chain and padlock wrapped in newspaper, on a desk and said it had been used to chain a man inside the city jail for 30 days." He declared, "Indian women had been in jail because they refused immoral advances by white men," and then he left.[30]

Working alone, Burnette shattered South Dakota's racial complacency and forced the state's population to confront their civil rights history. Unlike many of his tribal contemporaries who accepted accommodation, Burnette denounced discrimination. His angry messages and blunt tactics hit hard and occurred early in the state's civil rights movement, before an awareness had developed, and he therefore alienated many potential supporters. However, his outspoken defense of Indian civil rights caught the cresting radical civil rights wave that began with the 1961 African American summer freedom riders. That notoriety thrust him into the national Indian spotlight, since his actions found favor with the National Congress of American Indians (NCAI). At the Lewiston, Idaho, meeting of the NCAI in September 1961, delegates elected him executive director. By going to Washington, DC, Burnette took his vision of Indian civil rights and tribal sovereignty to a national level.[31]

The boundaries of South Dakota's civil rights investigations expanded after Burnette moved to Washington. In response to escalating national civil rights concerns and Burnette's 1959 congressional testimony and written statement, in which he gave examples of civil rights violations, the U.S. Senate Constitutional Rights Subcommittee of the Judiciary Committee held hearings in June 1962, at Pierre, South Dakota.[32] William A. Creech, chief counsel, presided, and Colorado senator John Carroll declared that he and his fellow committee members were "to ascertain whether Indians understand their basic rights under the Federal Constitution and whether these rights are adequately protected under existing law."[33] Donald Janson, a journalist for the *New York Times,* traveled to Pierre and wrote: "Complaints of gross mistreatment of Indians by white policemen dominated a recent hearing on constitutional rights." Indians accused local non-Indian law enforcement officers of brutality, claiming that lawmen had kicked, dragged, teargassed, and chained Indian inmates to jailhouse bunks. Martin, South Dakota, police chief Darrell King defended his actions, declaring that "the Indian is not a law-abiding person." He added, "As near as I can figure out, it's about like the Negroes down South: You can't let them get the upper hand."[34]

From Washington, DC, Burnette submitted a written statement to the U.S. Constitutional Rights Subcommittee conducting hearings in Pierre,

South Dakota; he alleged that "the practice in South Dakota is to arrest Indians on the pretense of intoxication or disorderly conduct and separate them from their money by fines, although non-Indians in the same place are not bothered." Such arrests occurred in many South Dakota towns, he noted, including Pierre, Rapid City, Winner, White River, Mission, Sisseton, Fort Pierre, Mobridge, and Chamberlain. Burnette added that some Indians did not know they could request an attorney, and those that did nonetheless would not do so because they feared "retaliation." He concluded, "I don't think there is anything that can be done" and added, "if you're suing a non-Indian in state court, you don't have a chance, so there's no use in spending a lot of money."[35] By 1963, Burnette had became the state's perennial Indian civil rights spokesperson.[36]

The Senate Subcommittee on Constitutional Rights returned to South Dakota in August 1963 to hold new hearings. Burnette concluded that these hearings were insignificant because the law officers accused of violating the civil rights of Indian prisoners had left their jobs. Furthermore, state residents were preparing to vote on a 1964 referendum to prevent the state from assuming jurisdiction on reservations. This referendum passed, ending some of the fears of state civil rights violations that many Indians associated with Public Law 280.[37]

Progress was being made, and evidence mounted that Burnette had been correct. The civil rights wave of the early 1960s had peaked, giving Indians and the government the legal support they needed to pursue evidence and to make charges of civil rights violations. In 1969, Office of Economic Opportunity (OEO) attorney William Janklow vindicated Burnette's civil rights charges, filing two class-action suits against the law officers of Mellette County. In one case, Janklow argued that the plaintiffs "were subject to cruel and unusual punishment, deprivation of rights, privileges, immunities, liberty and property" because the Mellette County jail was unsanitary and in a state of ruin, creating bodily risk and mental suffering. In the second lawsuit, White River and Wood Townships, Mellette County's clerk, auditor, and treasurer, and the state's attorney were all named as defendants, charged with "discriminating against American Indians by barring them from jury duty."[38]

Burnette, the man who had opened the door for civil rights in South Dakota, watched the final events of this early civil rights drama unfold from the NCAI's Washington, DC, office. He kept abreast of South Dakota issues, but practical concerns consumed much of his time as he sought funding to pay for the organization's work as the nation's Indian lobby. On an idealistic level, Burnette contributed to the defeat of the

1963 Indian Heirship Bill, which would have deprived heirs of their fractionalized allotments had it passed.[39]

Burnette left the NCAI in 1964, citing a "lack of co-operation from the tribes in solving Indian problems."[40] Now he had even greater doubts and misgivings about the practicality of his principles. The years spent in the nation's capital disheartened him, and he became skeptical about the American political process, which he had defended as a marine. He wrote that "the principles of liberty and justice were just a schoolboy's lesson, and the practical process of government pivoted on my social and political status, on whom one knew, and how much one could contribute."[41] In short, his years of dealing with intratribal disputes, a chronic shortage of funds, and federal red tape tarnished his idealism.

A disenchanted but more realistic Burnette returned to Rosebud in 1964 and reentered tribal politics, preserving what idealism remained by fighting government graft. He still believed that Rosebud could remain sovereign if tribal corruption ended.[42] His brother's resignation from the council provided Burnette an opportunity to return to tribal politics, and he asked the council to appoint him to complete his brother's unfinished term as a Swift Bear councilman. During his absence, politics on the reservation had changed. Cato Valandra, a moderate, was now chairman, and he opposed Burnette's request to complete his brother's unfinished council term, pointing to the tribal constitution's residency requirement. Following Valandra's prodding, the council denied Burnette's request.[43]

Though Valandra and Burnette had entered tribal politics together, they were now foes. Valandra's victory over Burnette in the council vote initiated a decade of historic electoral battles among Burnette, Cato Valandra, and Webster Two Hawk, another moderate, as each sought the tribal chairmanship. In these election struggles, Burnette the crusader argued that he was returning tribal government to the people by ousting corrupt politicians who preyed on their own tribespeople.[44] He declared that the OEO programs, which were part of the federal government's War on Poverty, employing Indians on temporary make-work projects, contributed to tribal corruption. According to Burnette, the downside of these temporary relief programs was that funding for the nation's War on Poverty escalated old reservation problems of corruption and fraud. These were issues he had once fought as tribal chairman, and now Valandra had used OEO funds to create new tribal work programs and build political support.[45] In an ironic twist, a federal court later convicted Valandra, in a civil suit, of taking tribal property for his own use.[46]

In January 1966, Rosebud tribal members voted on several tribal constitutional amendments in an election that was a prelude to Burnette's next bid for the tribal chairmanship. The amendments included a requirement that an individual had to have at least one-quarter Indian blood to be a tribal member, a tribal bill of rights, and provisions for electing the tribal president and vice president at large. Voters passed these resolutions, and the tribal council elected constitutional officers for the last time in January 1966.[47]

The 1967 Rosebud primary and general elections were historic, marking the first time the tribe voted at large for tribal president and vice president. In the August primary, Burnette (with 509 votes) defeated Valandra (with 496) and Lawrence Antonie (with 167). Then, Valandra beat Burnette by 40 votes in the October general election.[48] Burnette challenged the outcome, citing thirty-four election violations, ranging from an OEO worker improperly overseeing a polling place to violations of the tribal election code.[49] He carried his complaints to the secretary of the interior. This tactic was ironic, since Burnette had frequently accused the Department of the Interior of interfering in tribal affairs, but this was tribal politics, and he now sought outside support from the secretary of the interior.[50] Burnette's actions ultimately alienated the tribal election board members, and they eventually ruled against Burnette on all counts.[51] These elections revealed the growing distinction between Burnette the reformer, who demanded tribal autonomy, and Burnette the politician, who solicited the secretary of the interior and asked him to intervene in a tribal election matter.

Any hint of tribal graft within the tribal government put Burnette on the offensive. To him the ultimate cause of fraud was the nation's antipoverty program money, which enabled Valandra to employ people and in return expect favors from them.[52] Burnette took his story to "Newsfront" at WNDT television in New York City. On November 21, 1967, he informed the audience that tribal corruption included vote buying.[53] Valandra, to protect his own image, telegrammed program executive John K. Kiermair and claimed that Burnette's comments were nothing but political rhetoric.[54] Valandra then described Burnette as "a radical [who for] years has done our Indian people more harm than good."[55]

Nonetheless, when Burnette entered the August 1969 tribal presidential primary, he defeated the eight-year incumbent Valandra and newcomer Webster Two Hawk.[56] He credited his corruption charges against Valandra as the key to his primary victory, but Valandra threw his support behind Two Hawk, who then upset Burnette in the October general election.[57] As tribal president, Two Hawk's Republican leanings did not impress

Burnette, especially when the former became the director of President Nixon's National Tribal Chairmen's Association (NTCA). That made Two Hawk, who was an Episcopalian minister as well, "the definitive Uncle Tomahawk," according to Burnette.[58]

Two Hawk could not escape Burnette's political scrutiny. Even out of office, Burnette informed tribal members that their president was improperly transacting business. In October 1971, he charged that tribal officers were spending the tribe's funds without authority, in violation of the Rosebud constitution and federal statutes.[59] At the same time, a more contemptuous Burnette, along with Abraham Bordeaux, a former tribal employee, threatened to file a suit against tribal officers and OEO attorney Janklow for misuse of both tribal and OEO funds, but no suit followed.[60]

Burnette's criticism of these officials led the World War II veteran into sympathetic dealings with the American Indian Movement (AIM). Regional newspaper editors noted that Burnette was "an AIM sympathizer and yet [he] has denied AIM membership." Still wearing a crew cut, this former marine and tribal chairman now had more in common with younger activists than with his own generation. In the summer of 1972, several AIM members and Burnette gathered at Crow Dog's Paradise on Rosebud and discussed a preliminary agenda for a Washington, DC, demonstration that would change the American Indian's future. Burnette participated in the planning of the Trail of Broken Treaties, and he returned to Washington in the fall of 1972 as the AIM advance man. For the plan to work, Burnette cautioned the participants to "be on [their] finest behavior."[61] If successful, the Trail of Broken Treaties would give Burnette the potential to fulfill his dream "of having a force of . . . two hundred Indians in Washington, D.C., to demonstrate . . . until Congress and the president took notice."[62] His association with AIM damaged his prestige because, though he planned for hundreds of protesters, thousands converged on the capital, only to discover there were no accommodations. In a search for shelter, many blamed Burnette, but anger had its uses. Soon nonviolent demonstrators gravitated to the Bureau of Indian Affairs administrative building. The peaceful demonstrators refused to leave, then took control of structure and withstood a police assault.[63]

After the Washington demonstrations, Burnette confined his crusades to Rosebud politics, running again for tribal chairman in the 1973 tribal primary. This election exemplified Burnette's colorful career, featuring as it did a classic confrontation between two former chairmen who were political opposites. Burnette was the liberal AIM sympathizer, a Democrat challenging Two Hawk, the Republican incumbent and minister. Burnette was the community-conscious agitator opposed to tribal corruption in a race against the more conservative Two Hawk. Their styles also differed: Burnette never turned from confrontation, whereas Two Hawk favored accommodation.

In an upset, Burnette, who last served as chairman in 1961, defeated Two Hawk by nearly 150 votes. This election was important, and media from off the reservation covered the campaign. Newspapers reported that the campaign even included "rumors of threatened bodily harm and destruction of property."[64] Though there was no actual violence, Burnette's strong showing was helped by the support of the eighteen-year-old tribal members who were permitted to vote for the first time.[65]

His last term as tribal chairman and his subsequent reelection bid were both eventful. The council closed the reservation to hunting and fishing by anyone outside the tribe and forced the state of South Dakota to bargain on cooperative hunting and fishing regulations.[66] His reelection effort was stormier, and Edward Driving Hawk defeated Burnette by forty-eight votes. Burnette challenged the outcome in federal court, "citing alleged irregularities in the election." U.S. District Judge Robert J. Merhige eventually ruled in Driving Hawk's favor.[67]

Burnette spent the last years of his life defending his past actions and reflecting on tribal sovereignty. He completed two books in the early 1970s, *The Tortured Americans* and *The Road to Wounded Knee,* which are his personal reflections on the Indian in American history. A cursory reading of his works reveals a man caught between the divergent paths he traveled as a crusader and as a politician. At times these roles were at odds with one another, forcing Burnette to compromise his idealistic views to accommodate the necessities of political office. This inescapable dilemma was only aggravated by Burnette's confrontational style, which made his tasks more formidable because his opponents saw him as a radical and blamed his public outbursts on jealousy and his desire to see others fail so that he could succeed.

Ultimately, political reality tarnished Burnette's success but never the origins of his activism. He preserved his parents' teachings ("never forget your dignity and heritage"), the antipathy to power that he learned as a schoolboy, and the tolerance stressed in his military training. Collectively, these perceptions molded his civil rights crusade, which contributed to South Dakota's growing awareness of social inequalities in its midst. With Burnette's death in 1984, the Lakotas lost both a civil rights activist and a defender of tribal sovereignty.

Notes

1. Mellette County Centennial Committee, *Mellette County, South Dakota, 1911–1961* (White River, SD: Mellette County Centennial Committee, 1961), 33–36; Robert Burnette, *The Tortured Americans* (Englewood Cliffs, NJ: Prentice-Hall, 1971), 28; Robert Burnette, interview with Joseph H. Cash, August 25, 1971, American Indian Research Project, Library Cataloguing Service Date, Tape Number 799, transcript, p. 8, University of South Dakota, Vermillion.

2. *75 Years in Mellette County* (Mellette County Historical Society, 1986), 78–80.

3. Ibid.

4. Winnie Burnette to Karl E. Mundt, April 22, 1943, File Folder 3, Document Box 573, Record Group III, 1943, Karl E. Mundt Archives, Dakota State College, Madison, South Dakota.

5. Burnette, *Tortured Americans,* 27–28; Robert Philip Burnette, Life Membership Application, South Dakota Historical Society, September 5, 1961, Folder 19, Box 1, Harold Shunk Collection, Center for Western Studies, Augustana College, Sioux Falls, South Dakota.

6. *Todd County (SD) Tribune,* September 19, 1984.

7. "Today's World: South Dakota," n.d., File, Bob Burnette 1960, Box 127, E. Y. Berry Collection, Special Collections, Black Hills State University, Spearfish, South Dakota.

8. Burnette, interview.

9. Burnette, *Tortured Americans,* 45–49.

10. Ibid., 67.

11. *Pierre (SD) Daily Capital Journal,* April 6, 1960.

12. Burnette, *Tortured Americans,* 29.

13. Edward Lazarus, *Black Hills White Justice: The Sioux Nation versus the United States, 1775 to the Present* (New York: HarperCollins, 1991), 213–15; Burnette, *Tortured Americans,* 130–31.

14. "Indian Vote Seen as Big Factor," File, Bob Burnette 1960, Box 127, E. Y. Berry Collection; Alan L. Clem, *South Dakota Political Almanac* (Vermillion, SD: Dakota Press, 1969), 62.

15. "Indian Vote Seen as Big Factor"; Clem, *South Dakota Political Almanac,* 63.

16. Burnette, *Tortured Americans,* 64.

17. For a history of South Dakota efforts to assume criminal jurisdiction in Indian country, see Richmond L. Clow, "State Jurisdiction on Sioux Reservations: Indian and Non-Indian Responses, 1952–1964," *South Dakota History* 11 (Summer 1981): 171–84.

18. *Sioux Falls (SD) Argus-Leader,* February 19, 1957.

19. Ibid., February 11, 1957. The Johnson-O'Malley Act (1934) authorized federal assistance to school districts enrolling reservation children and burdened with a lack of resources.

20. Burnette, *Tortured Americans,* 57–58.

21. *New York Times,* March 25, 1959, 17.

22. *Sioux Falls (SD) Argus-Leader,* February 13, 1959.

23. Ibid., February 12, 1959.

24. E. Y. Berry to S. M. Stockdale, March 2, 1959, File, Burnette Testimony, 1959, Box 127, E. Y. Berry Collection.

25. *Todd County (SD) Tribune,* April 30, 1959.

26. *New York Times,* March 22, 1959, 43.

27. Ibid., March 25, 1959, 43.

28. "Air Cleared at Rights Hearing," May 10, 1959, File, Burnette Testimony, 1959, Box 127, E. Y. Berry Collection.

29. *Todd County (SD) Tribune,* April 20, 1960; *Pierre (SD) Daily Capital Journal,* April 14, 1960.

30. "Today's World, South Dakota," File, Bob Burnette 1960, Box 127, E. Y. Berry Collection.

31. Burnette, *Tortured Americans,* 68–69.

32. Ibid., 73.

33. *New York Times,* June 13, 1962, 37.

34. Ibid.

35. Ibid.

36. *Sioux Falls (SD) Argus-Leader,* April 27, 1963.

37. Burnette, *Tortured Americans,* 74–75; for a history of South Dakota efforts to assume criminal jurisdiction in Indian country, see Clow, "State Jurisdiction."

38. *Todd County (SD) Tribune,* August 21, 1969.

39. Burnette, *Tortured Americans,* 71–78.

40. "Burnette's Resignation Is Accepted," File, Bob Burnette 1960, Box 127, E. Y. Berry Collection.

41. Burnette, *Tortured Americans,* 78.

42. *Todd County (SD) Tribune,* September 19, 1984.

43. Burnette, *Tortured Americans,* 94–98.

44. Ibid., 86–87, 99–112.

45. Ibid., 94–98.

46. *Todd County (SD) Tribune,* October 21, 1971.

47. Ibid., January 20, 1966, and January 27, 1966.

48. Ibid., August 31, 1967, and November 2, 1967.

49. Affidavit, Robert Burnette, October 30, 1967, Folder 47, Box 17, Cato Valandra Papers, Special Collections, I. D. Weeks Library, University of South Dakota, Vermillion.

50. Robert Burnette and John Koster, *The Road to Wounded Knee* (New York: Bantam Books, 1974), see especially chapter 7, "The BIA: Big Brother Is Watching."

51. Tribal Election Board to Martin N. B. Holm, December 7, 1967, Folder 47, Box 17, Cato Valandra Papers.

52. Burnette, interview.

53. "Newsfront," November 21, 1967.

54. Cato Valandra to John K. Kiermayer, telegram, November 21, 1967, Folder 47, Box 17, Cato Valandra Papers.

55. Cato W. Valandra to Will, April 12, 1965, Folder 17, Box 1, Incoming Correspondence, Harold Shunk Collection.

56. *Todd County (SD) Tribune,* September 4, 1969.

57. Burnette, interview.

58. Burnette and Koster, *Road to Wounded Knee,* 269.

59. *Todd County (SD) Tribune,* October 28, 1971.

60. Ibid.

61. *Todd County (SD) Tribune,* October 25, 1973; Burnette and Koster, *Road to Wounded Knee,* 143.

62. Burnette and Koster, *Road to Wounded Knee*, 196.

63. Paul Chaat Smith and Robert Allen Warrior, *Like a Hurricane: The Indian Movement from Alcatraz to Wounded Knee* (New York: New Press, 1996), 139–166.

64. Ibid.

65. Ibid., October 30, 1973.

66. *Sioux Falls (SD) Argus-Leader*, September 21, 1974.

67. Ibid., January 24, 1976.

Suggested Readings

Burnette, Robert. *The Tortured Americans.* Englewood Cliffs, NJ: Prentice-Hall, 1971.

Burnette, Robert, and John Koster. *The Road to Wounded Knee.* New York: Bantam Books, 1974.

Cash, Joseph H. *The Sioux People (Rosebud).* Phoenix: Indian Tribal Stories, 1971.

Lazarus, Edward. *Black Hills White Justice: The Sioux Nation versus the United States, 1775 to the Present.* New York: HarperCollins, 1991.

Smith, Paul Chaat, and Robert Allen Warrior. *Like a Hurricane: The Indian Movement from Alcatraz to Wounded Knee.* New York: New Press, 1996.

13

Harvey Milk
San Francisco and the Gay Migration

Laura A. Belmonte*

Harvey Milk (1930–1978) was born on Long Island, New York, during the Great Depression. After an average childhood, he graduated from New York State College for Teachers and served in the U.S. Navy. Then came the social revolution of the 1960s. By 1970, Milk was a budding social activist and producer for such Broadway hits as *Hair* and *Jesus Christ Superstar.* He was also gay, and in 1972, he headed to San Francisco to settle permanently. For the next five years, Milk worked tirelessly as both a gay and community activist, demonstrating an adroit skill at forging political alliances in this cosmopolitan city. In 1977 his efforts were rewarded with his election as a city supervisor, making Milk the nation's first openly gay elected municipal official. One year later, however, he was assassinated in his own office. His death, along with the rise of the New Right movement of the late 1970s, reenergized the gay liberation movement, which itself would be sustained by the challenge of meeting the AIDS epidemic.

Milk's journey from the eastern seaboard to the Pacific Coast was a search for self-definition, one shared by many Americans of the politicized 1960s and the "me decade" of the 1970s. His story reinforces the argument that many parts of the West have always been places of diversity and cultural intersection, which sometimes leads to cooperation and innovation but at other times ends in violence.

Laura A. Belmonte teaches twentieth-century U.S. history at Oklahoma State University in Stillwater. Her research explores the connections between foreign policy, society, and culture. She is currently working on a manuscript entitled "Defending the American Way: National Identity, Propaganda, and the Cold War, 1945–1959."

On the morning of November 27, 1978, former San Francisco supervisor and ex-policeman Dan White loaded his .38-caliber pistol and filled his pockets with hollow-point ammunition. After getting a ride to

*I wish to thank Susan Goldstein and Tim Wilson for their generous assistance at the San Francisco History Collection. This essay is dedicated to Cece MacNaughton and to the memory of Brian MacNaughton.

city hall, he crawled in through a basement window and made his way to the office of Mayor George Moscone. When Moscone refused to reappoint him to his former post, White shot the mayor twice. He then walked over to the wounded man and pumped two dumdum bullets into his head. As he reloaded his gun, White walked to the offices of the supervisors. He asked Harvey Milk, his former colleague, to join him across the hall. After the two men entered the room, White closed the door. Seconds later, Milk shouted, "Oh no!" White shot Milk three times and then fired two dumdum bullets into Milk's head. He then ran from the building and went to a diner to call his wife. A devout Catholic, he asked her to meet him at Saint Mary's Cathedral. Shortly thereafter, he turned himself in to the police and confessed to the murders.[1]

The killings gained worldwide attention. That evening some 40,000 San Franciscans gathered for a candlelight march in honor of the fallen men. Both Moscone and Milk were hailed as committed politicians with promising futures. To gay and lesbian people everywhere, Milk represented unprecedented visibility and influence, but his fate also reminded them of the conflicts such power could engender.[2] Harvey Milk's life remains an example of progressive politics in America and of the continuing role of westward expansion in pursuit of individual happiness, community, and freedom.

Since World War II the Castro district of San Francisco has become a symbol of liberation for the gay community. Inspired by the New Left and the counterculture of the 1960s, gays and lesbians claimed an entire neighborhood as their own and forged a powerful cultural and economic force. They continued a long history of Americans who moved to the West in pursuit of individual fulfillment, but their motives obviously differed from those of the Mormons, the gold miners, or other pioneers. For the first time, emigrants moved westward seeking sexual freedom and identity—a lure that proved as powerful as religious freedom, potential wealth, or landownership.

Long before the gay migration of the 1970s, gay life in San Francisco was already a visible reality. During the height of the gold rush of the 1850s, the population of San Francisco was approximately 90 percent male, and it remained disproportionately male for decades. This environment proved conducive to homosexual activity—especially when one considers that the majority of these men were under forty years of age and isolated from women. There are legendary stories about all-male square dances in which the man dancing the "woman's" part was identified with a red bandanna on his arm. Extensive evidence about homosexual subcul-

Courtesy of the San Francisco History Center, San Francisco Public Library

tures among other predominately male groups—including sailors, pirates, and cowboys—can be extrapolated to San Francisco.[3]

Nonetheless public discussion of same-sex activities in San Francisco did not begin until the 1890s. Police arrested male prostitutes catering to military troops stationed at the Presidio. Stories of "passing women" who masqueraded as men in order to gain better jobs, political rights, or marry women appeared in local papers. In 1908 city officials closed down The Dash, San Francisco's earliest known gay bar. In 1933 the repeal of Prohibition sparked the emergence of new gay establishments, especially in North Beach, the predominantly Italian neighborhood that soon became a mecca for artists, Bohemians, and writers.[4]

No event transformed the lives of gays and lesbians more than World War II. Drawn together by military service or wartime employment, thousands of these individuals found each other in the sex-segregated environments created by the war. Because San Francisco served as one of the major dispatch points for troops heading to the Pacific theater, discharged soldiers often remained in the city rather than return to their hometowns with a "blue discharge."[5] By V-J Day, San Francisco's gay community burgeoned to unprecedented levels. The next decade, however, proved more challenging. Against the backdrop of Cold War rhetoric, the homophobia and anticommunism in the broader society created stereotypes of gays as predatory, contagious, and weak-willed. San Francisco authorities continued to raid gay clubs, theaters, and "cruising" spots. Despite the hostile climate, moderate homophile groups, including the male-dominated Mattachine Society (established in 1950) and the lesbian-controlled Daughters of Bilitis (founded in 1955), began challenging legal oppression. Meanwhile, gays and lesbians kept packing gay bars, and private house parties flourished. Long before Harvey Milk arrived, *Life Magazine* christened San Francisco the nation's "gay capital" in 1964.[6]

Little in Harvey Milk's early life portended his future role as a gay rights activist. Born in Woodmere, New York, on May 22, 1930, he was known for his quick wit and amiability, and he was a popular high school athlete. No one suspected that he led a secret gay life, but at seventeen he was arrested for being shirtless in a police raid of a "cruising" section of Central Park. Milk never told his family, but he always remembered the indignity of the incident. After graduating from college and serving in the navy, he settled into a comfortable job at an insurance company and a seven-year relationship with a young drifter named Joe Campbell. Milk paid little attention to McCarthyism's impact on gays or police harassment at gay establishments. He remained closeted to his family and coworkers. His politics were staunchly conservative.[7]

In the mid-1960s, however, Milk began to change. Bored with insurance, he became a researcher for a Wall Street investment firm. His math skills, memory, and charm enabled him to rise quickly through the ranks. After his relationship with Campbell ended, he began a romance with Jack

McKinley, another younger man. When McKinley became stage manager for avant-garde theater director Tom O'Horgan, Milk began socializing with artists whose lives were the antithesis of his own. Intrigued, he quit his job, grew his hair long, and became a producer for O'Horgan's hit shows *Hair* and *Jesus Christ Superstar.* He began adopting more liberal political views and abandoning the trappings of his buttoned-down life. When the *Hair* tour took McKinley to San Francisco, Milk followed. Although he got a job as a financial analyst there, he criticized the wealthy elites who controlled San Francisco politics and excluded gays, minorities, and the poor. In April 1970, following the U.S. invasion of Cambodia, Milk burned his Bank Americard in an antiwar rally at the Pacific Stock Exchange. Displeased by Milk's blooming radicalism, his employers fired him. He spent the next two years traveling with various O'Horgan productions.[8]

While Milk was changing, so were gay politics. In late June 1969 the Stonewall riots in New York raged for three days, sparking the gay liberation movement. By 1973 almost 800 gay and lesbian organizations had been formed all over the United States. More gay bars opened, but so did gay churches and synagogues, health clinics, community centers, and hosts of businesses and nonprofit services. Gay political clubs and newspapers proliferated. Urging their cohorts to "come out" and challenge antigay stereotypes and laws, gay liberation groups claimed homosexuals were an oppressed minority. Gays and lesbians began openly celebrating their sexuality and rejecting self-loathing and hiding in favor of pride and visibility.[9]

In the wake of Stonewall some San Francisco gay activists adopted more confrontational tactics. They questioned the homophiles' reliance on liberal politicians and working "within the system." They adopted the strategies of the Marxist, women's liberation, and radical political groups pervading the Bay Area. New gay militant groups formed.[10] In the early 1970s both militant and moderate gay activists scored victories in San Francisco. In 1969, California state assemblyman Willie Brown introduced legislation decriminalizing all sexual acts between consenting adults. Gay political groups provided crucial support in the elections of City Supervisor Dianne Feinstein and Sheriff Richard Hongisto. In 1972 the San Francisco Board of Supervisors passed an ordinance prohibiting antigay discrimination by city contractors.[11]

These gains were countered by the deep divisions within the city's estimated population of 80,000 gays in 1971. Moderate activists criticized radical attempts to include gays in a larger progressive coalition of minorities, the poor, and the elderly. Gay people of color accused white activists of racism. Lesbians, especially separatists, accused gay men of sexism. Poorer queers denounced elitism among wealthy gays. Drag, transgender, sadomasochistic, and leather groups felt marginalized. It would take a remarkable leader to unify such a diverse lot.[12]

No one would have guessed that Harvey Milk would become that leader. In 1972, Milk and his new lover, Scott Smith, returned to San Francisco. They moved to Castro Street in the heart of the Eureka Valley district, a deteriorating Irish neighborhood, and opened Castro Camera, living above the sprawling storefront. They joined an influx of gay men transforming the local demographics.[13]

To Milk, moving to Eureka Valley meant a chance to take part in city politics. Infuriated by the Watergate hearings, sales taxes, and underfunded schools, he decided to enter the 1973 election for the San Francisco Board of Supervisors.[14] Milk's answers to a questionnaire given to all candidates are quite revealing. He had no experience in local politics or community projects. He listed his net worth as "$2,000 in debt." He had no endorsements. He expected to "pass the hat for dollars and coins" in order to finance his campaign.

If Milk's resources were limited, his political vision definitely was not. He said he was running for the board to stop the waste of taxpayers' money and end prosecution for "victimless crimes," including prostitution, consensual sex, and marijuana use. When asked to specify the voters to whom he was appealing, Milk crossed out all of the subcategories and wrote, "I campaign for all." If elected, he intended to expand health care for the elderly and to create better job opportunities for minorities and the young. He denounced the city's increasing reliance on tourism and real estate development that displaced poor and minority San Franciscans. He advocated free public transportation and stricter environmental laws. Milk also outlined an ambitious civil rights agenda, supporting the aims of "all—especially gay, black, Mexican, Oriental." "For a city made of minorities," he added, "there is no excuse."[15]

The sweeping agenda of the audacious newcomer stunned local liberal politicians. Some thought that the ponytailed, mustached Milk was a crazy hippie. Even if they liked his personality and ideas, gay moderates worried that his unpredictable nature could harm the gay political movement. Having spent years building the local movement, they viewed Milk as an arrogant opportunist. They remained wedded to the idea that gays should rely on straight liberals to implement gradual civil rights reforms.

Milk emphatically rejected this logic. Believing that gays should run for office themselves rather than relying on anyone else, he launched impolitic attacks on moderate gay activists. Needless to say such tactics did not win him the endorsement of the Alice B. Toklas Memorial Democratic Club, the biggest gay political group in the city. But radicals loved him. Drag queens, bar owners tired of police raids, and marijuana users supported him in droves.

Milk combined his fiscal conservatism with fiery progressive oratory. He became skilled at the art of getting press coverage. Despite his hippie image and failure to secure gay political endorsements, he received 17,000 votes, finishing tenth out of thirty-two candidates. Even with a meager $4,500 campaign budget, Milk managed to win substantial support in heavily gay neighborhoods and counterculture enclaves. Convinced that gays would support one of their own, he decided to run again. Making two concessions to political reality, he cut his hair and vowed never to smoke pot or go to a gay bathhouse again. A populist was born.[16]

While Milk prepared for his political future, San Francisco's booming service economy drew gays from around the country. Beginning in 1973 the gay invasion of Eureka Valley skyrocketed. Drawn by inexpensive Victorian homes, gays began renovating scores of houses and opening new businesses. The neighborhood changed dramatically. The maternity shop became All-American Boy, a men's clothing store catering to gay styles. The historic Castro Theater reopened and showed the Hollywood classics beloved by many gays. The family florist evolved into a leather shop.[17]

Castro Camera served as the center of the changing community. Milk became known for his relentless efforts in advocating for the neighborhood at city hall. Old ladies facing eviction, troubled teens, and gay activists gathered in his storeroom. Local Teamsters leaders noticed Milk's growing influence and asked for his help in their boycott of six antiunion beer distributors. Milk agreed to help in exchange for a promise that the union would admit gay employees, and he quickly convinced gay bars to join the boycott. Five distributors agreed to settle. Thrilled at Milk's organizational skills and the success of their boycott, the Teamsters began hiring gay and lesbian drivers.[18]

Inspired by his success, Milk escalated his political activities. Insisting that gays had no right to complain about politics unless they participated, he registered 2,350 new voters. He tried to organize the neighborhood's gay and straight merchants. When the Eureka Valley Merchants Association refused to admit gay businesspeople, Milk organized the gay merchants into the Castro Valley Association (CVA). The subtle name change gained enormous significance as gay residents began referring to the neighborhood as the Castro instead of Eureka Valley. Throughout 1974, Milk promoted CVA and extolled the tremendous potential of gay economic power. To prove his point, he organized the Castro Street Fair in August. Over 5,000 people attended. Thrilled at the business created by the fair, some straight merchants joined CVA.

A number of older residents were appalled by the growing power of the Castro gays. Often, tensions erupted into violence. Gay bashings were frequent. Arsonists targeted gay establishments. Policemen shouted antigay epithets and harassed gays with unwarranted disorderly conduct tickets. Usually covering their badge numbers first, a few cops even beat gays. After a series of particularly brutal attacks over Labor Day weekend in 1974, gay attorney Rick Stokes filed a $1.375 million lawsuit against the San Francisco Police Department. Although the affair prompted a decline in police harassment, Milk used the melee to emphasize the need for gays to enter the San Francisco political establishment.[19]

He planned to lead the way himself. In March 1975, Milk announced his candidacy for a second run for the board of supervisors. He stressed his opposition to prosecution for victimless crimes and support for fairer taxation and improved schools. Although his work on the beer boycott had earned him scores of labor endorsements, gay moderates continued to shun him. Undeterred, Milk ran his campaign amid the chaos of Castro Camera. He relied on volunteers and often catapulted virtual strangers to positions of authority. Unable to afford expensive advertisements, he rose at 5:30 A.M. in order to shake hands with commuters. He spent his days campaigning in parks, churches, bars, and cafés. He was not always greeted warmly. Some people refused to take his leaflets, and in Golden Gate Park, someone shouted, "What are you running for, dairy queen?" Milk took such hostility in stride. "If I turned around every time somebody called me faggot," he explained to a local reporter, "I'd be walking backwards and I don't want to walk backwards."[20] Finishing just one spot short of the top six vote-getters elected to the board, he narrowly lost the election.

Nonetheless, Milk saw the election of 1975 as a victory. He established himself as a power broker for his neighborhood. Scores of gay-friendly and liberal candidates won office. District Attorney Joseph Frietas pledged to stop prosecution for victimless crimes. Promising to challenge the city's powerful real estate interests, George Moscone was elected mayor by a powerful coalition of the city's minorities, poor, elderly, and gays. Moscone recognized the importance of San Francisco's growing gay population. Accordingly, he rewarded Milk with an appointment to the city's board of permit appeals.[21]

Milk, however, had bigger plans. Just five weeks after being sworn in, he announced his intention to run for the Democratic nomination for the Sixteenth Assembly District seat representing east San Francisco in the state legislature. Moscone was furious. The mayor and most of the city's other Democratic leaders had already endorsed another candidate, Art Agnos. Milk was undeterred. After Moscone fired him, he launched a populist crusade against the wealthy and political elites. Agnos, he claimed, was the tool of a "machine" dominating city politics. The "Milk versus the Machine" campaign concluded with Milk losing to Agnos by 3,600 votes. He was, however, gaining substantial support, and he carried the Castro decisively.[22]

The Castro was undoubtedly becoming a force with which to be reckoned. By 1977, 20,000 gay men had moved to the neighborhood, and thousands more visited each weekend to experience the sexual energy pulsating through the district's bars. "The Castro was like Mardi Gras every weekend," one gay couple remembers. Gay softball leagues, a gay chorus, a tap-dancing troupe, and other gay clubs provided a host of community activities. The Castro Street Fair, Halloween, and Gay Freedom Day Parade drew massive crowds.[23]

Gays were also making striking gains nationwide. By 1977 almost forty cities had adopted ordinances outlawing antigay discrimination in housing, employment, and public accommodations. Eleven states were considering adopting statewide gay rights bills. And sodomy statutes were being repealed across the country.[24]

The gay community's growing power prompted a nationwide backlash as well. In January 1977, when Dade County, Florida, adopted a gay rights law, former Miss America runner-up and Florida Citrus Commission spokesperson Anita Bryant launched a campaign to rescind the law. On June 7, Dade County voters repealed the gay rights law by an overwhelming margin. A little-known California state senator, John Briggs (R-Fullerton), was inspired by Bryant's success. Hoping to advance his gubernatorial aspirations, he introduced legislation banning gays and lesbians from working in public schools.[25]

Throughout Bryant's crusade in Florida, reports of antigay violence in San Francisco soared. The attacks also took rhetorical forms. In August board of supervisors candidate Dan White released an ominous brochure proclaiming that he was "not going to be forced out of San Francisco by splinter groups of radicals, social deviates, and incorrigibles." White called for "frustrated, angry people" to "unleash a fury that can and will eradicate the malignancies which blight our beautiful city."[26]

The antigay backlash only increased Milk's determination to win election to the board of supervisors. In 1976, San Franciscans had voted to replace citywide elections with district elections. Neighborhoods—including the Castro—could now elect their own representatives. In November 1977, after his third campaign for election to the board of supervisors, Milk defeated sixteen other candidates and won the District Five seat. At a joyous victory party, he told his gay supporters: "This is not my victory, it's yours, and yours, and yours. If a gay can win, it means that there is hope that the system can work for all minorities if we fight." But Milk also recognized that his victory may have endangered his life. A week later, he taped a political will to be read in case he was assassinated. "If a bullet should enter my brain," he declared with chilling foresight, "let that bullet destroy every closet door."[27]

Whatever his personal safety concerns, Milk was determined to represent the Castro well. In January 1978 he was sworn in as the city's first gay supervisor, joining the first Chinese, the first unwed mother, and the first African American on the most diverse board of supervisors in San Francisco history. Dan White, a former policeman and fireman, was also inaugurated that day.

Milk quickly proved himself a hardworking legislator. At times he was abrasive and crude, but even his opponents admired his humor, eloquence, and dedication. He challenged corporate interests and defended minorities and the poor. Appalled by spiraling real estate prices, he pushed for a strict antispeculation tax. After his hilarious demonstrations of the city's "dog poop problem" gained wide media attention, Milk lobbied for legislation requiring pet owners to clean up after their pets. Although his colleagues defeated many of his proposals, he protected his constituents—gay and straight. He successfully fought for road improvements, street cleanings, and traffic signs in his district. He prevented closure of the community's elementary school and public library. In March, Milk won passage of the long awaited city gay rights law by a ten-to-one vote. Outlawing antigay discrimination in employment, housing, and public accommodation, the ordinance culminated decades of Bay Area gay activism.[28]

Milk thrived on the board, but Dan White found his own experience frustrating. Moody and inflexible, he was ill suited to the vicissitudes of politics. His biggest disappointment came when his colleagues voted six to five to construct a psychiatric facility in his district despite his vociferous opposition. At first, Milk had sided with White, but he changed his vote after learning more about the project. Enraged, White refused to speak to him for months and retaliated by attacking Milk's gay rights bill, casting the lone dissenting vote. In the months that followed, White opposed every gay-related issue put before the board. He also allied himself with the wealthy real estate developers whom Milk so disdained.[29]

Facing a continued antigay backlash, Milk paid little attention to White's ranting. Throughout early 1978, an organization called California Defend Our Children quietly gathered the 500,000 signatures needed for a statewide vote on the Briggs initiative, officially named Proposition 6. Gay activists were stunned at the breadth of the proposal. The bill not only barred anyone who engaged in "public homosexual conduct" from working in the public school system but also employed a sweeping definition of the word "public." Under Proposition 6, anyone "advocating, soliciting, imposing, encouraging or promoting private or public homosexual activity" in an educational setting could be dismissed. Attorneys warned that the Briggs bill posed a threat to the freedom of speech of *all* school employees regardless of sexual orientation. The news that voters in Saint Paul, Minnesota, Wichita, Kansas, and Eugene, Oregon, had repealed gay rights ordinances did little to cheer San Franciscan gays.[30]

Milk refused to be cowed. As his popularity increased, so did the number of death threats he received. Despite a morass of personal and financial problems, he continued to devote himself to his job. He also knew that gays could not ignore their increasingly powerful opponents. He emerged as the leader of several groups fighting the Briggs initiative. Putting aside their differences, gays and straights worked together to raise funds, canvass voters, and lobby politicians.[31]

Throughout the fall, Milk campaigned tirelessly against Proposition 6. He and Briggs made dozens of public appearances debating the proposal and the issue of homosexuality. The contests featured exchanges of various statistics and interpretations of the Bible. "This is not a civil rights question. This is not a human rights question. It is simply a question of morality," Briggs insisted. Milk shot back, "If Senator Briggs think he's better than Christ, that he can decide what's moral, then maybe we should have elected him Pope."[32]

Milk often used humor to deflect Briggs's outrageous charges. When Briggs argued that a quarter of gay men had over 500 sexual partners, Milk retorted, "I wish." Briggs repeatedly asserted that children needed good role models and should be protected from homosexuals who wished to "recruit them." "Children do need protection," Milk responded, "protection from the incest and child beatings pandemic in the heterosexual family." As for role models, he reminded his audiences that if children emulated their instructors, there would be "a helluva lot more nuns running around."[33]

Milk was not alone in opposing the Briggs initiative. When September 1978 polls showed that over 60 percent of California voters supported Proposition 6, many people realized Briggs could not be ignored and began publicly attacking his proposal. Gays realized that even in laid-back California, they could not take their civil rights for granted. In the weeks prior to the election, statewide polls showed Californians evenly split over Proposition 6. Briggs had proven himself an inept spokesman. Unable to persuade politicians to join him, he surrounded himself with fundamentalist preachers. Only three state groups—the Ku Klux Klan, the Nazi Party, and the Los Angeles County Deputy Sheriff's Association—endorsed Proposition 6.

On election day, California voters defeated the Briggs initiative by a significant margin. Seattle voters rejected an attempt to repeal the city's gay rights law. The antigay tide had turned. Milk was the nation's most prominent gay activist. Supported by a progressive coalition of gays, minorities, and the poor, he expected easy reelection. Life was good for Supervisor Milk.[34]

Dan White was not so lucky. Unable to work as a fireman while serving on the board, he struggled to support his wife and newborn son on his $9,600 supervisor's salary. After he closely aligned himself with local real estate interests, a developer helped him attain a potato stand at Pier 39, the city's newest tourist attraction. White and his wife, Mary Ann, worked long hours to make ends meet. White grew depressed and distant. He stopped shaving and stayed in bed for days. Citing his financial problems, he resigned from the board on November 10, 1978. Six days later, he changed his mind. He explained that his sixteen brothers and sisters had offered financial assistance and that his supporters had urged him not to quit. Returning White's letter of resignation, Moscone proclaimed, "As far as I'm concerned, Dan White is the supervisor from District 8. . . . A man has the right to change his mind."[35]

But then Moscone exercised the same prerogative. He announced that the city's attorneys had advised him that White could not rescind his resignation. Although he could legally reappoint White, the mayor hesitated. Citing several complaints about the former policeman, Moscone stated that he would not reappoint White unless he provided evidence of substantial support in District 8. At the same time, an "unnamed supervisor" told reporters that White was "a nice guy" but a poor supervisor who opposed gays and minorities in order to curry the favor of the wealthy.

It did not take a genius to figure out that White's critic was Harvey Milk. Behind the scenes, Milk reminded Moscone that White had been the swing vote on many six-to-five defeats. Milk also let the mayor know that San Francisco's gays would not look favorably on the reappointment of the homophobic White. With gays now composing a quarter of the city's electorate, Moscone knew he could not afford to alienate the city's 100,000 gays and lesbians or his liberal constituents. Distracted by the news that 900 members of the San Francisco–based People's Temple had committed suicide in jungles of Guyana, few citizens paid much attention to Moscone's dilemma. They were about to receive another shock.[36]

On November 27, Dan White murdered Moscone and Milk. For the next week the stunned city mourned its fallen leaders. Flags were lowered to half-staff. Businesses closed. President Jimmy Carter expressed "a sense of outrage and sadness at the senseless killing." Thousands attended memorial services for Moscone and Milk. While the city grieved, police booked White on two counts of first-degree murder. His confession left no doubt who had committed the crimes. His colleagues and neighbors portrayed him an intensely moral and competitive man who had snapped under the pressure of financial problems. Yet his jailers noted White's eerily calm demeanor.[37]

Although several details about the murders emerged in the next few months, nothing prepared San Franciscans for White's dramatic trial. He pleaded not guilty and faced a possible death sentence. Jury selection began in April 1979. Douglas Schmidt, White's attorney, questioned potential jurors about the death penalty, gay organizations, psychiatry, and Moscone and Milk. After only three days of selection, Schmidt and Assistant District Attorney Thomas F. Norman accepted an all-white, all-straight jury.[38]

In his opening argument on May 1, Schmidt presented White as "a good man" who "cracked" after a long struggle with depression. White was, he said, an "honest and fair" public servant who "tried very hard to be tolerant of different lifestyles." "Good people—fine people with fine backgrounds," Schmidt concluded, "simply don't kill people in cold blood."[39] Norman's bland recounting of the murders proved no match for Schmidt's sympathetic portrait of White.[40]

Norman was no more adept at challenging Schmidt's psychiatric experts. Three of the four defense experts claimed that White lacked the mental capacity to commit premeditated murder. He was, they said, a conflicted man who lacked friends and confidants. Furthermore, White's frequent episodes of deep depression were exacerbated by a diet made up exclusively of junk food.[41]

The so-called Twinkie defense made legal history, and Norman's prosecution was lackluster and ineffective. After Schmidt made an eloquent closing argument imploring the jury to spare White's life, Norman embarked on a four-and-a-half hour summation that put jurors, bailiffs, and even District Attorney Joseph Frietas to sleep.[42] On May 21, after thirty-six hours of deliberation, the jury convicted White of two counts of voluntary manslaughter. He would serve a maximum sentence of seven years and eight months.

The lenient verdict generated an enormous uproar. An incredulous Mayor Dianne Feinstein declared, "As far as I'm concerned, these were two murders." Many San Franciscans agreed. The evening after the verdict was announced, 5,000 predominantly gay demonstrators marched from the Castro to city hall. Invoking Milk's fervent belief in nonviolence, several speakers attempted to calm the crowd, but their pleas fell on deaf ears. A riot erupted. Flinging a lighted match into a police car, one demonstrator told a reporter, "Make sure to put in the paper that I ate too many Twinkies." By the time the White Night Riots ended, demonstrators destroyed $1 million of city property. Dozens of gays and cops were injured. Over fifty people were arrested.[43]

Fears that Milk's death would stymie the gay community's growing political power proved groundless. On May 22, 1979, the night after the White Night Riot, a peaceful crowd of 4,000 gathered in the Castro to commemorate Milk's forty-ninth birthday. The event became an annual celebration of the activist's life. In the 1980s, when AIDS began to decimate San Francisco's gay male population, the city became a worldwide model for its educational and medical response to the epidemic. The crisis prompted unprecedented cooperation between gay men and lesbians. By the 1990s gay people held prominent positions throughout San Francisco government, politics, and business. Confronting increasingly hostile national opposition, the city's queer community worked to overcome its racial, ethnic, economic, and sexual divisions. Although Milk would have disdained the Castro's evolution into a pricey gay tourist trap, he would have been thrilled that the neighborhood embodies the visibility and power he wanted for gays everywhere.[44]

Harvey Milk's life and death continue to inspire human rights advocates throughout the world. His colorful lifestyle and courageous message have been depicted in books, an Oscar-winning documentary, plays, a television show, a musical, and an opera. His progressive vision and concern for justice stir all people who hope for a world in which diversity and dignity triumph over discord and derision.

Notes

1. The definitive account of Harvey Milk's life and assassination is Randy Shilts, *The Mayor of Castro Street: The Life and Times of Harvey Milk* (New York: St. Martin's Press, 1982). See also Mike Weiss, *Double Play: The San Francisco City Hall Killings* (New York: Addison-Wesley, 1984).

2. See Shilts, *Mayor of Castro Street.*

3. Susan Stryker and Jim Van Buskirk, *Gay by the Bay: A History of Queer Culture in the San Francisco Bay Area* (San Francisco: Chronicle Books, 1996), 13–19.

4. The San Francisco Lesbian and Gay History Project, " 'She Even Chewed Tobacco': A Pictorial Narrative of Passing Women in America," in *Hidden from History: Reclaiming the Gay and Lesbian Past,* ed. Martin Duberman, Martha Vicinus, and George Chauncey Jr. (New York: Meridian Books, 1989), 183–94; Stryker and Van Buskirk, *Gay by the Bay,* 18–19.

5. "Blue discharge" refers to the paper on which dishonorable discharges for homosexuality were printed. Such discharges often prevented gays from attaining private employment. See Allan Bérubé, *Coming Out under Fire: The History of Gay Men and Women in World War Two* (New York: Free Press, 1990).

6. On the impact of McCarthyism on gays, see John D'Emilio, "The Homosexual Menace: The Politics of Sexuality in Cold War America," in *Passion and Power: Sexuality in History,* ed. Kathy Peiss and Christina Simmons (Philadelphia: Temple University Press, 1989), 226–40; Geoffrey Smith, "National Security and Personal Isolation: Sex, Gender, and Disease in the Cold-War United States," *International History Review* 14 (May 1992): 307–35; and Bérubé, *Coming Out under Fire,* 255–79. On the homophile movement, see John D'Emilio, *Sexual Politics, Sexual Communities: The Making of a Homosexual Minority in the United States, 1940–1970* (Chicago: University of Chicago Press, 1983), 121–22, 177–95; Stryker and Van Buskirk, *Gay by the Bay,* 43–47.

7. Shilts, *Mayor of Castro Street,* 3–22. On Milk's interest in the arts and his life with Joe Campbell, see Harvey Milk–Susan Davis Alch correspondence, San Francisco History Collection, San Francisco Public Library (hereafter cited as SFHC, SFPL).

8. Shilts, *Mayor of Castro Street,* 24–46.

9. Martin Duberman, *Stonewall* (New York: Plume, 1994).

10. On these protests, see *San Francisco Chronicle,* July 2, 1969, November 1, 1969, November 4, 1969, and November 19, 1969.

11. Ibid., October 18, 1971; Shilts, *Mayor of Castro Street,* 60–65.

12. On these divisions, see Stryker and Van Buskirk, *Gay by the Bay,* 54–62. The term "queer" is not used pejoratively; rather, it is used to reflect the wide diversity of the gay community, encompassing gay, lesbian, bisexual, and transgendered people.

13. Shilts, *Mayor of Castro Street,* 43–46, 65.

14. For Milk's motivations in running for office, see Shilts, *Mayor of Castro Street,* 69–72.

15. San Francisco Board of Supervisors Study, August 7, 1973, Vertical File on Harvey Milk, SFHC, SFPL.

16. Shilts, *Mayor of Castro Street,* 69–80. See also 1973 Campaign Brochure, Vertical File on Harvey Milk, SFHC, SFPL.

17. On the development of the Castro and reaction of residents, see Peter L. Stein, *The Castro* in the series *Neighborhoods: The Hidden Cities of San Francisco,* produced by Peter L. Stein (San Francisco: KQED Books and Tapes, 1997), videocassette; Shilts, *Mayor of Castro Street,* 112.

18. Shilts, *Mayor of Castro Street,* 81–84.

19. Ibid., 87–93; Stein, *Castro.*

20. *San Francisco Chronicle,* March 17, 1975, and October 23, 1975. See also 1975 Campaign Brochure, Vertical File on Harvey Milk, SFHC, SFPL.

21. Shilts, *Mayor of Castro Street,* 95–110; *San Francisco Chronicle,* January 30, 1976.

22. Shilts, *Mayor of Castro Street,* 127–152; *San Francisco Chronicle,* March 10, 1976, June 9–10, 1976; 1976 Campaign Brochure, Vertical File on Harvey Milk, SFHC, SFPL.

23. Stein, *Castro*; Frances Fitzgerald, "The Castro—I," *The New Yorker,* July 7, 1986, 34–54.

24. For a chronology of these developments, see Mark Thompson, ed., *Long Road to Freedom: The Advocate History of the Gay and Lesbian Movement* (New York: St. Martin's Press, 1994).

25. Stein, *Castro*; Shilts, *Mayor of Castro Street,* 155–58; *San Francisco Chronicle,* April 21, 1977, and June 8–10, 1977.

26. *San Francisco Chronicle,* June 23, 1977, and July 1, 1977; Shilts, *Mayor of Castro Street,* 161–63.

27. Shilts, *Mayor of Castro Street,* 169–85.

28. Ibid., 189–97, 203; *San Francisco Chronicle,* March 21, 1978.

29. On White's temperament, see Shilts, *Mayor of Castro Street,* 198–200.

30. *San Francisco Chronicle,* January 12, 1978, and April 27, 1978; Thompson, *Long Road to Freedom,* 163.

31. Shilts, *Mayor of Castro Street,* 204–6, 214–18, 221–26.

32. Ibid., 229–30.

33. Ibid., 230–31.

34. Ibid., 242–51.

35. *San Francisco Chronicle,* November 11 and 18, 1978, and, on White's behavior prior to his resignation, May 2, 1979.

36. Ibid., November 21–22, 1978; Shilts, *Mayor of Castro Street,* 254–55.

37. *San Francisco Chronicle,* November 28 and December 2, 1978.

38. Ibid., February 10, 1979, April 20, 1979, April 22, 1979, and April 28, 1979.

39. Ibid., May 2, 1979.

40. Ibid., May 4, 1979.

41. Ibid., May 8–10, 1979.

42. Ibid., May 12, 1979, and May 15–16, 1979.

43. Ibid., May 22–23, 1979.

44. Ibid., May 23, 1979; Stryker and Van Buskirk, *Gay by the Bay,* 85–142; Stein, *Castro.*

Suggested Readings

Bérubé, Allan. *Coming Out under Fire: The History of Gay Men and Women in World War Two.* New York: Free Press, 1990.

D'Emilio, John. *Sexual Politics, Sexual Communities: The Making of a Homosexual Minority in the United States, 1940–1970.* Chicago: University of Chicago Press, 1983.

Shilts, Randy. *The Mayor of Castro Street: The Life and Times of Harvey Milk.* New York: St. Martin's Press, 1982.

Stryker, Susan, and Jim Van Buskirk. *Gay by the Bay: A History of Queer Culture in the San Francisco Bay Area.* San Francisco: Chronicle Books, 1996.

Index

ISBN 0-8420-2860-9
90000 >
9 780842 028608